Success in Elements of Banking

Success Studybooks

Success in

ELEMENTS OF BANKING

David Cox, A.I.B.

Lecturer in Business Studies,
Worcester Technical College.

John Murray

First published 1979 by
John Murray (Publishers) Ltd
50 Albemarle Street, London, w1x 4BD

Filmset by
Northumberland Press Ltd, Gateshead, Tyne and Wear
Printed in Great Britain by
Fletcher & Son Ltd, Norwich

British Library Cataloguing in Publication Data

Cox, David
    Success in elements of banking.
    1. Banks and banking – Great Britain
    I. Title
    332.1′0941   HG2990

    ISBN 0-7195-3703-7

Foreword

Banking is a career which has become increasingly attractive to young people in recent years. It is a profession where there are excellent opportunities for promotion and where, from the beginning, employees are given full facilities to follow part-time courses of study leading to higher levels of professional qualification.

This book provides a new, self-contained course designed to give all students a thorough grounding in the main aspects of banking. It covers the historical background of the development of money and banking, and goes on to consider the present-day role of banks and the controls under which they operate. The more important bank services are all described in detail as are the various aspects of bank lending.

Success in Elements of Banking is appropriate to the following examinations: BEC National Certificate and Diploma in Business Studies (recognized by the Institute of Bankers); Bankers' Conversion Courses (recognized by the Institute of Bankers); the Stage 1 Examination set by the Institute of Bankers, London, for overseas students, and all similar examinations of other Institutes of Bankers and colleges. It is suitable for students working for any professional examination which contains a paper on banking, and for those following correspondence courses.

Certain sections of Units 16, 17 and 18 go a little beyond the strict requirements of the Elements of Banking syllabus. This is because the topics concerned relate directly to what has gone before and the interested student will want to pursue logical lines of thinking. It seems more satisfactory, therefore, from everyone's point of view, to round off a subject at its natural boundary rather than to chop it off at·some arbitrary point. It also follows that students working towards the Stage 2 Examinations set by the Institute of Bankers, London, or similar papers of other Institutes of Bankers, will find these, and other Units, beneficial as background or revision reading.

The Questions set at the end of each Unit are designed either for self-testing or for use in class. They are invaluable for helping to assess a student's progress, and for giving practice in answering the kind of question that will be encountered in the actual examination. Many are chosen from past papers set by the Institute of Bankers.

Teachers and students following BEC courses will find the Assignments on page 257 will fully complement their own requirements and will provide valuable guidelines for individual work and research.

D. C.

Acknowledgments

In writing this book I have been helped by many people, especially those teachers, lecturers and professional bankers who appraised and criticized it at different stages. I am particularly grateful to Eric Glover, Peter Spiro and John Mortimer of the Institute of Bankers; to Bill Harrison, Leslie Harfield, Peter Gutmann, Geoffrey Parkinson, Stephen Green and Gerald Klein.

My sincere thanks also go to Jean Macqueen for her patient editing work on the typescript; to Irene Slade, editor of the 'Success Studybooks' series; and to her assistant, Rosemarie Burston, who researched the illustrations and helped with everything.

The assistance of the following organizations is gratefully acknowledged: the Bank of England, for permission to reproduce material taken from the Bank's *Quarterly Bulletin*; the Central Statistical Office, for permission to quote material from the *Monthly Digest of Statistics*; the *Financial Times*, for permission to quote share prices (page 77); the Institute of Bankers, London, for permission to use questions from past examination papers; Lloyds Bank Limited, for permission to reproduce their balance sheet, bank giro credit and specimen cheques (pages 141 and 142); Midland Bank Limited, for permission to reproduce export documents from their booklet *Services to Exporters* (pages 197, 199 and 200); National Westminster Bank Limited, for permission to reproduce their 'shopping basket' advertisement (page 117); Oyez Communications Group, for permission to reproduce their Bill of Exchange form (page 124).

Cartoons were kindly provided by: *Accountancy* (pages 15, 36, 48, 97, 119, 145, 151, 156, 170, 176, 236 and 252); Bank Education Service (page 9); *The Building Societies Institute Journal* (pages 55, 62 and 73); *Journal of the Institute of Bankers* (pages 4, 115, 122, 137, 164, 181, 185, 194, 214 and 227).

D. C.

Contents

xiv Contents

The Business of Banking

1.1 What is a Bank?

If you mention a bank most people in England and Wales will think only of the branches of the 'big four' banks—Barclays, Lloyds, Midland and National Westminster—that are found on every High Street. They are commonly known as *clearing banks*, because they are members of the London Bankers' Clearing House through which many thousands of cheques and credits are 'cleared' or sorted daily (see Unit 10.9). These, with other, smaller, clearing banks and a range of more specialized banks such as merchant banks, foreign banks and savings banks, together with the central bank, the Bank of England, make up the varied structure of British banking. (The Bank of England—which, despite its name, controls all aspects of banking throughout Britain—and the present-day British banking structure are considered in Units 4 and 5 respectively.)

Every bank performs three basic functions:

(i) it accepts and safeguards deposits of money from customers;
(ii) it permits money to be withdrawn or transferred from one account to another;
(iii) it lends the surplus of deposited money to customers who wish to borrow.

The word that is common to these functions is *money*, and the development of money is discussed in Unit 2.

1.2 Responsibilities of Banks

A sound banking system depends partly on the control exercised by the central bank and, to a large extent, on trust: that is, the customer's trust that his deposits will be looked after in the best possible way and that when he wishes to withdraw his money, the funds will be available. The banks have a major responsibility to behave like good citizens in business: while profitability remains a major consideration, this must sometimes be set aside in favour of an informed and ethical judgement that takes account of the interests of others. In Britain in the early 1970s, for instance, some banks made errors of judgement in lending too much to certain sectors of the business community, notably in the property market. Several of the smaller banks would have failed if it had not been for assistance organized by the Bank of England, funded mainly by the clearing banks.

Whenever banks lend money it is their customers' money that is being advanced, so it is important that they should lend where there is a minimal risk of non-repayment. They have often been criticized for not lending more freely, but a high risk of loss will frequently deter them from granting an advance, even if the highest rates of interest could be charged.

1.3   The Role of the Banks

In Unit 1.1 we saw that the basic functions of any bank are to accept, safeguard and lend the surplus funds of its customers while permitting the withdrawal of funds, or their transfer from one account to another. Nowadays, the banks have come a long way from their origins in the London goldsmiths of the late seventeenth century (see Unit 3.1), and while some specialize in meeting the needs of particular groups of customers, such as companies or small savers, the clearing banks provide a range of services to satisfy the financial needs of all types of customer, from the smallest personal account holder to the largest company. These services can be grouped under the following headings:

(i) deposits and savings;
(ii) advances;
(iii) money transmission;
(iv) financial and advisory services;
(v) foreign services.

We shall consider the scope of these services briefly, one by one, though each is dealt with in greater detail later in this book.

(i) **Deposits** are the funds that customers leave in their accounts, whether these are current accounts, which are for 'current' money that is not intended to be saved, or deposit or savings accounts which are for money that will not be required immediately. Customers with a current account are usually issued with a cheque book which enables them to *draw* or write out cheques that instruct the bank to pay cash from the account or to make payments to other people. Deposit and savings account holders do not have the benefits of a cheque book; instead they are paid interest on monies left with the bank.

(ii) **Advances** are the monies lent by a bank, generally in the form of an *overdraft* on a current account, by which the customer draws out more money than he has put in to the account. They may also be made by means of a *loan* or *personal loan*. Interest is charged on all advances, the rate varying with the method of granting the advance, the creditworthiness of the customer and the length of time for which the funds are borrowed. Advances represent that part of customers' deposits which the bank consider may safely be lent, while the remainder is retained in the form of cash and other assets.

(iii) **Money transmission** enables customers to make payments without having to carry around large sums of cash, because the cheque is a convenient method of settling a debt. Equally a customer can pay in money at any bank branch for the credit of an account at another branch by completing a simple form known as a *bank giro credit*. He may also instruct his bank to *debit* or deduct amounts from his account to make regular payments to meet recurring debts, such as club subscriptions, life assurance premiums or mortgage repayments, by means of the *standing order* or *direct debit* systems (see Unit 11).

Besides enabling customers and, to some extent, non-customers to transfer funds quickly and easily by means of a piece of paper, the banks physically move many thousands of pounds worth of notes and coin from branch to branch each day. This is to ensure that branches which regularly pay out more notes and coin than they receive will never be short of cash. For instance, some denominations of coin are in constant demand by shopkeepers, and other coins are needed by private customers for gas and electricity meters. So some branches, particularly those where gas and electricity boards and bus companies pay in, regularly have surpluses of coin needing to be transported to other branches that have a deficit.

(iv) **Financial and advisory services** cover a wide range of facilities that can be tailored to suit the individual needs of the customer. Financial services vary. One form is the *cheque guarantee card* for personal customers, which can be used to guarantee or 'back up' a cheque when paying for goods in a shop or drawing cash at branches other than that at which the account is maintained. Another might be a business service such as *factoring*, in which the bank administers a client's sales ledger and enables a company to obtain an advance against debts which are due to it. The major banks are always willing to give advice, from suggesting suitable investments to a customer with a few hundred pounds, to advising a private limited company of the best time to 'go public', that is, to have its shares quoted on a stock exchange. These services are discussed more fully in Units 14 and 15.

(v) **Foreign services** of the banks include travellers' cheque and currency services; they also make international payments. All large banks have links with overseas banking groups, so payments of this kind can easily be made. Some banks have linked more formally with a number of overseas banks to form consortia which are able to provide large-scale finance to suit the needs of multi-national corporations. Foreign banking services are discussed more fully in Units 11 and 16.

1.4 The Economic Importance of Banks

Britain has a highly developed banking and financial system: over 60 per cent of the adult population have a bank account of some kind. The most popular bank account is the *current account*, and nearly 50 per cent of adults have such an account. The London clearing banks have between them nearly 12 000 branches, mainly in England and Wales, while in other parts of the United

Kingdom branch networks are maintained by the Scottish clearing banks and the Northern Ireland banks. The result is that anywhere in Britain it is difficult to be more than a few miles from a bank. A developed banking system permits payments by one person to another to be made safely at reasonable cost both in Britain and overseas. Such payments enable trade and industry to function more efficiently and the role of the banks in assisting exporters with the financial side of their business is a considerable contribution to the economy of Britain.

The banks are important economically because they act as intermediaries between the large number of depositors and those who wish to borrow: in this way they encourage savings by providing the means of attracting and collecting funds through the various types of accounts they offer and their extensive branch network, while at the same time they put such funds to effective use. In January 1979 their total deposits in sterling amounted to £31 122 million, and their sterling advances to customers to £20 822 million, much of this being lent to help finance the commerce and industry that is so important to a trading and manufacturing nation such as Britain. The provision of finance to businesses encourages enterprise and leads to the provision of extra jobs, increased production and less reliance on the import of foreign goods. Lending to personal customers, on the other hand, stimulates demand for goods which again helps to increase production. The banks are able to 'create' money by granting loan or overdraft facilities to a customer to buy goods, since paying for these goods effectively produces new money as soon as the borrower's cheque is paid into the seller's bank account. Thus by allowing an advance,

'No, you *tell them the Board has refused the loan, and I'll keep the engine running*'

a bank deposit has been created; this process is known as the *credit-creation multiplier* (see Unit 2.10).

During the nineteenth century London developed into a major financial centre of the world, and today still plays an important part in the provision of worldwide financial services. All major world banks are represented in London and in few other cities is it possible to find such a wealth of expertise. British banking, by providing services overseas and to overseas customers, contributes greatly to the nation's balance of payments (the account which records imports and exports of Britain in money terms). Banking and other financial services provided by the City of London are known as *invisible exports* because they are services rather than tangible goods. In 1977 banking services contributed £254 million to the nation's invisible earnings.

Everybody in Britain is affected by the work of the banks, whether as a personal deposit customer, as a borrower or simply in working for a business that benefits from a bank advance and the expertise of British banking services. It follows that, with such an important role in the economy, there should be adequate supervision and control of the banking system and this is provided by the central bank, the Bank of England, which is considered in detail in Unit 4.

1.5   Questions

1. What are the basic functions of any bank?

2. How does a sound banking system contribute to the prosperity of a country?
(*The Institute of Bankers*)

3. What are the main services provided by the banks?

4. What is meant by 'deposit banking', and in what ways does it contribute to the expansion of trade and industry?
(*The Institute of Bankers*)

The Development of Money

2.1 A Definition of Money

We saw in Unit 1.1 that *money* is the word common to all the basic functions of a bank. Money can be defined as *anything which passes freely from hand to hand and is generally acceptable in the settlement of a debt.* Although most countries now use a system of bank notes and coins, many different commodities have been used as money by people in various parts of the world and at various times in history: precious metals such as gold and silver, base metals such as iron, beads, stones, seashells and paper, while even cigarettes, soap and chocolate were used in Austria and Germany during and after the Second World War. All of these, at the time of their use as money, passed freely from hand to hand and were generally acceptable in the settlement of a debt.

We are all pleased to receive money as a birthday present and expect to be paid a sum of money at the end of a week's or month's work. This is not because we like the pictures on the bank notes or the colour of the coins: money by itself gives us no benefit—only by spending it can we obtain the things we want. Without some form of money in circulation, the range of goods and services available to us would be considerably reduced and business transactions would be difficult to carry out.

2.2 The Development of the Money System

Although we should find it difficult to manage without money nowadays, people once used to get by without it. The present system, with notes and coins as money, has been arrived at in three distinct stages.

(a) Direct production

This means obtaining or making all the goods you need entirely by yourself without help from others. This was the way in which people lived in Britain right up to the end of the Old Stone Age around 3000 B.C.; during this period each man and his family unit were completely independent of others. Everything that was needed had to be made or obtained by the family: if they were hungry, they had to go out and catch food; if they wanted somewhere to live, they had to build it themselves. In our technological society, direct production of all goods is wholly impracticable: think how difficult it would be if you had to make your own transistor radio or your own clothes and shoes.

(b) Indirect production using barter as the medium of exchange

Indirect production means producing goods for others as well as for yourself. It develops when a man has more than enough goods for his own family and decides to barter or exchange his surplus with someone who has other goods available. For example, a man who is skilled at fishing but poor at catching rabbits can exchange his surplus fish with a man who is a clever rabbit-catcher but an incompetent fisherman. With indirect production goods are exchanged for other goods—an arrangement that was common throughout Britain from the beginning of the New Stone Age (about 3000 B.C.) until the arrival of the Romans in A.D. 43.

There are several drawbacks to barter:

(i) **Double coincidence of wants.** This is the problem of finding someone who wants what you have on offer *and* who also has available what you want. The fisherman seeking a change of diet might try to find someone with eggs to offer, but having found such a person he might be disappointed to learn that he isn't anxious to exchange his eggs for fish but instead wants some cooking pots.

(ii) **Exchange rates.** The difficulty here is in fixing the relative values of the two commodities being bartered: for example, how many fish is one rabbit worth?

(iii) **Giving change.** With small items like fish and rabbits, this is not much of a problem. However, imagine a man who, having worked for days making a table, now wants a rabbit for his dinner. He realizes that his table is going to be worth a considerable number of rabbits but, if he only wants one, what will the rabbit-catcher give him for 'change'? It is rather like going into a baker's shop for a loaf of bread with only a £10 note, and finding that the baker can't give you change in the form of money and you have to take the 'change' in extra bread and cakes!

Thus bartering makes it possible for a person to obtain the goods or services that he has not the skill or the time to produce for himself, but it is beset with problems and is a slow and inefficient way of trading.

(c) Indirect production using money as a medium of exchange

This is the stage of monetary development that we have now reached in Britain and in all other developed countries; in this system money overcomes the problems inherent in barter, and acts as the medium of exchange. In these countries indirect production is carried to a high degree so that people specialize in their own jobs. The economist Adam Smith in his book *The Wealth of Nations*, which was published in 1776, pointed out the benefits of specialization and the division of a production process into separate tasks each performed by a different person. A modern factory is an example of this: as the item being manufactured passes along the production line, each worker in turn adds the parts or performs the tasks that are his contribution to the finished product. This specialization and division of labour is a part of almost everybody's experience, whether or not he works in a factory: bank clerks, doctors, nurses, teachers, secretaries and shop assistants are all specialists in their own particular skills and make their own contributions to trade and society.

In return for doing our specialist jobs, we each receive money at the end of the week or month. Some people are paid in cash, but many of us have our earnings paid direct into our bank accounts: we then withdraw whatever we require in the form of cash. When we pay for goods and services, money acts as the medium of exchange: just as we are prepared to accept money in exchange for our work, a shopkeeper is prepared to accept it in payment for goods.

2.3   Functions of Money

Whether it is in the form of shells or sovereigns, iron bars or paper bank notes, the functions of money are the same.

(a) A medium of exchange
Money forms the intermediary in a trading transaction. If we want to sell something, we are prepared to accept money from the buyer; if we want to buy, we know that the seller will accept money in payment.

(b) A unit of account
This function of money enables prices to be directly compared. One of the problems of the barter system lies in the agreement of a rate of exchange between commodities: how many fish is one rabbit worth, or how many rabbits should be paid for a cooking pot? When all rates of exchange have a common denominator—money—it is easy to compare the prices of different commodities.

A unit of account also enables us to keep accounting records, such as bank statements, invoices and ledgers, by using money amounts.

(c) A store of value
Money should, ideally, remain reasonably stable in value so that if we save we know that, when we come to spend our savings, we can buy a similar amount of goods as we could have done at the time when we put the savings aside. In times of inflation, money does not perform this function very well. For example, something that could have been bought for £1 in Britain in 1951 would have cost £4 in 1977.

For money to be a store of value it is not necessary for it to be valuable in itself; the fact that money does buy, and will buy in the future, a certain quantity of goods gives it the value. A Bank of England £5 note by itself has

little value—it is only a printed piece of paper—but provided there are goods to purchase in the future, it acts as a store of value.

(d) A standard for deferred payments

Money acts as the measure in which deferred or future payments are to be made. For example, a bank loan agreement states that the borrower will repay a certain amount of money each month for a number of months: these deferred payments, to be received by the bank in the future, are stated in terms of money.

2.4 The Qualities of Money

In order to perform the functions of money satisfactorily, the money in use must have certain qualities.

(a) Acceptability

This is the most important quality of money: people must be prepared to accept the money in use. Otherwise it will cease to be regarded as money, and either the barter system will return, or some other acceptable commodity will take over as money.

(b) Cognizability

To assist in acceptability, money should be cognizable—that is, people should recognize it easily as the money in use.

(c) Divisibility

As we said in Unit 2.2, one of the drawbacks of the barter system was the difficulty of giving change. As an aid to acceptability, money should be easily divisible with a range of denominations in issue to ensure that goods of different prices can be purchased with the exact money or that change can easily be given where money of a higher denomination is offered.

(d) Durability

It is a help if the money in circulation is durable—that is, it should last for a reasonable time without deterioration. If dead rabbits were acceptable as money they would soon start to go bad and there wouldn't be much incentive to save. In Britain, bank notes have an average life of about twelve months and coins usually last about twenty years.

(e) Portability

Money should be easy to carry in both large and small amounts. If blocks of granite were used as money, you would find it difficult to carry your life savings with you and such a currency would soon be replaced by something more portable.

(f) Scarcity

To be generally acceptable, the supply of money must be restricted. If money consisted of stones picked up from the ground or shells washed up on the seashore, the supply would be relatively unlimited and people would not be prepared to accept them in exchange for goods. For many years, precious metals such as gold and silver were used to make coins and because such metals were relatively scarce the supply of money could not increase suddenly. Nowadays most coins are tokens that are worth less as metal than as coins, while for larger denominations we use paper bank notes that are intrinsically almost worthless. However, the quality of scarcity is maintained because the money stock is controlled by the Government and the central bank of the country. In Britain the Treasury (the Government department concerned with finance) and the Bank of England exercise these controls (see Unit 2.8).

(g) Homogeneity

This means that every coin or note has the same buying power and is identical in all respects to every other coin or note of the same denomination. A coin that was minted ten years ago, when it would have bought more than it can today because of the effects of inflation, nevertheless has the same buying power now as a brand-new coin of the same denomination. Equally one new ten-pence piece buys the same amount of goods and services as any other, and all ten-pence pieces look alike, weigh the same and are just the same size. Older coins still circulate in Britain, however, such as the one- and two-shilling pieces, which are regarded as equal in buying power to the five- and ten-pence coins respectively and are of the same weight and size as their post-decimalization counterparts.

2.5 A History of Coins in Britain

In Britain coins can be traced back to the first century B.C. when iron bars were used as currency in the Midlands and south-west, while at the same time some gold and silver coins imported from Gaul (northern France) were also circulating alongside the iron bars in the south. The first true coins to be minted in Britain were crudely made from copper and tin and were in use during the half-century before the arrival of the Romans. When the Romans arrived in A.D. 43 they brought with them their own coins, which were usually made of silver, and gradually the iron bars and the old copper and tin coins went out of circulation. During the third century A.D. the Romans started to mint their own coins in London.

Following the departure of the Romans in A.D. 410, many people in Britain must have reverted to barter for a time. The minting of coins was restarted during a time of prosperity in the Anglo-Saxon period when the local rulers in each area minted their own silver coins. During the reign of Offa, king of Mercia, in the eighth century, a coinage was introduced based on a pound weight of silver. The Latin words for pound by weight were *libra pondo*, hence our present word 'pound'; from this weight of silver was made 240 coins named 'denarii' after a Roman coin of similar value. Until the end of the thirteenth century the denarius (or penny as it later became known) was virtually the only coin in circulation in Britain. William the Conqueror continued the development of the silver coinage by introducing a new silver standard, known as *sterling silver*, which had 925 parts of pure silver in every 1 000. This standard was to remain in use almost continuously up to 1920.

The Norman kings established the pounds, shillings and pence system which was to remain unchanged until the decimalization of the British currency in 1971. The Normans used the Roman system of accounting with the *libra* (one pound weight of silver) as the major unit of currency. The *libra* was divided into twenty *solidi* (later to become the shilling), and these were further subdivided into twelve *denarii* (pennies). This currency was based on the weight of silver and it was not until the thirteenth and fourteenth centuries that gold coins started to re-appear.

Henry VII introduced the gold sovereign in 1489, with a money value of one pound—the first time that a pound coin had been issued. By 1504, he had also introduced the silver shilling, which remains in circulation today as a cupro-nickel five-pence piece. During the reign of Charles II the silver penny was withdrawn and copper coins were introduced (in 1672). One of the problems of gold and silver coins was the ease with which unscrupulous people could 'clip' scraps of the precious metal from their edges, a difficulty that was overcome when Charles II introduced a machine designed by a Frenchman to manufacture coins with milled edges. Even today the British cupro-nickel five- and ten-pence coins retain the milled edge.

Gold and silver coins circulated in Britain for hundreds of years and silver continued to be used in the coinage until 1947. The silver standard, with the *pound 'sterling'* based on one pound weight of silver, continued until the recoinage of 1816 when the country 'went on to the gold standard', that is, the currency became linked to the price of gold and all bank notes could be exchanged for gold (see Unit 2.7). Since 1947, coins in circulation in Britain have had no precious metal content, and their metal content is worth less than their face value.

The Royal Mint, which is under the control of the Chancellor of the Exchequer, manufactures coins for use in Britain and other countries. The metal is purchased in the market and British coins are sold at face value to the Bank of England, which arranges for their distribution to the banks. As most coins are token coins the Royal Mint makes a considerable profit each year, and this passes to the Government.

2.6   A History of Bank Notes in Britain

The history of the bank note is bound up with the development of the banking system in Britain. Here we are concerned only with the bank note itself; Unit 3 deals in detail with the history of banking services.

From Roman times onwards, coins were the only form of money in Britain until the second half of the seventeenth century, when London goldsmiths started to hold gold and silver coins for safe-keeping on behalf of their clients. In exchange for these coins they would issue receipts promising to repay the amount deposited on demand. As the goldsmiths were well-known and trusted, their promissory notes soon began to circulate among merchants as a form of currency in the settlement of debts. To encourage this the goldsmiths began issuing their receipts in convenient denominations, such as £10 and £50, and made them payable to bearer rather than to a named individual—this helped to make them more easily transferable. In 1694 the Bank of England was founded and, from the start, had the right to issue notes (see Unit 4).

Outside London there were few goldsmiths, and banking and bank notes were slower to develop. During the eighteenth and early nineteenth centuries, however, wealthy industrialists and merchants in most parts of the country formed a large number of small private banks. Nearly all of these banks issued their own notes which circulated freely in their respective localities.

A series of Acts of Parliament in the nineteenth century gradually established the monopoly of the note issue in England and Wales in the hands of the Bank of England. The most important of these, the Bank Charter Act of 1844, was to extinguish the note issues of the private banks as they went bankrupt or merged with the developing joint-stock banks, which have become the present-day clearing banks. The monopoly of the note issue in England and Wales was not achieved until 1921 when the last private bank with its own note issue (Fox, Fowler & Company of Wellington in Somerset) was absorbed by Lloyds Bank Ltd.

A further provision of the 1844 Bank Charter Act gave the Bank of England the authority to make a *fiduciary issue* of bank notes. A fiduciary issue (or *trust issue*) is backed solely by Government securities and not by gold and silver. The Act permitted the Bank of England to make a fiduciary issue of £14 million, with every note issued above this amount being backed pound for pound by gold and silver held in the vaults. The issue was to be increased by two-thirds of the amount of the note issue of any private bank that merged with a joint-stock bank or went bankrupt.

The fiduciary issue has increased greatly over the years, largely as a result of two world wars and the general inflationary trend. In 1939, at the outbreak of the Second World War, the remaining stock of gold backing the note issue was transferred to pay for imports and since that date there has been no gold backing the note issue; that is, it has all been a fiduciary issue backed entirely by Government securities. From £14 million in 1844, the fiduciary issue had increased to £8 850 million by February 1979. Nowadays, the amount of notes in circulation depends in practice on public demand: the Treasury and the Bank of England are less concerned with the value of notes in circulation than with controlling the growth of the money stock (see Unit 2.8).

In Scotland, the Bank of England's monopoly of the note issue did not apply, and there were no restrictions at first on the growth of joint-stock banking as there were in England and Wales (see Unit 3.2). Such banks developed early and each issued its own notes. In 1845, an Act of Parliament was passed regulating Scottish note issues: no new note-issuing banks were to be allowed

Table 2.1   Notes and coins circulating in Britain (£ millions)

Date	Total	Bank of England	Scottish Clearing banks	Northern Ireland banks	Estimated coin	Held by banks	Estimated circulation with the public
December 1966	3 428	3 063	135	9	221	737	2 690
December 1968	3 735	3 338	146	13	238	787	2 947
December 1970	4 199	3 670	160	20	349	903	3 296
December 1972	4 955	4 380	189	28	359	865	4 090
December 1974	6 325	5 631	248	31	415	1 159	5 166
December 1976	7 906	7 075	310	38	483	1 180	6 726
December 1977	9 058	8 144	362	43	509	1 232	7 826
December 1978	10 349	9 306	424	49	570	1 458	8 891

Source: *Monthly Digest of Statistics*, Central Statistical Office

and a fixed fiduciary issue was imposed on the nineteen issuing banks already in existence. Amalgamations have reduced the number of Scottish banks retaining their own note issue, and now only three remain: the Bank of Scotland, the Clydesdale Bank and the Royal Bank of Scotland. Nowadays the note issues of the Scottish banks are comparatively small and, apart from the fiduciary issue, are largely backed by holdings of Bank of England notes. A similar scheme operates in Northern Ireland where a few joint-stock banks also retain the right to issue their own notes. Table 2.1 compares the currency circulation of Bank of England notes with those issued by the Scottish and Northern Ireland banks.

2.7   The Gold Standard

When Britain went on to the gold standard in 1816, the gold sovereign became the legal standard coin. In a country that is on the gold standard the currency is worth a fixed amount of gold and bank notes may be exchanged for the gold at which they are valued. In Britain the Mint price of gold was fixed at £3. 17s. 10½d. (£3.89) per standard ounce, eleven-twelfths fine (this means a purity of eleven parts of pure gold in every twelve parts of metal).

The convertibility of bank notes into gold continued almost without a break until it was suspended at the outbreak of the First World War in 1914, when gold sovereigns were withdrawn from circulation and replaced by special bank notes issued by the Treasury which circulated alongside Bank of England notes.

The gold standard remained suspended until 1925 when the gold bullion standard was introduced. This was different from the gold standard in that individual bank notes were not convertible, but gold bullion (the metal in the form of bars) was obtainable at the Bank of England in a minimum quantity of a 400-ounce bar at a cost of approximately £1 500, so that the currency was still technically convertible into gold. Naturally, few people took advantage of this arrangement; it was abandoned in 1931 and the currency has been inconvertible ever since. After their withdrawal in 1914, gold coins were never reintroduced for use in Britain.

2.8   The Money Stock

The growth of the fiduciary issue in Britain from £14 million in 1844 to £8 850 million by February 1979 (see Unit 2.6) does not reflect the even bigger increase in the growth of bank deposits. We use notes and coin to pay bills and make purchases: these obviously form part of the money stock. We also use cheques to make payments: cheques are not money in themselves but are a claim on the money in a bank account and are normally accepted as a medium of exchange. Therefore, when calculations are made about the size of the stock of money in a country, the balances of bank current accounts must be included. A further calculation of the money stock also includes other items, such as the balances of deposit accounts that are not generally accepted as money in the narrow sense of being a medium of exchange because they are subject to a period of notice of withdrawal. These are included because they affect the growth of bank lending and credit creation (see Unit 2.10). Both bank current and deposit account balances, although not money in the form of notes and coin, can be called *near-money* (see Unit 2.9).

'It's not so much the money supply that worries me—it's the credit card supply'

At present three definitions of the money stock are in official use in Britain: M1, sterling M3, and M3. (There was once an intermediate definition, M2; but its use was discontinued at the end of 1971, following the changes in the banking structure that took place in that year (see Unit 4.11) which made it a misleading figure.)

(i) M1 consists of notes and coin in circulation with the public plus sterling sight deposits held by the private sector only. (*Sight deposits* are funds available on demand, such as bank current account balances, including money at call and money placed overnight; the *private sector* means individuals, companies and institutions not owned by the state; the *public sector*, on the other hand, includes all Government departments and state-owned corporations.)

(ii) Sterling M3 comprises notes and coin in circulation with the public together with all sterling deposits, including certificates of deposit, held by United Kingdom residents in both the public and private sectors. (Certificates of deposit are a special type of long-term bank deposit and are discussed in Unit 7.11.)

(iii) M3 consists of sterling M3 together with all deposits held by United Kingdom residents in other currencies.

In all these definitions the deposits considered are confined to those with institutions included in the United Kingdom banking sector as defined by the Bank of England, but 60 per cent of the net value of sterling transit items (cheques and credits passing through the bank clearing system) is deducted. Fig. 2.1 shows the growth of M1 and sterling M3 from 1972 to 1978.

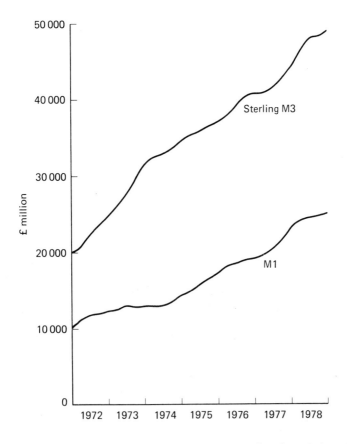

Fig. 2.1   Money stock: amounts outstanding, seasonally adjusted (from data given in the Bank of England Quarterly Bulletin)

2.9   Near-money

Near-money may be defined as assets that are transferable and therefore can be passed in the settlement of a debt, but which have not achieved all of the qualities and functions of money mentioned in Units 2.3 and 2.4. The definitions of money stock given in Unit 2.8 include several types of near-money found in the banking sector.

(i) **Sight deposits.** These are generally current accounts from which money may be withdrawn on demand.

(ii) **Deposits subject to notice of withdrawal.** These include deposit accounts where a minimum notice of withdrawal of seven days is required, and term deposits and certificates of deposit where funds are placed for a fixed period of time and may not normally be withdrawn before the expiration of the time.

(iii) **Money at call, overnight and short notice.** These terms generally refer to the surplus funds of banking and other financial institutions that are deposited with other banks for short periods of time.

The definition of near-money can be widened to include funds deposited with building societies, National Savings Certificates, Premium Savings Bonds, postal orders, shares in companies, bills of exchange and so on. It could also include items such as trading stamps and luncheon vouchers which are from time to time acceptable as money. However, the definition is generally considered to be restricted to the assets and liabilities of the banking system. The reason for this is because of the ability of the banks to 'create' more money as a result of the credit-creation multiplier.

2.10   How the Banks 'Create' Money

In January 1979, notes and coin estimated to be in circulation with the public in Britain totalled £8 382 million, M1 was £25 730 million and sterling M3 was £50 390 million. How is it that the money stock, M1 and M3, can exceed the value of notes and coin in circulation?

This happens because of the way in which the banks are able to create money in the form of bank deposits. It has been said that every bank loan creates a bank deposit: whenever a manager grants overdraft or loan facilities, the customer will have a reason for wishing to borrow—to buy a new car, perhaps—and will draw a cheque on his account to pay for it. The cheque will be paid into another bank account (that of the garage selling the car) thus creating a new deposit, and when it has passed through the clearing system will take up the facilities granted by the manager. Therefore, by granting an advance, a new deposit has been created somewhere in the banking system and the money stock increased.

The banks generally lend between 60 and 70 per cent of their total deposits, the remainder being held in the form of easily realizable assets so that the banks will always have sufficient resources to enable them to repay their depositors. Every loan creates a new deposit, and a proportion of every new deposit may be re-lent to create still further deposits. This process can continue until the total of the new deposits created is several times the amount of the original advance.

An example will show just how this process works. Bank *A* grants its customer, *M*, an overdraft of £500 to buy some new furniture. *M* writes out a cheque and hands it to the seller of the furniture, *N*, who pays it into his account with bank *B*. This bank keeps 35 per cent of the deposit as reserves and re-lends the other 65 per cent, £325, to customer *O* to pay for his holiday. *O* gives a cheque for this amount to the travel agent *P*, who pays it into his account with bank *C*. This bank lends 65 per cent of the deposit, £210, to customer *Q*, who issues a cheque for this amount, which creates another deposit within the banking system, and so the process goes on (see Fig. 2.2).

The amount by which the banks can create further bank deposits, and thus increase the money stock, is measured by the *credit-creation multiplier*. From Fig. 2.2 it can be calculated that an original advance of £500 has created deposits totalling £1 410. In this example there is, therefore, a multiplier effect of

$$\frac{\text{Total amount of new deposits created}}{\text{Amount of original advance}} = \frac{£1\,410}{£500} = 2.8.$$

The multiplier is easy to calculate if you know the percentage of deposits

Original overdraft granted for	£500
Cheque drawn and deposit created	£500
Overdraft granted: 65%[†] of £500	£325
Overdraft granted: 65% of £325	£210
Overdraft granted: 65% of £210	£135
Overdraft granted: 65% of £135	£90
Overdraft granted: 65% of £90	£60
Overdraft granted: 65% of £60	£40
Overdraft granted: 65% of £40	£25
Overdraft granted: 65% of £25	£15
Overdraft granted: 65% of £15	£10

[†]assumes that 35% of all deposits is kept in the form of reserves

Fig. 2.2   The credit-creation process

retained as reserves and not re-lent. In the example, 35 per cent was retained as reserves. Divide the reserves percentage (35 per cent) into 1 (100 per cent) and the answer, 2.8, is the multiplier effect.

Of course, a bank manager does not have to wait for deposits to be paid in before he can grant loan or overdraft facilities; but the bank as a whole must consider its total deposits when formulating its lending policy.

2.11   Legal Tender

Legal tender may be defined as the notes and coins which must be accepted when offered in payment. In Unit 2.8 we saw how cheques are a claim on the money in a bank account; while they are usually acceptable as a medium of exchange, they are not legal tender and the person being paid can, if he wishes, refuse to accept a cheque in settlement. He is, however, legally bound to accept notes and coin within certain limits: in Britain, Bank of England notes are legal tender up to any amount, fifty-pence pieces are legal tender up to £10, five- and ten-pence coins up to £5 and bronze coins up to 20p. Scottish and Northern Ireland bank notes are not legal tender, although in their own areas they enjoy a status equal to that of Bank of England notes.

2.12   Questions

1. Give a definition of money; describe the main functions of money.

2. What are the qualities of money? How well does the money in use in your country today meet these qualities?

3. Trace the development of (i) notes and coin, and (ii) paper money in England and Wales.

4. Define any *two* of the following, giving illustrative examples as appropriate: (a) near-money; (b) legal tender; (c) the fiduciary issue.
   (*The Institute of Bankers*)

5. What are the disadvantages of the barter system?

6. Trace the development of paper money in England and Wales from gold-smiths' receipts to the present-day bank note.
   (*The Institute of Bankers*)

7. Whatever comes into use as money must possess certain qualities. Discuss these qualities as found in present-day forms of money.
   (*The Institute of Bankers*)

8. What are the main functions of money? What effect does inflation have upon money's ability to perform these functions?
   (*The Institute of Bankers*)

The Development of Banking in Britain

3.1 Origins

In the days before the London goldsmiths of the seventeenth-century began accepting deposits of coin and other valuables (see Unit 2.6), city merchants and other wealthy people kept such items at the Royal Mint, which at that time was situated in the Tower of London. In 1640 King Charles I needed money to pay for his army and, unable to persuade Parliament to vote him the cash he wanted, he seized £200 000 of bullion belonging to the merchants. This, of course, meant that the Mint could no longer be used as a public safe-deposit so the merchants began to search for other places where they could keep their valuables. The goldsmiths, because of their trade, had excellent strongrooms, so they became an obvious choice.

As an acknowledgment for deposits the goldsmiths issued receipts and soon found that their receipts were being passed from one trader to another in the settlement of debts. This saved a trader with a debt to pay from having to go to his goldsmith, present the receipt, draw out the coins required and then hand them over to his creditor, who would immediately deposit them with his own goldsmith: it was much simpler just to transfer the receipt. To help in this, the goldsmiths began to issue receipts in convenient denominations and to make them payable to bearer so that the title to the receipt would 'pass by delivery'. Present-day British bank notes are payable to bearer in the same way and whoever is in possession of a note, provided he came by it honestly, has the legal title to it and may pass that title on by *delivering* or negotiating the note to another person.

The goldsmiths began to concentrate on the banking side of their business and soon found that, at any one time, only a small proportion of the coins they were holding for safe-keeping would be required to meet demands for repayment of their receipts. They began to lend the surplus monies and to charge interest for doing so; other services were developed such as deposit accounts, discounting (or 'cashing') bills of exchange before the date for payment, and dealing in bullion and foreign currencies. By 1677 there were forty-four gold-smith–bankers operating in London.

3.2 Formation of the Bank of England

The Bank of England was founded in 1694 with a capital of £1·2 million by a group of wealthy London merchants and financiers. It was established under royal charter, which gave it *joint-stock* status, a rather quaint phrase implying that its standing was equivalent to that of the present-day limited company. At that time there was no concept of the company; the most usual forms of business unit were the individual and the partnership. When a group of people wished to pool their money in a common venture it was necessary to obtain a special charter from the Crown. The King, William III, was only too pleased to grant a royal charter to the Bank of England, because in return the capital subscribed of £1.2 million was lent to him to finance his war against France. The charter, which was to be periodically renewed, also gave the new bank the right to issue notes, payable on demand, up to the amount of the loan to the King.

The Bank of England Act of 1709 renewed the Bank's charter, and also laid down that, as long as the Bank continued in business, no other corporation or partnership of more than six persons could issue bank notes payable on demand or within six months in England and Wales. This clause gave the Bank an effective monopoly of joint-stock banking which was to last until 1826 (see Unit 3.4).

In 1715, for the first time, the Bank acted as agent for the issue and management of a British Government loan, which we know today as the National Debt, and during the first half of the eighteenth century it became banker to the principal Government departments. Both of these functions are still performed by the Bank today.

The London goldsmith–bankers, together with a number of new firms, continued to issue their own notes until 1770 when they decided to abandon their own issues in favour of Bank of England notes. The withdrawal of their notes brought about a more general use of cheques in London and in 1773, for their mutual convenience, they established the London Bankers' Clearing House to provide a central place where cheques could be exchanged between themselves. As time went by, they opened accounts with the Bank of England, in which they deposited their spare funds: they came to regard these funds as their ultimate reserves and, when necessary, would ask the Bank for loan facilities to help them overcome a financial crisis. This helped to establish the Bank as a 'lender of last resort' (see Unit 4.8).

3.3   Rise of the Private Country Banker

Outside London the business of banking was slower to develop: the goldsmiths did not attempt to open branches in the provincial cities because of the problems of transport and communications in the late seventeenth and early eighteenth centuries. There were also restrictions on the size of banking firms imposed by the 1709 Act (see Unit 3.2). Nor, at this time, did the Bank of England open any branches in the provinces. It was left to the wealthy merchant to found a bank in his own locality. Thus, just as the goldsmiths had done, the merchants added banking to an already established trade and the numbers of country banks grew rapidly, especially in the second half of the eighteenth century (see Table 3.1).

Table 3.1　Numbers of private and joint-stock banks (excluding the Bank of England and foreign banks) in England and Wales, 1750–1978

Year	Number of private banks outside London	Joint-stock banks Number of banks	Number of branches
1750	12	—	—
1776	150	—	—
1797	230	—	—
1800	350	—	—
1810	721	—	—
1825	554	—	—
1833	430	50	not known
1844	273	105	486
1884	172	118	1 621
1904	35	65	4 414
1934	nil	16	10 131
1978	nil	6	11 600

Most banks printed their own bank notes and nowadays these old notes are in demand as collectors' items. From 1808, a private bank needed a licence before it could print money, but this only cost £30 per year and the bank was then free to print and issue as many notes as the public could be persuaded to accept, the only restriction being that the value of the minimum-denomination note was to be £1. Some country banks also issued their own coins, but this practice was prohibited by Parliament in 1812. Outside London the cheque did not start to come into general use before the development of the joint-stock banks in the 1830s (see Unit 3.4), and until this time most payments for substantial amounts were made using the notes of the private banks.

A major problem of the private country banks was that, if they wished to issue notes, the 1709 Act restricted their size to a maximum of six partners—in practice many were smaller. This meant that they were unable to set up large branch networks, such as those maintained by the major clearing banks today, and few developed beyond their immediate neighbourhoods. Moreover, there was the additional difficulty that a small local bank was unable to spread its risks: if it operated in an agricultural area, a farming crisis could result in failure of the bank; similarly, in an industrial town, the collapse of one or two large businesses could affect it severely. A further probelm was that banking had developed initially as a sideline to other businesses—rather like the present-day sub-post office and stores—and there was often a lack of professional banking expertise and sometimes a conflict of interest in decision-making. Since, apart from the licensing system, there was no central control of the note issue, a bank could issue as many notes as it could put into circulation. With the country on the gold standard from 1816 onwards, anybody holding bank notes could demand to be paid in gold: there only had to be a rumour that the local bank was in difficulties and it would be besieged by crowds of people demanding payment, almost certainly leading to the bank closing its doors and possibly failing.

3.4   Development of the Joint-stock Banks

In 1825 there was a severe financial crisis, resulting in the failure of ninety private banks. This led the Government to pass legislation in 1826 in an attempt to stabilize the banking system. The opening of joint-stock banks, with their own note issue, was to be allowed outside a radius of sixty-five miles (105 km) from London, although they were not to be permitted to set up offices within the area around the capital. In addition, the Government persuaded the Bank of England to establish a number of provincial branches; they were opened as follows:

    1826: Gloucester, Manchester, Swansea
    1827: Birmingham, Leeds, Exeter, Liverpool, Bristol
    1828: Newcastle upon Tyne
    1829: Norwich, Hull
    1834: Plymouth, Portsmouth

(Today the Bank, with its head office in Threadneedle Street in the City of London, has branches in Birmingham, Bristol, Leeds, Liverpool, Manchester, Newcastle upon Tyne and Southampton, together with a representative office in Glasgow.)

For a time the development of a branch network by the Bank of England delayed the establishment of joint-stock banks and the first was opened outside the area covered by the Bank, at Lancaster in 1826, followed shortly by others at Norwich, Bristol and Huddersfield. By 1833 nearly fifty joint-stock banks had been established and, in the same year, the Act of Parliament renewing the Bank of England's charter permitted joint-stock banking within the London area provided that the new banks did not issue notes—a restriction that hastened the development of the cheque as a means of money transfer. The Act also made Bank of England notes legal tender.

The success of the 1826 and 1833 Acts is demonstrated by the rise in the number of joint-stock banks and the simultaneous fall in the number of private country banks shown in Table 3.1. In 1844, following further severe financial crises, the Bank Charter Act was passed; it had three main provisions:

(i) the note-issuing function of the Bank of England was to be separated from the Bank's other activities by forming two departments: the Issue Department and the Banking Department.

(ii) the establishment of a fiduciary issue (see Unit 2.6) of £14 million; beyond this amount, all notes had to be backed pound for pound by gold and silver held by the Bank.

(iii) ultimately to centralize the note issue of England and Wales in the hands of the Bank of England: the Act prohibited banks already issuing their own notes from increasing the number in circulation. As private banks merged with the developing joint-stock banks or went bankrupt, they were to lose their rights of note issue.

By 1844 the number of joint-stock banks had reached 105 and few new banks were established after this date; by this time also, as Table 3.1 shows, the decline of the private banks had set in. The next sixty years saw the virtual extinction of the private bank, a reduction in the number of joint-stock banks as they merged with one another, and the growth of branch networks. The development of large banks with branches throughout the country was helped by an Act of Parliament in 1862 which extended the privilege of limited liability to banking concerns and opened the way to the establishment of large limited company banks as we know them today. In 1882 the Bills of Exchange Act brought together in one statute the law relating to bills of exchange and cheques. It contained specific provision for crossed cheques and gave protection to banks and customers against loss through theft and fraud, so increasing the usefulness of the cheque and giving banks greater scope for developing their current account business. A series of amalgamations between 1890 and 1914 brought most commercial banking into the hands of sixteen banks; a further series of mergers in 1917 and 1918 reduced the numbers to five large clearing banks, each with a nationwide branch network, and a few smaller banks. There were fears that any continuation of this trend would lead to monopolies in commercial banking that would leave little or no choice for the customers. A Treasury Committee was set up to look into the situation, and its report in 1918 suggested that Government approval should be required for any further amalgamations. Though this recommendation was not given the force of law, the banks concerned entered into a general undertaking not to consider further amalgamations without seeking Treasury approval.

In Scotland joint-stock banking developed much faster than in England, because although the Bank of Scotland was originally granted a monopoly of joint-stock banking similar to that of the Bank of England, this privilege was not continued when its charter was renewed in 1716. Thus the first half of the eighteenth century saw the rapid development of the Scottish banking system along the lines that still exist today.

3.5 The Bank of England Develops as a Central Bank

With the development of the joint-stock banks, the importance of the Bank of England as a commercial bank started to decline. As it strengthened its hold over the note issue, there was a fall in the circulation of private bank notes;

all the other banks opened accounts with the Bank of England and settled their indebtedness with one another by drawing cheques on these accounts.

The emergence of the discount market as a market for discounting bills of exchange (see Unit 7) in the second half of the nineteenth century helped to consolidate the Bank's position as a central bank: in 1890 the Bank announced that it would always in future rediscount approved bills for the discount market at Bank Rate (see Unit 4.9(c)). This meant that the Bank would act as 'lender of last resort' to the discount market and thus, because of the inter-relationships between this market and the banks, indirectly to the banking system.

During the twentieth century the Bank has steadily strengthened its position as a central bank. Early in the century it took the decision to decline new private business of a kind that would put it in direct competition with the other banks. During the First World War, while the Government was borrowing on a substantial scale to finance the war, the Bank was entrusted with the responsibility of raising many loans. In the Second World War it played a large part in devising and implementing measures to deal with the financial and economic consequences of the war effort, and again had the task of covering the Government's wartime borrowing requirements. Interest rates were kept low and the bank rate, to which at that time all bank overdraft rates were related, was held at 2 per cent for the whole of the war, except for a few months in late 1939 when it stood at 4 per cent. In the immediate post-war period the Bank had the task of restoring the country's financial and economic machinery by means of its monetary policies.

Ever since its foundation in 1694 the Bank had remained a company owned by private stockholders, despite its increasing involvement in the financial and economic affairs of the country. In 1946 the Government felt that so important an institution should be brought under its own control, and in that year the Bank of England Act nationalized the Bank. The private stockholders were compensated by the issue of Government stock and the composition of the Court (or board) of Directors, appointed by the Crown, was widened to include representatives of industry and trade unions (previously it had been composed mainly of bankers). The Act gave the Bank wide powers: if the Bank thought it in the public interest, it could request information from bankers and make recommendations to them which, if authorized by the Treasury, could be turned into directions using the force of law, although in such a case the banker would always first be given the opportunity to make representations and explain his position. However, the Bank has no power to make requests and recommendations with respect to the affairs of any particular customer of a banker. Thus the Act gave the Bank legal powers to control the banking and financial systems; previously the Bank had relied on the voluntary co-operation of bankers, and in practice, even today, much of the control is still carried out on an informal and voluntary basis.

Changes are currently taking place to bring all banks under the closer jurisdiction of the Bank of England by a system of statutory control. To bring Britain into line with the banking directive of the European Economic Community (EEC), of which Britain is a member, a Deposit Protection Fund is provided for by the Banking Act, 1979. It will partly insure those who deposit money with recognized banks and licensed deposit-taking institutions, the scheme being paid for by the banks and institutions themselves (see Unit 4.10).

3.6   Emergence of the 'Big Four'

For nearly fifty years after the general undertaking given in 1918 by the clearing banks to obtain Treasury approval of further amalgamations, there was a period of stability in the British banking structure. The only changes from 1918 until the late 1960s were the absorptions of some of the smaller banks by the larger banks: the system in England and Wales became dominated by the 'big five'— Barclays, Lloyds, Midland, National Provincial and Westminster banks. It was a time of consolidation: branch networks were built up, new services were introduced, and affiliations were developed with banks in Scotland and Northern Ireland.

In 1967 a report on bank charges was published by the National Board for Prices and Incomes, which had been set up by the Government to make recommendations about price increases of goods and services and about wage rises. The report, besides considering bank charges, was critical of the 'wasteful' nature of bank competition, and in particular of the spread of new branches of all five of the major clearing banks. The report contained the historic statement:

> Further amalgamation among the banks, carried through to the appropriate point could permit some rationalization of branch networks. The Bank of England and the Treasury have made it plain to us that they would not obstruct some further amalgamation if the banks were willing to contemplate such a development.

Thus the go-ahead was given for further amalgamations, and within a few months the Westminster Bank and the National Provincial Bank (which already owned Coutts & Co. and the District Bank) announced plans for a merger. The proposed merger could have been referred to the Monopolies Commission for investigation to determine whether it would bring about a monopoly and, if so, whether or not it would be detrimental to the public interest; the Government chose not to do this and allowed the merger to take place. The new company became the National Westminster Bank, while Coutts & Co. continues to trade under its own name.

Almost at the same time, Barclays, Lloyds and Martins announced plans to merge into one bank: this would have created a huge banking group which would have had 5 500 branches in England and Wales (out of a total of some 12 000 branches at that time for all the clearing banks). The Government referred this proposal to the Monopolies Commission, which rejected the proposed merger of the three banks, but agreed that Martins, the smallest of the three, could be absorbed either by Barclays or Lloyds; shortly after this, Martins was absorbed into Barclays. In their rejection of the amalgamation of all three, the Monopolies Commission was critical of the way in which the clearing banks did not have to disclose their true profits, and of the joint fixing of interest rates. Both of these matters have now been dealt with: by mutual agreement the banks started to disclose true profits from 1969 and the collective agreement on interest rates was abandoned in 1971 under the terms of the Bank of England's document *Competition and Credit Control* (see Unit 4.11).

In 1970 some of the smaller clearing banks—Glyn, Mills & Co., Williams Deacon's Bank and the English branches of the National Bank—merged to form Williams and Glyn's Bank. In Scotland too, there were mergers to form three large banking groups: the Bank of Scotland, partly owned by Barclays, the Clydesdale Bank, wholly owned by Midland, and the Royal Bank of Scotland which forms part of the National and Commercial banking group, which also owns Williams and Glyn's Bank.

Commercial banking in Britain is now dominated by the London clearing banks, the Scottish clearing banks and the Northern Ireland banks, which together have some 13 500 branches and sub-branches across the country and employ nearly 300 000 staff. During recent years the British banking structure has been enhanced by a range of newer banks: some from overseas, some formed to meet specialist financial needs and some developing new areas of work as the sophistication of their customers increases. The present structure of banking in Britain is considered in detail in Unit 5.

3.7   Questions

1. Outline the history and development of the Bank of England.

   (The Institute of Bankers)

2. What effect did the report of the National Board for Prices and Incomes on bank charges in 1967 have on the development of British banking?

3. Trace the development of commercial banking in England and Wales from the London goldsmiths of the seventeenth century to the 'big four' London clearing banks of the 1970s.

4. What were the main provisions of the 1844 Bank Charter Act?

The Bank of England

4.1 What is a Central Bank?

Every country with an established banking system has a central bank which acts as banker to the Government in the widest sense. It liaises with and advises the Government on monetary policy and ensures that the necessary steps are taken to carry it through.

Central banks differ from commercial banks in certain respects:

(i) they do not aim to maximize profits, which is traditionally an objective of a commercial bank owned by shareholders (central banks are normally nationalized institutions);

(ii) those who govern them are much more closely involved with the work of Government departments than are their counterparts in commercial banking;

(iii) they have a supervisory role over the commercial banks which usually has the backing of law;

(iv) they are able to influence the actions of the commercial banks and other financial institutions, particularly with regard to lending;

(v) they control the issue of notes and coin;

(vi) they do not compete for business with the commercial banks, but they usually maintain the Government bank accounts;

(vii) they act as 'lender of last resort' to the banking system;

(viii) they do not provide a full banking service for personal and commercial customers.

In Britain, the central bank is the Bank of England.

4.2 The Weekly Return

The 1844 Bank Charter Act (see Unit 3.4) divided the Bank of England into two principal departments: the Issue Department and the Banking Department. It also specified that the Bank had to issue a *Weekly Return* showing the assets and liabilities of each department: this is still published today and Table 4.1 shows a modern return.

The liabilities of the Issue Department are notes in circulation and notes held in the Banking Department ready for issue to the other banks as required. As the note issue is now entirely fiduciary (see Unit 2.6) the assets backing

Table 4.1   Bank of England Weekly Return for 21 February 1979

LIABILITIES	Issue Department	ASSETS	
	£ million		£ million
Notes issued:			
In circulation	8 843	Government securities	7 552
In Banking Department	7	Other securities	1 298
	8 850		8 850

LIABILITIES	Banking Department	ASSETS	
'Capital'	15	Government securities	951
Public deposits	25	Advances and other accounts	212
Special deposits	255	Premises, equipment and	
Bankers' deposits	404	other securities	173
Reserves and other accounts	644	Notes and coin	7
	1 343		1 343

Source: *Bank of England Quarterly Bulletin*

it comprise Government and other securities—Government debt in the form of stocks, Treasury bills and other advances, together with local authority debt and other securities.

The liabilities of the Banking Department are the capital, reserves and deposits of the Bank. The *capital* is the amount subscribed by the original stock-holders, together with accumulated interest and reserves; it has been held by the Treasury since the nationalization of the Bank in 1946. *Public deposits* are the balances of the Government accounts maintained at the Bank (see Unit 4.4(*a*)), *special deposits* are those which banks and certain finance houses are required to maintain from time to time with the Bank of England as part of the Government's monetary policy (see Unit 4.9(*b*)) and *bankers' deposits* are the balances which the London clearing and other banks maintain at the Bank as a part of their reserves. The balances of the Bank of England's other customers, together with undistributed profits and reserves, are included in *reserves and other accounts*.

The assets of the Banking Department consist mainly of holdings of Government securities—stocks and Treasury bills; included among *advances and other accounts* are loans made to the discount houses (see Unit 7.3) and other customers of the Bank; *premises, equipment and other securities* are miscellaneous other assets. The final item *notes and coin* comprises notes ready for issue to the other banks, as an opposite entry to the liability amount on the Issue Department's return, together with the holding of coin for the Bank's own use.

4.3   The Functions of the Bank of England

The Bank of England's roles are widely varied and far-reaching in their significance.

(i) It acts as banker to:
the Government,
the banks and other financial institutions,
some overseas central banks and international financial organizations,
a few private sector customers, and
its own staff.
(ii) It is the note-issuing authority in England and Wales.
(iii) It serves as registrar of Government and other stocks.
(iv) It administers exchange control and manages the Exchange Equalization Account.
(v) It acts as lender of last resort to the discount houses.
(vi) It carries out the Government's monetary policy.
(vii) It supervises the banking institutions of the United Kingdom.

These functions, which are discussed one by one on the next few pages, are shared between a number of specialized departments working under the general control of the Court of Directors (Fig. 4.1).

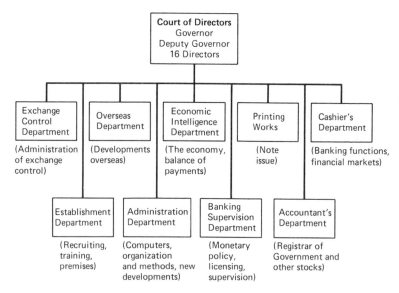

Fig. 4.1   *Organization of the Bank of England*

4.4 The Bank of England as a Banker

(a) Banker to the Government
Although the Government maintains a large number of small accounts with the commercial banks, its main accounts are kept with the Bank of England. The Exchequer account ultimately receives all Government revenues, in the form of taxes and other income, and all Government expenditure originates from it. Other accounts are those of the National Loans Fund, the National Debt Commissioners and various dividend accounts that enable the Bank to pay interest on the Government stocks for which it acts as registrar.

While the Bank was originally founded to make a loan to the Government, this is not a major part of its work nowadays. The only direct lending is of a very short-term nature, usually overnight. However, the Bank arranges all the Government's borrowing—short-term through the issue of Treasury bills and longer-term through the issue of Government stocks. It advises the Government on terms and the state of the market, and provides other services as well (see Unit 4.6).

(b) Banker to the banks and other financial institutions
The Bank acts as banker to the commercial banks, the discount houses, accepting houses and a large number of the overseas banks operating in London. The London clearing banks usually maintain a sum equal to at least $1\frac{1}{2}$ per cent of their eligible liabilities (see Unit 8.5(a)) in their accounts with the Bank of England and from these balances they settle the daily cheque clearing and other inter-bank indebtedness. When the commercial banks require new bank notes and coins these accounts are drawn upon and they are increased when surplus or soiled or damaged notes and coins are paid in. The balances are regarded as being as good as cash and may count towards a bank's eligible reserve assets.

(c) Banker to overseas central banks and international financial organizations
Accounts for a number of overseas central banks, principally of countries of the British Commonwealth, are maintained by the Bank together with those of such bodies as the International Monetary Fund, the International Bank for Reconstruction and Development and the Bank for International Settlements.

(d) Banker to private sector customers and its staff
Although the Bank ceased to compete for business with the commercial banks in the early years of this century, it still maintains some private sector accounts for companies and individuals that have close associations with the Bank. These accounts are said to give the Bank practical experience of commercial banking. In early 1978 the Bank suggested that it would like to increase its range of private sector customers by taking on new business. It also maintains accounts for the members of its own staff.

4.5   The Note-issuing Authority

The Bank of England, as Unit 2.6 explained, has the monopoly of the note issue in England and Wales. Nowadays it is a major task to withdraw worn and soiled notes, which are sent to the Bank from other banks throughout the country for destruction, and to print new notes. Each working day at the Bank's printing works, some eight million old notes are burnt in the furnaces which power the heating system—certainly the most expensive heating system in the country! A similar number of notes are printed each day and, in terms of staff, this is the Bank's biggest undertaking.

4.6   Registrar of Government Stocks

In 1715, just twenty-one years after its foundation, the Bank acted for the first time as an agent for the issue and management of a Government loan (see Unit 3.2). This function continues today and a glance at the *Financial Times* in the closing prices section headed 'British Funds' will indicate some of the stocks currently managed by the Bank—Exchequer and Treasury Stocks. The Bank arranges to issue the stock to cover the Government's longer-term borrowing requirements and then fulfils the role of a company registrar, attending to recording the transfer of stocks from one holder to another and to the payment of dividends and interest at the right time and, when a stock is due for repayment, sending cheques to the stockholders.

In addition to dealing with British Government stocks, the Bank acts as a registrar for stocks issued by the nationalized industries, some local authorities, public boards and Commonwealth governments.

4.7   Administration of Exchange Control

The Bank acts as agent for the Government in administering the requirements of the Exchange Control Act 1947, which aimed to protect and conserve Britain's official reserves of gold and foreign currencies. Bank of England permission is required to transfer funds to residents outside the Scheduled Territories, and this is usually freely given for trading and similar transactions. (The Scheduled Territories consist of the United Kingdom, including the Isle of Man and the Channel Islands, together with the Republic of Ireland and Gibraltar.) Transactions between United Kingdom residents and residents of the Scheduled Territories may be made without restriction and do not require Bank of England permission. The Bank delegates many of the powers to deal with exchange control application to the commercial banks, these banks being designated *authorized banks.* Other, more limited, powers are delegated to solicitors and stockbrokers in connection with transactions in securities—stocks and shares—and they are known as *authorized depositaries.*

The Bank manages, on behalf of the Treasury, the Exchange Equalization Account, which holds Britain's official reserves of gold, foreign exchange and Special Drawing Rights on the International Monetary Fund. It is through this account that the Bank sometimes intervenes on the foreign exchange market —where currencies are bought and sold—to prevent undue fluctuations in the exchange value of sterling against other currencies.

4.8   Lender of Last Resort

Most central banks act as 'lender of last resort', so that if there is a general shortage of funds, the central bank is always prepared to lend. In Britain, the Bank of England is a direct lender of last resort to the discount houses (see Unit 7) and, as these act as an intermediary between the central bank and other banks, last-resort lending is available indirectly to the banks. While the Bank is prepared to act in this way, it does so on its own terms, often charging a higher rate of interest than that prevailing on the money markets and requiring lending to be backed by securities on which there will be no possibility of loss. By taking these precautions, the Bank ensures that, while it is prepared to make funds available, they will only be requested 'as a last resort' after every other possible source has been approached.

4.9   The Government's Monetary Policy

All central banks liaise with and advise their governments on monetary policy and act as the link between the government and the banks and other financial institutions in carrying out the policy. In Britain, the Treasury and the Bank of England—collectively referred to as *the Authorities*—are concerned in controlling the growth of the money stock and the ability of the banks and other financial institutions to create credit.

At present there are five ways in which the Bank of England is able to carry out the Government's monetary policy in controlling the lending of the banks. It may issue directives to the banks or it may call on them to make special and supplementary special deposits, it may vary the minimum lending rate in order to influence market interest rates, it can engage in open-market operations and funding, and it can increase or decrease the required reserve asset ratios.

Each of these ways will now be considered in detail.

(a) Directives
The Bank of England is in the unique position in Britain of having authority conferred on it by the Bank of England Act 1946 (see Unit 3.5) to direct a bank to take a certain course of action using, if necessary, the force of law. This legal force is rarely required, but the Bank frequently issues directives to the banks and deposit-taking institutions telling them of action they are

required to take to implement the Government's policy on bank advances. Fig. 4.2 illustrates a recent directive and others may be seen in issues of the *Bank of England Quarterly Bulletin*.

Directives used to take one of two forms: either quantitative or qualitative. *Quantitative directives* required the banks to limit the total amount of their lending to a certain figure. For example, the Bank of England might issue a directive saying that during the next six months advances must not increase by more than 5 per cent: thus a bank with advances of £5 000 million would only be able to increase its lending by a maximum of £250 million, whatever the growth of its deposits during that time. In the 1971 credit control proposals, however, the Bank agreed to abandon quantitative directives (see Unit 4.11). *Qualitative directives*, which are still used, advise the banks and other institutions which types of customers they should or should not lend to, for instance, to lend to manufacturing industry but not to property companies.

(b) Special and supplementary special deposits
Special deposits were first used in 1960 and are a call on the whole banking system to deposit a certain percentage of their eligible liabilities (basically their deposits; the term is explained fully in Unit 8.5) with the Bank of England. The effect is to take money out of the banking system, which means that the

---

Credit control

Notice to banks and deposit-taking finance houses, issued by the Bank of England on 22 July 1976.

In his Parliamentary statement today, the Chancellor of the Exchequer reaffirmed his intention to restrain the growth of the money supply while ensuring that industry is not denied essential finance. In this context, banks and finance houses are asked:

1   to provide, within the bounds of banking prudence, finance required for both working capital and fixed investment by manufacturing industry and for the expansion of exports and the saving of imports;

2   in order to ensure their ability to meet the requirements in (1) above during the next two years, to exercise strict restraint on lending or provision of facilities for other purposes;

3   in particular, to maintain existing restraint on lending and the granting of facilities to persons, property companies and for purely financial transactions, and to continue to observe the existing request on terms of personal loans.

Fig. 4.2   Bank of England Credit Control Notice

banks must restrict or reduce their lending in order to maintain the required reserve asset ratio (see Unit 4.9(e)). When the Authorities wish to increase bank lending, they will make a repayment of special deposits, knowing that money put back into the banking system will quickly be lent out by the banks. Interest is usually paid on special deposits at the Treasury bill rate but at certain times, when the Authorities wish to penalize the banks, lower interest or even no interest at all may be allowed.

The *supplementary special deposits scheme* was introduced in December 1973 as an attempt by the Authorities to control the ease with which the banks were able at that time to increase their deposits and consequently their lending. This scheme, which is nicknamed the Bank of England's 'corset', works by placing a restriction on the rate of growth of a bank's 'interest-bearing eligible liabilities' (IBELs): these are, in the main, the bank accounts on which interest is paid—deposit accounts and all funds obtained from the money markets (see Unit 7) through certificate of deposit issues and inter-bank transactions—but excluding certain long-term deposits. When the scheme was first introduced the base level of IBELs was established from the average for October, November and December 1973. The banks were told that IBELs for each bank were not to increase by more than 8 per cent over the base level during the next six months. If they did exceed the limit, then a proportion of the excess had to be placed with the Bank of England at a nil rate of interest, as supplementary special deposits. The proportion to be deposited with the Bank varied according to the amount of the excess: the highest penalty was for a bank that exceeded the ceiling by more than 3 per cent, when 50 per cent of the excess had to be deposited. The arrangement was suspended in February 1975 but was re-introduced in November 1976 with a 3 per cent growth limit of IBELs for the first six months and 0.5 per cent each month for a further two months. For increases over the limit a further proportional scheme applied with a maximum penalty of 50 per cent being applied to banks that exceeded the ceiling by more than 5 per cent; this scheme was suspended in its turn in August 1977, and a new 'corset' scheme was introduced in June 1978. Under the new arrangements the growth of IBELs from the average amount outstanding in the six months from November 1977 to April 1978 to the average for the three months of August, September and October 1978 was not to exceed 4 per cent. Where the growth was above this level, non-interest-bearing special deposits had to be made on a proportionate basis; for instance, where the excess growth was more than 5 per cent above the specified level the special deposit consisted of 50 per cent of the excess. This scheme was extended in August 1978 for a further eight-month period to June 1979, but was modified by an allowance for a 1 per cent growth per month in IBELs.

The supplementary special deposits scheme looks like becoming a permanent feature of the Authorities' credit control methods because by withdrawing funds from circulation it strikes directly at the banks' means of creating credit. The penalties for exceeding the set limits and having to make deposits with the Bank of England at a nil rate of interest are especially damaging to profitability because the banks still have to pay interest to their depositors.

(c) Minimum lending rate

Ever since the Bank of England developed the role of a central bank acting as lender of last resort to the discount houses, it has had the ability to influence market interest rates by changing the rate at which it is prepared to lend. In theory, interest rates affect the demand for loans and overdrafts which will have subsequent repercussions on the ability of the banks to create credit: high interest rates lead to a reduction in demand for advances, whereas low rates create a demand. This theory works well while inflation is low, but during periods of high inflation in Britain in the 1970s, bank customers were prepared to borrow money at rates of up to 18 per cent or more (November 1976); exactly twelve months later the rates would have been 8 or 9 per cent.

Prior to October 1972, the minimum rate at which the bank was prepared to lend was known as *bank rate*, but in that month a change was made. Bank rate was considered to have become too much of a 'market leader', since it was rigidly followed by other interest rates, particularly those of the banks and building societies. It was announced formally each week and changes received major press and television coverage: a rise in the rate was thought to indicate a period of credit restriction and a fall a period of economic expansion. It was felt that a more flexible rate was required that could respond more easily to the changing conditions of the money market. *Minimum lending rate* accordingly replaced bank rate in October 1972. It changes more frequently than did bank rate, and the changes do not reflect major alterations in monetary policy, but instead follow the trends of market interest rates. While the banks do not rigidly tie their deposit and overdraft rates to minimum lending rate, these rates do tend to follow its variations, although an individual bank is always free to set its own rates. Until May 1978 minimum lending rate was usually calculated by means of a formula linked to the Treasury bill rate:

> Take the average rate of discount at the Friday Treasury bill tender;
> add half per cent;
> round up to the next quarter per cent.

For example: on 2 December 1977 £500 million of Treasury bills was offered for tender and applications amounted to £737 million. The average rate of discount on allotment was 6.4912 per cent.

Average rate of discount	6.4912	per cent
add half per cent	0.5	per cent
	6.9912	per cent
round up to the next quarter per cent	7.0	per cent

Thus minimum lending rate for the week was 7 per cent.

The Authorities could vary minimum lending rate without reference to the Treasury bill rate if they wished. This meant that the formula was temporarily suspended and, when this was done, it usually happened that, within the next week or two, the Treasury bill rate came into line with minimum lending rate so that the formula could be re-introduced. The Authorities took this action when they wished to influence the general level of interest rates rather than to allow it to be settled by market forces.

In May 1978 the Authorities decided to abandon the formula and the Bank announced that minimum lending rate would, in future, be set by administrative action. Although the formula had in general worked well, it was clear that the Government had become unhappy with a system which appeared to follow the market rather than lead it. On occasions the close automatic link with the Treasury bill rate had led to undesirable erratic movements in interest rates. In setting the new-style minimum lending rate the Authorities still respond to the situation in the market. While the banks do not automatically adjust borrowing and lending rates with changes in minimum lending rate, it is likely that they will make a move within a few days of any change. An announcement of a change in minimum lending rate is made at 12.30 p.m. on Thursdays and requires the approval of the Chancellor of the Exchequer.

Fig. 4.3 shows the changes that have taken place in the rate since it was introduced in October 1972.

(d) Open-market operations and funding
Open market operations are the buying and selling of long-term Government stocks in the gilt-edged market by the Authorities in order to increase or restrict bank lending. When the Authorities buy stocks on the market, the Bank of England makes payments to the individuals and institutions from whom it has purchased them. When the payment cheques are banked, additional deposits are made in the banking system and the banks are then able to 'create' more money by increasing their lending (see Unit 2.10). The reverse happens when the Authorities sell Government stock in the market: the Bank of England receives payment and a transfer of money from the banking system is made when the cheques of the individuals and institutions purchasing the stock are cleared through the Clearing House: this withdrawal of funds from the banking

system reduces the ability of the banks to create credit. Open-market operations in short-term securities are also conducted in the bill markets, where the Bank buys and sells Treasury bills to influence rates and/or maintain stable conditions. In the United Kingdom dealings in long-term stock are more important from the point of view of controlling credit.

Funding refers to the translating of short-term debt previously raised to cover Government borrowing, into longer-term debt. The Bank may reduce the issue of Treasury bills (short-term debt) and increase the issue of Government stocks and bonds with medium to long periods before repayment. These longer-dated stocks and bonds are more likely to be purchased by individuals and institutions outside the financial sector than are Treasury bills, most of which are held by banks and discount houses.

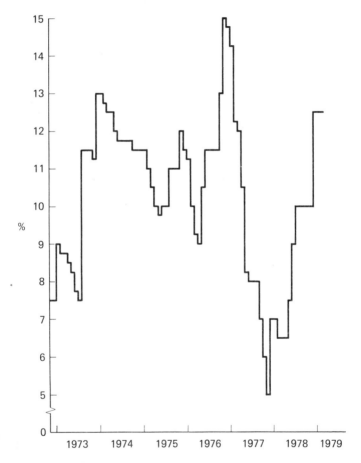

Fig. 4.3   Bank of England minimum lending rate (end-of-month rates) (from data given in the Bank of England Quarterly Bulletin)

The effects of issuing more longer-term and less short-term debt are twofold. Firstly, the purchase of longer-dated stocks by non-bank holders reduces the deposits of the commercial banks in the same way as in open-market operations, causing the banks to reduce their lending. Secondly, reducing the issue of Treasury bills, which count as part of a bank's reserve assets (see Unit 4.9(*e*)), puts a 'squeeze' on the availability of these assets, and if this becomes acute the banks may have to reduce their lending by calling in overdrafts. However, there are other reserve assets apart from Treasury bills and in practice the Authorities' control of the credit base through reserve assets is neither precise nor reliable. As a result they have tended to rely on direct weapons—notably the 'corset'—for controlling advances and deposits.

(*e*) Reserve asset ratios

Since the changes brought about by the 1971 *Competition and Credit Control* document, all banks are required to maintain a minimum of $12\frac{1}{2}$ per cent of their eligible liabilities in the form of eligible reserve assets. This is known as the *reserve asset ratio* (see also Unit 4.11(*b*)). The Authorities have the power to alter the required reserve assets ratio and so directly affect the banks' ability to create credit. An increase in the ratio would mean that the banks would have to switch some of their funds away from lending and transfer them to reserve assets. A decrease in the ratio would have the opposite effect in that the banks would reduce the proportion of reserve assets and increase their lending.

4.10 Supervision of Banking Institutions

As the central bank in Britain, the Bank of England has the task of supervising the banks that operate in the country. It has certain powers conferred on it by the Bank of England Act 1946, but in addition the European Economic Community required Britain to introduce a new basic banking law as part of moves towards standardizing Community controls. The Banking Act, 1979, which, at the time of writing, has not yet been implemented, contains three major provisions:

(i) the recognition or licensing of deposit-taking institutions;
(ii) stricter controls over the use of the word 'bank'; and
(iii) the setting up of a 'Deposit Protection Fund'.

Recognition and licensing will be under the direct control of the Bank of England which will have the right to withdraw recognition or a licence. The objective of this is to prevent careless or unscrupulous operators from taking deposits from the public. The major banks, such as the clearers, will be *recognized* and will form the primary banking sector. In order to avoid licensing, however, they will be subject to a stiff test of capital and reserves. 'Second division' banks will be *licensed*; but it is expected that before a licence is granted, an examination would be made of their balance sheet ratios, liquidity position, the risk involved in the assets they hold, together with a breakdown into sectors of loans (so as to avoid an over-concentration in any one area, such as property). The senior management of the institution would also be considered.

The words 'bank', 'banker' and 'banking service' will only be available for use by recognized banks that have passed the stiffer examination. Other deposit-taking concerns will be barred from calling themselves banks in any form. It is hoped that, as time goes by, the distinction between a bank and any other kind of deposit-taking institution will become clearer, especially in the minds of depositors.

The Deposit Protection Fund will consist of a central pool contributed to by all banks and deposit-taking institutions, and this will be used to repay 75 per cent of the 'protected deposits' of the depositors of any failed institution. There will be a limit of £10 000 on the amount of the 'protected deposits' of each depositor. Therefore depositors will bear some loss, but not all, if the worst happens and an institution is unable to meet its obligations. The pool will be formed in the first instance from levies ranging between £2 500 and £300 000 drawn from each recognized and licensed institution on the basis of its deposit base: the pool will amount to about £6 million in cash. In addition the Authorities have the right to call on each bank for up to 0.3 per cent of its total sterling deposit base to produce a second-line fund of about £125 million.

Criticisms have already been made of the provisions for the way in which the public sector banks—the National Savings Bank, the Trustee Savings Bank and National Girobank—and the building societies are excluded from the regulations. (However, National Girobank will lodge with the Treasury a contribution equal to that which it would have paid had it been a member of the Deposit Protection Fund.) Also, because of the size of their sterling deposits (see Unit 8.7) the clearing banks, which have traditionally been the safest sectors of the banking system, feel that they will be contributing the largest part of the Deposit Protection Fund and will be underwriting the bulk of the risks.

4.11   Competition and Credit Control

The changes that took place in 1971 have been briefly mentioned already. They were concerned with the stimulation of competition among the various banking institutions and the provision of a better framework within which the Authorities could control the ability of the banks to create credit. It is now appropriate to consider in more detail why these changes were needed, what they were, and how successful they have been.

(a) The need for the changes

The 1967 report on bank charges of the National Board for Prices and Incomes had already criticized the lack of competition amongst the banks. At that time, the major banks had a collective agreement on deposit interest rates—they all paid the same rates and there was no benefit in the customer's 'shopping around'. There was a further agreement among them that no interest should be paid on current accounts.

As far as credit control was concerned there were, prior to the 1971 arrangements, two minimum reserve ratios, applying only to the clearing banks: an 8 per cent cash ratio and a 28 per cent liquidity ratio. Both these ratios were expressed as percentages of deposits; 8 per cent of deposits had to be held in the form of cash, either in the bank's tills or at the Bank of England, and a further 20 per cent in the form of liquid assets that could easily be turned into cash, the two amounts together making up the 28 per cent liquidity ratio.

The system was criticized for several reasons. The main problem was that the minimum reserve ratios applied only to the clearing banks and not over the whole range of banking institutions. They financially penalized the banks to which they applied, because those banks were forced to keep too high a percentage of their assets in low-yielding form. Another problem was that the Authorities did not fully control the assets making up the liquidity ratio. This meant that, if the Authorities wished to 'squeeze' bank lending by restricting the supply of these assets, the banks simply increased their holdings of private sector liquid assets, thus by-passing the intended squeeze. Moreover, the quantitative and qualitative controls on bank lending and special deposit requirements similarly did not apply to the whole of the banking sector, and in times of credit squeeze institutions outside the Authorities' control were able to continue lending without restriction. It was in order to attempt to rectify these faults that the Bank of England produced a consultative document entitled *Competition and Credit Control* in May 1971. After a few months of consultation and discussion the measures it proposed were introduced in the following September.

(*b*) **The nature of the changes**
The major change was the scrapping of the liquidity and cash ratios and the introduction of the *reserve asset ratio*, with a minimum of $12\frac{1}{2}$ per cent of eligible liabilities to be held in the form of eligible reserve assets to apply to all banks. (A full list of eligible liabilities and eligible reserve assets is contained in Unit 8.5 and is discussed there in the context of a banker's balance sheet.) At the same time, finance houses became subject to a 10 per cent reserve asset ratio.

The special deposit requirements were also to apply to the whole of the banking system and similar requirements were introduced for finance houses. Quantitative directives were ended: the Authorities decided that in future they would control only the total amount of credit, and individual banks should compete among themselves for shares of that total. Qualitative directives were to remain and their scope was extended to cover all banks and deposit-taking finance houses.

The banks agreed to abandon their collective policy on interest rates. Each bank was to establish its own base rate (to which overdrafts are now related) and its own deposit rate. Previously overdraft and deposit rates had been fully linked with the Bank of England's bank rate (which became minimum lending rate in 1972; see Unit 4.9(c)) and any movement in this automatically meant changes in deposit and overdraft rates. The Authorities also reserved the right to place limits on the terms offered by the banks on deposit accounts; this was to ensure that in periods of high interest rates the banks should not attract too much money away from building society and savings bank accounts. This power was used for many months between 1973 and 1975 to restrict interest paid on bank deposit accounts under £10 000 to $9\frac{1}{2}$ per cent.

As a part of the new arrangements the Authorities also announced in May 1971 new tactics in the 'gilt-edged' securities market of the Stock Exchange (see Unit 6.12). Previously, in order to create a stable market in 'gilts'— Government and other stocks—both from the point of view of prices and interest rates, the Authorities had invariably supported prices by buying on the market if selling pressure was forcing them down. This action was to assist in the Bank's role in financing Government debt. The result of the Authorities buying Government stock was to pump money into the banking system (see Unit 4.9(d)): support for the gilt-edged market had the same effect, often at times when the Authorities did not wish to increase the credit-creation ability of the banks. Under the new provisions, they would no longer support the market in stocks of over one year to maturity, although they reserved the right to intervene if they wished. This meant that interest rates in such stocks were free to fluctuate without intervention and also that the Authorities were no longer obliged to put money into the banking system at inappropriate times.

Competition and Credit Control applies to all banking and deposit-taking institutions in Britain and special arrangements were introduced for the discount market (see Unit 7.4). The position of the Northern Ireland banks is dealt with differently from other banks in Britain because a part of their business is conducted in the Republic of Ireland, outside the control of the Bank of England. They maintain the same $12\frac{1}{2}$ per cent minimum reserve asset ratio as do other banks, but that part of their business conducted in the Republic outside the United Kingdom) is excluded from the calculations.

(c) How successful have the changes been?

In their observance of the $12\frac{1}{2}$ per cent reserve asset ratio, the clearing banks soon found that they were able to reduce their liquid assets from those held under the pre-1971 arrangements; they could hold less cash and fewer liquid assets and consequently more was available for lending. Although the size of the reduction from a 28 per cent liquidity ratio to the $12\frac{1}{2}$ per cent ratio appears considerable, cash in the bank's tills is excluded from eligible reserve assets, so that the new $12\frac{1}{2}$ per cent is brought effectively up to about $16\frac{1}{2}$ per cent. Some items, too, which were significant in the liquidity ratio (export and ship-building credits, and money at call with institutions other than members of the London Discount Market Association) no longer count as reserve assets.

Almost at once, each bank established its own deposit and base rate, although in practice all the major banks use the same rates and change them by the same amount at the same time. The reason for such similarity can be explained by saying that all these banks operate in very similar environments: they have the same sources of deposits, repayable on similar terms; their borrowing customers require funds for similar reasons and for similar periods of time; the cost of their operations, branch network, staff and so forth are similar. However, with the abandonment of fixed rates for deposits, the banks were able to develop a market for larger deposits, particularly certificates of deposit (see Unit 7.11), offering higher interest rates fixed for periods from three months to five years. The Authorities became concerned at the ease with which banks were able to increase their deposits in this way, because of the effect this was having on the growth of advances and hence, through increased deposits, on the money supply. Consequently the supplementary special deposits scheme (see Unit 4.9(*b*)) was introduced in December 1973: as a result of the restrictions imposed on the growth of 'interest-bearing eligible liabilities' by the scheme there was a fall in the amount of certificates of deposit outstanding in 1974. The damage had been done, however, and corrective action was taken too late. The considerable increase in deposits, helped by the new reserve asset ratios, enabled the banks to step up their lending, particularly to the 'secondary' banks and the property market, and the increase in lending was fuelled by the credit-creation multiplier. When the property market collapsed in late 1973 and 1974 most banks 'got their fingers burnt'; several smaller banks found themselves in severe financial difficulties and were only rescued with assistance organized by the Bank of England and provided by the clearing banks.

Thus the changes of 1971 have certainly had a far-reaching effect on the British banking system. One of the good points to come from the arrangements is that *all* banks, deposit-taking institutions and finance houses are now required to maintain reserve asset ratios. Similarly directives and special and supplementary special deposits are spread over a wider range of financial institutions than before. It should be said, however, that *Competition and Credit Control* has failed to produce much difference between interest rates among the banks, even though the old collective agreement has been abandoned. Its most serious fault was that it prepared the way for a considerable increase in the growth of bank lending which ultimately led to the secondary banking crisis of 1974. There were also problems with minimum lending rate, which was supposed to fit in with the overall philosophy of *Competition and Credit Control* by reflecting market forces, and indeed, as we saw in Unit 4.9(*c*), the Authorities have found it necessary to revert to the old system of fixing this key rate.

4.12 Questions

1. Outline the functions normally carried out by a central bank.

(The Institute of Bankers)

2. Describe the ways in which the Bank of England exercises control over bank lending.

3. What is the significance of the Bank of England's minimum lending rate?

4. What were the reasons for the introduction of the provisions of *Competition and Credit Control*? What changes were brought about and how successful have they been?

5. Describe the main functions of the Bank of England.

6. In most countries, a central authority has responsibility for licensing banks and for regulating banking activities, quite apart from the administration of credit controls. What institution usually has this responsibility and by what means would it seek to exercise effective supervision and regulation of the banking system?

(The Institute of Bankers)

7. What were the main features of the Bank of England's publication on *Competition and Credit Control* (1971) in so far as it affected the clearing banks?

(The Institute of Bankers)

The British Banking Structure

5.1 Introduction

Although the 'big four' clearing banks are by far the best known of the British banks, they are only a part of today's banking structure: Fig. 5.1 classifies the whole range of banks under appropriate headings. In recent years distinctions between the various types of bank have become blurred as a result of the diversification of services and the acquisition of interests in other banks and financial institutions.

The whole United Kingdom banking structure is, of course, supervised and controlled by the central bank, the Bank of England.

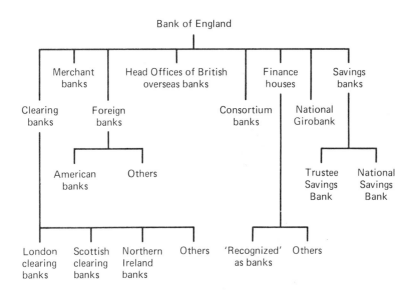

Fig. 5.1   British banking structure

5.2   Clearing Banks

These comprise the London clearing banks, the Scottish clearing banks, the Northern Ireland banks and a few smaller banks owned by the clearers. They are called *clearing banks* because they are members of a clearing house through which cheques and credits are exchanged between other member banks. These banks are also often called *commercial banks* because they are owned by shareholders and intend to make a profit. Through their large branch networks, they offer a 'retail' banking service to their many thousands of personal and business customers.

(i) **The London clearing banks** are the members of the London Bankers' Clearing House. They are the 'big four'—Barclays, Lloyds, Midland and National Westminster—together with the Co-operative, Coutts & Co., and Williams and Glyn's. All these banks offer similar services, which are considered later in this book. The Central Trustee Savings Bank is also a member of the Clearing House, representing the eighteen regional Trustee Savings Banks: these banks are organized differently from the other clearing banks and are currently extending the range of their services (see Unit 5.9).

(ii) **The Scottish clearing banks** are three in number: the Bank of Scotland, the Clydesdale and the Royal Bank of Scotland, each of which retains the right of note issue. These banks are partly owned by the London clearing banks; they have close links with them and, in Scotland, perform similar functions.

(iii) **The Northern Ireland banks** provide similar services in their own areas of operation to those of the London and Scottish clearing banks. There are four member banks of the Northern Ireland Bankers' Association: the Northern Bank, the Ulster Bank, the Allied Irish Banks and the Bank of Ireland. The first two have their head offices in Northern Ireland, have close connections with the London clearing banks, retain the right to issue their own notes and operate branch structures both in Northern Ireland (which is of course a part of the United Kingdom) and in the Republic of Ireland, outside the United Kingdom. The last-named two banks have their head offices and main branch structures in the Republic of Ireland, issue their own notes and maintain a number of branches in Northern Ireland.

Banks operating in Northern Ireland come under the control of the United Kingdom Authorities just as do the London and Scottish clearing banks, although some exceptions in control are allowed because of the fact that they operate both in Northern Ireland and the Republic of Ireland, and also because of the disturbed political situation in the province.

(iv) **Other banks** include a few banks such as the Isle of Man, C. Hoare & Co., Lewis's and the Yorkshire. Most are owned by London clearing banks, and in terms of numbers of branches and total deposits they are very small;

they perform similar functions, in their restricted localities, as those of the larger clearing banks. As they are not members of the London Bankers' Clearing House, their cheques are cleared through a clearing bank acting as their agent.

5.3 Merchant Banks

It is difficult to define the work of a merchant bank briefly: but in essence they are financial institutions providing specialist services which generally include the acceptance of bills of exchange, corporate finance, portfolio management and other banking services. There are perhaps some 100 institutions in Britain that call themselves merchant banks.

Several of the present-day merchant banks started in business during the late eighteenth and early nineteenth centuries. Their origins are similar to those of the private country banks in that their founders were merchants, but they traded overseas rather than in Britain. As world trade expanded during the nineteenth century these merchants grew in reputation and soon found themselves being asked to lend their name to lesser-known traders by *accepting* bills of exchange (see Unit 10.3). By accepting a bill they guaranteed that the holder of the bill would receive full value at the date of payment. This *acceptance* business continues today and the banks most actively engaged in it form the seventeen members of the Accepting Houses Committee. A bill of exchange that has been accepted by a reputable bank can be discounted or sold before maturity—the due date of payment—at *finer* or lower rates of discount than a commercial bill which bears only the acceptance of a trader.

In the nineteenth century, 'the bill on London' became the main instrument of payment for all goods and produce moving internationally. A bill drawn on a London accepting house was often the preferred means of international payment, despite being almost invariably expressed in sterling. Meanwhile the merchant bankers also helped to increase the volume of international trade by developing the documentary *letter of credit* (see Unit 16.7). This was opened by the bank at the request of the buyer of the goods and authorized the seller to draw his bill of exchange on the merchant bank, with an undertaking that, provided the bill was accompanied by specified shipping and other documents relating to the goods, the merchant bank would accept it. The seller of the goods was satisfied because he knew he would be drawing a bill of exchange on a reputable merchant bank and could therefore sell the bill to someone else and thus receive its present value in cash immediately. The buyer was satisfied because, subject to arrangement with the merchant bank, he was receiving a period of credit. The merchant banker was satisfied because he could charge a commission for the use of his name. By thus specializing in the financing of international trade, the merchant banks were able to build up a store of information on traders throughout the world which further enhanced their expertise in international finance.

As their overseas business developed, the merchant banks began to be recognized as bankers and consultants not only by traders and overseas private customers, but also by overseas local and central governments. Many countries sought their advice in raising loans, and as a result London became the major world financial centre for the issue of foreign government bonds. This business flourished throughout the second half of the nineteenth century and early twentieth century, coming to an abrupt halt with the outbreak of the First World War in 1914.

After the war ended in 1918, the merchant banks attempted to restore their business to that of the pre-1914 world. Not only were they hampered by exchange control regulations which restricted the movement of money around the world, however; the clearing banks and the foreign and London-based overseas banks also moved into the market for overseas trade, as their competitors. A shrinkage of world trade in the early 1930s hit the merchant banks hard, and sterling declined as a world currency.

In the 1930s the merchant banks accordingly began to look for other areas of business; in particular, their role in the share issue function developed (see below). Also the late 1920s and early 1930s saw the founding of a number of investment trusts, and the merchant banks became involved in the management of their investments.

Since the end of the Second World War, merchant banks have considerably expanded their range of services and most are now active in the field of *corporate finance*, that is, providing companies with financial expertise. They assist their company customers to find suitable sources of finance often by arranging to sell or *issue* the company's shares to members of the public and obtain a stock

'One day, young man, you could be wearing this suit!'

exchange quotation for the shares—hence the name *issuing houses* for the banks involved. Such a task may last for several years from the first contact between company and bank to the date of 'going public', and requires considerable financial skill. The banks most concerned with the issuing of shares make up the sixty or so members of the Issuing Houses Association which represents the interests of its members by maintaining standards and liaising with the Council of the Stock Exchange, from whom permission has to be sought before a share may be 'quoted', and with the Bank of England.

Merchant banks also advise and assist companies in other aspects of corporate finance ranging from making a rights issue, under the terms of which existing shareholders are offered additional shares at an attractive price, to advice on merging with or taking over another company. Some banks act as company registrars, as the Bank of England acts as the registrar of Government stocks.

Besides the two main areas of acceptance of bills and corporate finance the merchant banks are specialists in the investment of clients' funds—*portfolio management*—on behalf of pension funds, investment trusts, unit trusts and private individuals. Pension funds collect contributions from people during their working lives and pay them a pension when they have retired; investment and unit trusts bring together sums of money from thousands of individual savers and invest the funds on their behalf. All these require expert investment management, and this can be provided by the merchant banks (see also Units 6.11 and 6.12).

They also offer banking services such as current, deposit and fixed-term deposit accounts, mainly for the company customer. In recent years some have developed factoring (a sales ledger accounting service which may include the granting of an advance against the debts owed to the company), leasing (the 'renting' of machinery and other assets), hire purchase (instalment finance for capital equipment) and insurance broking (see Unit 15). The merchant banks differ from the clearing banks principally in that they have few, if any, branches and are mainly 'wholesale' bankers accepting large sums on deposit, chiefly for fixed terms, from financial institutions, companies and individuals. When they lend it is usually to companies and for medium or long periods of time. Unlike the clearing banks, they may purchase shares in a company customer and play a direct part in its management.

Since the early 1960s, the merchant banks have become involved in dealings on the developing international money or Eurocurrency market and the international capital or Eurobond market (see Unit 7.14). In both these markets, merchant banks act for United Kingdom and foreign companies and state enterprises to assist in the raising of medium- and long-term finance in a range of currencies.

During the last two decades the major clearing banks have all developed an interest in merchant banking and each has either bought its way into an established merchant bank or set up a new one. Many of the corporate services of the clearing banks described in Unit 15 are offered through their merchant banking subsidiary.

5.4 Foreign Banks

Some 300 different foreign banks are now operating in Britain, together employing about 20 000 staff. Most banks are situated in London although some are beginning to establish branch networks. During the nineteenth century the merchant banks helped to establish London as the principal financial centre of the world and ever since the 1860s, banks from other countries have established themselves here, with the largest number arriving during the last twenty years. Most initially set up a representative office which does not transact normal banking business but provides a business contact service; later, as business develops, a branch providing a full banking service will be established.

The reasons for wishing to be represented in Britain are:

(i) to develop trade between Britain and the overseas country;

(ii) to provide financial services to businessmen from the overseas country while visiting Britain;

(iii) to provide a banking service to immigrants and foreign nationals from the overseas country, living and working in Britain;

(iv) to act as international bankers in a major world financial centre on behalf of businesses from the overseas country.

The foreign banks are dominated by some sixty American banks, most of them having arrived since 1965—there are now more American banks in London than there are in New York. They are particularly attracted to Britain because London is the centre of the market in Eurocurrencies, of which the Eurodollar is the most important (this is a market in lending and borrowing currencies outside their country of origin and is considered in detail in Unit 7.14). They are also here because of the development of North Sea oil and the increasing inter-country investment that is taking place between Britain and America. Surprisingly, almost 30 per cent of bank advances to United Kingdom manufacturing industry are made by overseas banks (see Table 5.1).

Some American banks are currently establishing branch networks and competing more directly with the clearing banks by introducing services aimed particularly at the personal customer. In addition, a number of 'ethnic' banks, such as Allied Irish Banks, Bank of Cyprus, Bank of Baroda and the State Bank of India, have set up domestic branches in competition with the big banks in districts where people from their own countries have settled in Britain.

5.5 Head Offices of British Overseas Banks

Just as overseas banks have established representative offices and branches in the United Kingdom, so British banks have been established overseas. The major development overseas took place at the height of the British Empire's power during the second half of the nineteenth century. Instead of setting up one branch in each capital city, 'retail' branch banking structures, modelled

Table 5.1 Bank advances to British manufacturing industry, 16 August 1978

	£ million	per cent
London clearing banks	4 852	45.9
Scottish clearing banks	539	5.1
Northern Ireland banks	109	1.0
Accepting houses (members of the Accepting Houses Committee)	361	3.4
Other British banks	1 507	14.3
American banks	2 064	19.6 ⎫
Japanese banks	53	0.5 ⎬ 29.3
Other overseas banks	976	9.2 ⎭
Consortium banks (see Unit 5.6)	100	1.0
	10 559	100.0

Source: *Bank of England Quarterly Bulletin*

on those operating in Britain, were developed in the countries of the Empire, particularly in Africa, the Middle and Far East. Since 1945, as these countries have gained their independence, so more control of the banking system has been taken by their new leaders. Some banks have been nationalized, while others have been obliged to establish separate companies in the overseas country with the resultant problems of remitting profits back to Britain. The 1960s and 1970s have seen an escalation in the costs of administering a scattered retail branch network and it has not been unknown for a bank head office in London to make higher profits than all of the overseas branches of the bank put together.

Five major British banking groups with large overseas branch networks still remain:

Barclays Bank International, which is wholly owned by Barclays Bank, and has branches in Africa, the Caribbean, and more recently, California and New York;

Lloyds Bank International, controlled by Lloyds Bank, has a large branch network in South America (formerly belonging to the Bank of London and South America) and, more recently, branches in a few towns and cities in Europe (formerly owned by Lloyds Bank Europe);

Grindlays Bank, which is partly owned by Lloyds Bank, has branches in India, Pakistan and Africa:

Standard and Chartered Bank, an independent, has branches throughout Africa and the Far East.

The Hongkong Bank Group, which includes the British Bank of the Middle East, has recently transferred its headquarters to Hongkong, where its business is centred.

With the changes in branch structures as a result of independence or altered politics in host countries, the British overseas banks have sought new areas of profitable business and their head offices in London have become active in the London money markets, particularly the Eurocurrency and certificate of deposit markets (see Unit 7).

5.6   Consortium Banks

As the name suggests, a consortium bank is formed by a group of other banks, usually from several different countries. The Bank of England defines it as a bank which is *owned by other banks but in which no one bank has a direct shareholding of more than 50 per cent and in which at least one shareholder is an overseas bank*. The first consortium bank to be formed was Midland and International Banks in 1964, the shareholders being the Midland Bank, Toronto–Dominion Bank, Standard and Chartered Bank and the Commercial Bank of Australia. There are now some thirty such banks operating in London.

These banks are formed in order to be able to put together large loan 'packages' to meet the financial requirements of large multi-national companies for long periods of time. They are also able to arrange *syndicated loans*: this means sharing out large loans amongst syndicates of banks. The bank that is organizing the loan, called the *lead bank*, contacts up to fifty other banks inviting them to participate.

Consortium banks obtain their funds partly from the parent banks, but mainly from the Eurocurrency markets.

5.7   Finance Houses

The idea behind the services of a finance house or hire purchase company is that items are purchased on an instalment basis: the goods are supplied after payment of a deposit and the balance outstanding, together with interest, is paid by means of agreed instalments. In Britain, hire purchase companies date back to the second half of the nineteenth century when they were established to finance the purchase of railway wagons for colliery companies—the word *wagon* still features in the names of some of the companies operating today. With the coming of the motor car in the early twentieth century, the companies turned their attention to financing the purchase of vehicles and during the period between the two world wars widened their interests to include other consumer goods such as furniture, carpets and radios. During the 1960s and 1970s all the major clearing banks established an interest in finance houses and the facilities they offer now include company services such as industrial hire purchase, factoring and leasing (see Unit 15).

A recent development of the finance houses has been the opening of 'money shops': these are usually situated in shopping centres and, in contrast to the imposing buildings of the banks, look like normal retail shops. Their hours of business are linked to shopping hours rather than the more limited banking hours, and their aim is to provide, in relatively informal surroundings, a range of services including the provision of hire purchase 'packages' for a wide range of consumer purchases, acceptance of deposits, a current account service and other banking activities. The money shops owned by subsidiaries of the clearing banks also provide a cheque encashment service, backed by a cheque card, for personal customers of the parent bank.

Finance houses obtain their funds by borrowing from banks and other financial institutions, and by accepting deposits from industrial and commercial companies and private individuals. A number of the larger finance houses have been recognized as banks by the Bank of England: the advantage for them is that, while they are subject to the same reserve ratio and special deposit requirements as all other banks, they can borrow on the inter-bank money market (see Unit 7.8) and issue their own certificates of deposit. Those finance houses that are not part of the banking sector are required to maintain a reserve ratio of 10 per cent of eligible liabilities in the form of eligible reserve assets.

The Authorities are able to exercise control over the amount of credit granted by the finance houses, by specifying a minimum deposit and a maximum repayment period: for example, to purchase a car on hire purchase at the time of writing, the minimum deposit required is $33\frac{1}{3}$ per cent of the cost and the maximum repayment period is two years. Most personal hire purchase contracts are for the purchase of 'consumer durables' such as cars, washing machines, carpets, furniture or television sets; when the Authorities wish to expand credit and make such items more readily available, they reduce the minimum deposit and extend the maximum repayment period. If, on the other hand, they wish to restrict credit and reduce sales of these items—perhaps to enable more to be exported or, more probably, to reduce the number of goods being imported—minimum deposits will be increased and maximum repayment periods will be reduced.

5.8   National Girobank

National Girobank, the money transfer system of the Post Office, was established in 1968 in an attempt to provide a simple, cheap and efficient banking service for people who had not previously had a bank account (even in 1978, 40 per cent of the adult population in Britain remained 'unbanked'). National Girobank also enables certain bills, such as those for electricity, gas and telephone, to be paid by both account holders and non-account holders at any of more than 20 000 post offices. When a Girobank account holder wishes to pay another account holder he fills in the appropriate form and posts it, using the special envelope supplied, to the National Girobank's Computer Centre at Bootle in Merseyside, where all accounting transfers are effected. As all the accounts are maintained in one place there is no clearing system to delay payment, and the transaction is carried out immediately upon receipt of the transfer form. Payments to people who do not have a Girobank account may be made by Girocheque which can be paid direct into a bank account;

alternatively an open Girocheque without a crossing (see Unit 10.8) may be cashed at a post office after authentication at the Girobank Centre. Cash may be withdrawn by the account holder at certain post offices nominated by him, or at any post office if he has a Girobank guarantee card (which operates in a similar way to a cheque card). In either case the amount that may be withdrawn is restricted, but larger amounts may be drawn in cash if prior arrangements are made. At present the bank makes no charges for operating personal accounts provided that they remain in credit.

Other services include hire purchase facilities arranged through a finance house, overdrafts and loans, deposit accounts (see Unit 6.5) and the supply of travellers' cheques and foreign money. Services recently introduced for personal customers include bridging loans (a short-term loan used during house purchase to 'plug' the gap which occurs between paying for the new house and receiving the sale proceeds of the old one; see Unit 17.10(a)), budget accounts (a method of spreading the cost of bills more evenly over the year; see Unit 13.7) and cash dispensers (see Unit 14.5). Bridging loans, overdraft facilities and the cheque guarantee card are normally only available to those who have their salary paid directly into their Girobank account.

Customer balances at present total about £200 million, the customers including local authorities, Government departments, nationalized industries, mail-order firms and other businesses and some 660 000 personal account holders. National Girobank, like any bank, maintains some of its assets in the form of notes and coin, and balances at the Bank of England. It lends some of its funds to the discount market 'at call' (that is, the money is repayable on demand); the remainder of its assets are largely invested in the public sector in local authority loans, bills and bonds and British Government securities.

In September 1978 National Girobank was given 'listed' status by the Bank of England. This means that the bank now has to comply with the various banking ratios including the maintenance of the $12\frac{1}{2}$ per cent reserve asset ratio, the maintenance of special deposits with the Bank of England and 'corset' provisions. National Girobank will not be required to take part in the Deposit Protection Scheme included in the Banking Bill; it will, however, have to lodge with the Treasury a contribution equal to that which it would have paid were it not for this exemption.

5.9   Trustee Savings Banks

These make up one category of savings bank in Britain today; the other comprises the National Savings Bank, discussed in Unit 5.10.

Trustee Savings Banks (TSBs) were founded in Scotland in the early eighteenth century to provide non-profit-making savings facilities for working people. At that time the joint-stock and private banks were only interested in wealthy customers and provided no services for the small saver: they required a minimum deposit of £10 to open an account and this was the equivalent of a year's earnings for most workers. The idea was to collect people's savings, pool them and then place them on deposit with a joint-stock bank at a rate of interest. The interest thus earned could be passed back to the savers in proportion to their deposits.

The 1817 Savings Bank Act marked the beginning of a period of development for these banks and provided that savers' funds could be placed in a Government fund called the Fund for the Banks for Savings, where it could earn interest. The fund was guaranteed by the Government (in contrast to the unreliability and frequent failures in the private sector at that time) and the banks were to be managed by unpaid local trustees—hence the name given to the banks— acting on behalf of the National Debt Commissioners who control the debt of the central Government. The TSBs remain in the hands of local trustees (still, at the time of writing, unpaid) and each bank continues to operate in its own locality, although in 1975 mergers took place to reduce the number of banks.

Since 1964, TSBs have developed a wide range of banking services far removed from the old 'savings bank' image, beginning with the introduction of current accounts. The changes have been particularly marked as a result of the publication in 1973 of the report of the Committee to Review National Savings which was chaired by Sir Harry Page. The Page Committee Report, as it has become known, recommended that the TSBs should be allowed to develop as a 'third force' in banking in the private sector, and since then the TSBs have made several moves to expand their services. The Central Trustee Savings Bank was established in 1973 to co-ordinate and supervise the activities of the local TSBs and to provide the central organization necessary to enable them to develop away from the savings bank image, and three years later it

'It's part of our policy of diversification'

became a member of the London Bankers' Clearing House, so enabling the banks to clear their own cheques and credits. In 1975 the then seventy-three local TSBs operating throughout Britain were merged into nineteen (now eighteen) larger regional units, together controlling a total of 1 650 branches and 14 million active accounts. The funds of these regional banks range in size from £48 million (North Staffordshire TSB) to £712 million (North West TSB), while the number of branches varies from eight (Channel Islands TSB) to 228 (South East TSB). All the regional banks are regulated by the 1976 Trustee Savings Banks Act, which embodies the Page Committee recommendations and permits the banks to withdraw their monies from the Fund for the Banks for Savings and to invest them in the best interests of their depositors. At present withdrawals are taking place from the Fund and the Bank of England will increasingly assume control over the TSBs, just as it controls all other banks operating in Britain. Like other banks, the TSBs will no longer have Government backing for their funds and will have to build up reserves; the present preferential tax position on savings account interest (see below) will cease, and the TSBs will come into line with other banks as from November 1979.

TSB accounts and services

The savings account was the account that attracted the small saver of the nineteenth century and that until the 1960s represented the bulk of depositors' funds. The deposits of this type of account are currently placed with the Fund for the Banks for Savings although as withdrawals take place from this (see above), the savings account will be phased out. At present there is a tax concession for savings account holders: the first £70 of interest earned each year is free from all United Kingdom income tax.

Investment accounts were started in the 1880s and offer a higher rate of interest than that on savings accounts, although there is no tax concession. Funds from these accounts are invested in Government securities.

Cheque accounts were introduced in 1964 and there are now some 1.5 million of these accounts. Besides a cheque book service, facilities offered to cheque account customers include cheque guarantee cards, credit cards, standing orders, direct debits, personal loans and temporary overdrafts (see Units 11 and 14 for further details of these services). Most cheque account holders are personal customers and there are plans to introduce secured loans, backed by the deposit of security (see Unit 17), bridging loans, budget accounts and possibly mortgage facilities. The TSBs are considering attracting business customers by offering them loans.

Term deposits are accepted by most TSBs from customers who are prepared to leave larger deposits for a pre-arranged period of time, the rate of interest being fixed for the term of the investment.

Services offered to savers and investors by the TSBs are more fully discussed in Unit 6.5. Other services offered to all customers include safe custody (the keeping of valuables at the bank on behalf of customers), the provision of travellers' cheques and foreign money, insurance facilities, and the sale of National Savings securities such as Premium Savings Bonds, British Savings Bonds, National Savings Certificates and Government stocks and bonds on the National Savings Stock Register (National Savings securities are discussed in Unit 6.6). In 1968 the TSBs launched a unit trust which, under the management of the TSB Trust Co. Ltd., has developed schemes to enable investors to take advantage of various savings plans linked to life assurance.

5.10 National Savings Bank

This bank was established under the name of the Post Office Savings Bank by an Act of Parliament in 1861. It was re-named in 1969 when it was separated from the Post Office and came under the control of the Government's Department of National Savings. As its original name suggests, it is operated through post offices and has the advantage of 20 000 post office 'branches' with far longer opening hours than clearing banks. It is the largest organization of its kind in the world, with some 21 million active accounts and total deposits amounting to £3 043 million in December 1977.

Depositors' funds are lodged with the National Debt Commissioners and are invested in Government securities; thus the funds are guaranteed by the Government. There are two types of account: the *ordinary* and the *investment accounts* which are almost identical to the savings and investment accounts of the Trustee Savings Banks. The ordinary account carries a tax concession in that the first £70 of interest earned each year is free of all United Kingdom income tax; it seems that this concession will continue after it ceases to apply to TSB savings accounts in 1979. NSB accounts are discussed more fully in Unit 6.5(*b*).

The Page Committee report recommended that the NSB should continue to provide a savings and banking service for the individual.

5.11 Questions

1. Outline the types of bank that make up the present-day British banking structure.

2. In what broad respects does the role of a clearing bank differ from that of: (*a*) a merchant bank; (*b*) a building society?

(The Institute of Bankers)

3. Trace the development of merchant banks and outline their present-day functions.

4. What services do Trustee Savings Banks offer and to what extent are they in direct competition with the clearing banks?

5. What are the services offered by the National Girobank?

Unit Six

Savings and Investment

6.1 Why Save?

Saving may be defined as *not spending income on consumption.* Therefore that part of our after-tax income that we have not spent on consumption or expenditure on goods and services is saved.

Why do we save? There are two main reasons: we may save for a specific purpose, such as to pay for a holiday or a motor-cycle, or we may save for an unspecific purpose, such as 'for a rainy day' or to have something to fall back on in the event of some unexpected expense occurring in the future.

To save for either of these reasons would involve refraining from spending a part of our income and putting it on one side. We could put it in a jug on the mantelpiece or, more sensibly, into a bank or building society account or some other form of savings scheme: the length of time before the savings are likely to be needed determines the most suitable place for them.

The definition includes another form of saving that does not involve the task of transferring money into an account and can be called 'unconscious' saving because it takes a form that most people would not acknowledge as saving: examples of this kind of saving are payment of premiums on a life assurance policy and the repayment of a mortgage on a house. In each of these, money from present after-tax income is not being spent on consumption but is being put aside for the future. At some stage the life assurance company will pay out a lump sum of money on their policy and the mortgage will be repaid, the cash value of the house representing savings.

While most saving is voluntary—each individual takes his own decision to save—some saving is compulsory, such as National Insurance, which pays for sickness and other benefits, and contributions to pension funds.

In Britain in the 1970s, despite the high rates of inflation, it is estimated that we now save about 14 per cent of our after-tax income, compared with 8 per cent in the late 1960s.

The clearing banks with their nationwide network of branches are able to provide a first-class money transfer service in which they have few competitors; they also offer various savings and investment facilities to their customers, but in this area they meet competition from a whole range of institutions offering numerous schemes with a bewildering array of differing interest rates and conditions. The objective of this Unit is to consider the range of savings and investment facilities provided by banks and other financial institutions. As rates of interest offered to savers are subject to fluctuations, none are quoted in the text, but Table 6.3 in Unit 6.14 gives those of the major savings institutions at the time of writing (February 1979). A column of the table has been left blank for you to enter the current rates.

6.2   Clearing Banks

They directly offer the following savings and investment facilities:

(*a*) deposit and/or savings accounts,
(*b*) fixed-term deposits, and
(*c*) their own unit trusts.

Indirectly they offer the facilities of their associated finance houses (see Unit 6.3) and act as agents in the provision of most of the savings and investment schemes mentioned in this Unit.

(*a*) **Deposit and/or savings accounts**
The operation of these accounts is fully considered in Units 13.3 and 13.4. They are ideal places in which to keep savings that are temporarily not needed. The money is readily available: normally seven days' notice of withdrawal is required, but in practice it is usually possible to make withdrawals without prior notice. Interest is calculated on a day-to-day basis and is usually credited to the account twice a year, often in June and December. It is paid *gross of tax* (that is, without deduction), and account holders who are taxpayers have to declare the amount of interest received to the Inland Revenue so that the correct amount of tax is charged.

(*b*) **Fixed-term deposits**
Where a customer has £10 000 or more to invest, all clearing banks can offer improved interest rates if the sum of money can be deposited for a set period of time. The period of deposit may range from a few days up to five years and the rate of interest, which is paid gross of tax, is fixed for the term. Interest is usually paid twice a year and the fixed rate depends upon the time period and how the bank views the trends in interest rates in the future: usually the longer the time period, the higher is the rate of interest paid. The customer benefits in that the interest rate is fixed for the period but, balanced against this must be the consideration that none of the funds can be withdrawn before the end of the term.

(*c*) **Unit trusts**
These provide a way for a saver to invest in stocks and shares indirectly; units may be bought or sold easily by dealing direct with those who run the trust—the unit trust managers—without the need to go through stockbrokers. Most people do not have sufficient time, experience or capital to be able to invest directly in stocks and shares; a unit trust solves this problem by collecting together

a pool of money subscribed by a large number of individual savers and then buying and selling stocks and shares with this money, using the expertise of professional investment managers. In return for his funds, the individual saver receives a certificate stating that he holds a certain number of units in the trust. The income of the trust consists of dividends paid by the companies whose shares the trust has bought and after deduction of certain management expenses, this is divided between the investors on the basis of the number of units held by each, and either distribution cheques are sent to them or the income is used to buy more units on their behalf.

The value of units in a trust varies with the changes in value of the shares purchased by the investment managers, and prices at which units may be bought and sold appear in most daily newspapers. While such transactions can be carried out by dealing direct with the unit trust, any bank is able to make purchases or sales for its customers. An investment in a unit trust should always be regarded as long-term because of the changes which may take place in the value of the trust's shares owned as a result of fluctuating stock exchange prices; such changes will, of course, affect the value of the units.

While in Britain, the concept of the unit trust dates back to 1931, the clearing banks and the Trustee Savings Banks did not establish their own trusts until the 1960s and 1970s. All the banks had previously built up considerable expertise in managing the investments of their customers (see Unit 14.8) and some had acted as trustees to unit trusts. There are at present a large number of different unit trusts—some connected with banks, others with insurance companies, and a number with professional savings companies. Most unit trusts have some declared objective: one may hope to invest its funds to achieve long-term capital growth (that is, so that the value of the units will rise over a period of time); another may concentrate its investments into shares which will pay high dividends, so that large distributions may be made to unitholders; yet another may concentrate on small companies, or overseas companies, or on certain groups of shares such as those of financial or oil companies. Most banks operate more than one unit trust and can usually supply leaflets giving details; they should also be able to give information about other trusts that are not directly connected with the bank.

While an intending investor can buy units of certain trusts from the bank, he can buy others direct from insurance companies and the professional savings companies. There is a variety of purchase schemes such as *straight purchase* (a sum of money is paid and a certain number of units received), *regular instalments* (monthly or other regular payments are made to the trust managers to be applied in the purchase of units) and *share exchange schemes* (an exchange of units for shares already held). There are certain tax advantages in the regular savings schemes linked with life assurance which are offered by a number of trusts, including those operated by the banks. The terms and conditions vary, particularly with the age of the unitholder: details are readily available from banks, unit trust managers and life assurance companies.

In law a unit trust is constituted by a trust deed made between the managers and the trustee, who must be independent of each other. The *trustee* of the fund—usually a bank or an insurance company—safeguards the interests of the purchasers of units who are beneficiaries of the trust fund, controls the issue of units, maintains a register of holders and generally watches over the management of the trust. The *managers* are the promoters of the unit trust, having the task of persuading the investing public to entrust its money to them for managing, and are responsible for the day-to-day management of the fund and for making a market in the units. They aim to make a profit out of promoting the trust from the charges they are entitled to levy for their services. The trustee will not interfere with the day-to-day management of the trust unless the actions of the managers are in conflict with the interests of unitholders.

6.3 Finance Houses

Most banks have a finance house as a subsidiary or associated company and there are a number of houses not connected with a bank (see Unit 5.7). All of these offer, among other facilities, hire purchase to personal and business customers. Most accept deposits from members of the public as a source of a part of their funds and pay interest at rates that vary with the amount of money and the time period. Where larger amounts, commonly more than £1 000, can be deposited for fixed terms of between one and three years, higher rates of interest can usually be obtained. Interest on accounts is usually paid gross of tax but sometimes the finance house will give the depositor the option of receiving interest net of tax. Depending on the type of deposit, notice of withdrawal will vary between one month and twelve months.

6.4 Building Societies

Building societies are non-profit-making organizations that attract funds from savers and then lend them to people who wish to buy a house. With branch networks, longer opening hours (including Saturday mornings) and a range of savings accounts, the building societies are the banks' biggest competitors for 'High Street' deposits. Many savers compare the interest paid by building societies and the banks: any advantage of one over the other is quickly noticed and funds are soon transferred across the 'High Street'. If, after allowance has been made for tax, bank deposit rates are higher than those offered by the building societies, the Government may place a maximum limit on the rates offered by the bank: in 1973, for instance, bank deposit rates for amounts less than £10 000 were pegged at $9\frac{1}{2}$ per cent to prevent a flow of funds away from the building societies who were unable to raise their rates to compete at a time of 'dear' money because it would have made mortgage repayments from borrowers excessively high.

There are currently some 400 different building societies operating in Britain, with total shares and deposits of £26 109 million at December 1976: they range from local societies with a few branches to the largest societies with countrywide branch networks. Most belong to the Building Societies Association, which imposes certain conditions on its members with regard to the maintenance of minimum ratios of cash to invested funds, and also advises them on rates to be allowed to investors and charged to borrowers. The tax position on interest paid to society investors differs from the banks, in that there is no standard-rate income tax to pay on the interest received—the society accounts directly to the Inland Revenue in respect of this tax. The interest should always be declared to the tax authorities because there may be a liability in respect of tax at rates above the standard rate. The banks, on the other hand, always pay interest on their deposits gross of tax. When comparing rates between building societies and banks, therefore, it is essential to compare like with like: either the gross equivalent of society rates (as displayed in their offices) should be compared with the deposit rates of the banks or, alternatively, tax at standard rate should be deducted from the rates of the banks to make them directly comparable with society net rates. Under the arrangements that the societies have with the Inland Revenue, tax already paid by a society cannot be reclaimed by investors if they do not normally pay tax—so, for a non-taxpayer, such as a person living only on a State pension, a building society is not the best place to keep savings.

Most societies offer a range of accounts which will usually include a share account, deposit account, Save-As-You-Earn (SAYE) scheme, regular savings account and a term share account. The terms of these accounts—minimum deposit, notice of withdrawal required, maximum 'on demand' withdrawal amount and so on—vary from one society to another; it would be useful for you to obtain some leaflets from different societies and make a comparison.

'It's something of a needle match between the Bank Manager and the Building Society Manager'

(a) Share account

This is the commonest type of building society account. The account holder, who may deposit up to a maximum of £15 000 (£30 000 for a joint account), is deemed to be a member of the society and holds a share, but unlike shares of companies quoted on the Stock Exchange, he may withdraw his share or increase it at will, subject only to the society's regulations. Interest is calculated on a day-to-day basis and is normally paid twice a year, and most societies give the investor the option of either having his interest credited to his account or receiving it by cheque. Withdrawals can be made either in cash or by cheque, subject to any limitations imposed by the society.

(b) Deposit account

The deposit account offers the same facilities as a share account but with even greater security: a depositor only lends his money to the society whereas a share account holder has a share in the society. In the unlikely event of a society meeting financial difficulties, the depositor would be repaid in full before the share account holders. The additional security is recognized by the payment of a slightly lower rate of interest on deposit accounts than on share accounts.

(c) Save-As-You-Earn scheme (SAYE)

This is a contractual saving scheme under the terms of which regular monthly savings of up to £20 a month are paid for a period of five years, after which payments cease. At the end of this period a tax-free bonus is earned and if the total savings plus bonus are left for a further two years, the tax-free bonus is doubled. The rate of interest on this type of account is fixed, and is higher than that offered on share and deposit accounts, although the rate is reduced if the terms of the scheme are not maintained.

(d) Regular savings account

This account is for people who wish to save a part of their income regularly without the constraints of the SAYE scheme. The saver agrees to make monthly payments into the account of, usually, between £1 and £50 (£100 for a joint account)—the amount can be altered, subject to the maximum and minimum limits, if financial circumstances should change. The time period for saving is not fixed and limited withdrawals are permitted; alternatively, the account may be closed when the funds are required. Interest rates are higher than for share and deposit accounts, but lower than that paid under the SAYE scheme.

(e) Term share account

Building societies offer higher rates of interest if funds can be deposited for a fixed period of time, rather like the fixed-term deposits of the banks. Unlike the bank deposit rates, however, the interest rates are subject to fluctuation but are usually 0.5 to 1 per cent above the offered on share accounts, depending on the length of the period for which the funds are deposited; but minimum deposits are much lower than those required by the banks and may be as low as £100, although this varies from one society to another.

Perhaps the biggest advantage that the building societies have over the banks is their ability to give special consideration to their investors for a mortgage. Some societies have devised special accounts for first-time home buyers whereby they will guarantee a mortgage after a set period of regular savings, subject to certain conditions. However, not all investors are interested in obtaining a mortgage and building societies offer a safe, convenient place to keep savings with a range of accounts to suit most requirements.

6.5   Savings Banks

There are two principal types of savings bank operating in Britain today: Trustee Savings Banks and the National Savings Bank, discussed briefly in Units 5.9 and 5.10. National Girobank has also recently started to offer a deposit account service.

(a)   Trustee Savings Banks
The TSBs offer savings accounts, investment accounts, term deposits and unit trusts.

The savings account is intended for day-to-day savings and may be opened by individuals, clubs and societies; any amount may be kept in the account and there is no maximum balance. Interest is calculated on a monthly basis from the 21st of each month and applied to the account on 20 November each year. For many years the first £70 of interest earned was free of all United Kingdom income tax, although this facility will be phased out from November 1979. Withdrawals are normally made in cash from the branch where the account is maintained although cash may usually be withdrawn at other branches upon presentation of the pass book, subject to a maximum of £30. Withdrawals may also be made in the form of a cheque, although a small charge is usually made for this service.

The investment account earns a higher rate of interest, paid gross of tax, the interest being calculated and credited to accounts in a similar way to savings accounts; but there is no tax concession. A period of notice of withdrawal is usually required, and although cash may be taken out of the account on demand, interest will be deducted relating to the period of notice that has been forgone.

Term deposits are accepted by TSBs, the minimum amount being £1 000 for two years at a fixed rate of interest, which is paid gross.

Unit trusts. Like the clearing banks, TSBs have their own unit trusts which offer a direct investment scheme, as well as a variety of insurance-linked monthly savings plans.

(*b*) **The National Savings Bank**

The National Savings Bank, which is run by the Government's Department for National Savings, offers two accounts for savers—the ordinary account and the investment account.

Ordinary accounts may be opened by anyone aged seven or over, clubs and societies, and any amount from 25 pence may be deposited up to a maximum balance of £10 000. Interest is calculated on a monthly basis from the first day of each month. It is credited to the account on 31 December each year and is paid gross of tax. A tax concession applies in that the first £70 of interest is free of all United Kingdom income tax. A depositor may withdraw up to £50 cash on demand at any savings bank post office but the pass book may be retained for checking at Savings Bank Headquarters. Larger amounts may be withdrawn in cash or by crossed warrant (which is similar to a cheque) by completing a notice of withdrawal form, but it takes a few days for the transaction to authorized. An emergency service for withdrawals of up to £75 is available; it involves telegraphing Savings Bank Headquarters asking them to authorize payment of the amount at a named post office.

Investment accounts are intended for longer-term savings. The interest rate is higher than that on ordinary accounts; it is calculated in the same way but is paid gross of tax with no tax concessions. Accounts may be opened on similar terms to the ordinary account but the minimum deposit is £1 and the maximum balance is £50 000. One month's notice of withdrawal is required and this is effected by completing a withdrawal form, the payment being made either in cash at a named savings bank post office or by crossed warrant.

(*c*) **National Girobank**

The Post Office's banking division has recently started to offer a deposit account service. The interest is paid gross of tax and a bonus (currently 1 per cent each year) is paid on the minimum balance over six months. Withdrawals may be made by completing a form and sending it to Girobank Headquarters. The funds can either be credited to a Girobank current account or collected from a named post office within a few days.

6.6   National Savings

The Department for National Savings offers a variety of savings facilities, besides the National Savings Bank. These include National Savings Certificates, British Savings Bonds, Premium Savings Bonds and the Save-As-You-Earn Scheme; all may be bought at most banks and all savings bank post offices. Certain Government stocks and bonds may be bought through the Department at low rates of commission (see Unit 6.7). Table 6.1 shows the total of national savings at 31 August 1978, together with amounts for each type of savings.

Table 6.1   United Kingdom National Savings at 31 August 1978

	£ millions
National Savings Bank:	
Ordinary accounts	1 783.5
Investment accounts	1 187.5
Trustee Savings banks:	
Ordinary departments[1]	1 736.5
New department[2]	3 136.7
Premium Savings Bonds	1 311.7
Save-As-You-Earn	419.0
National Savings Certificates	4 686.7
British Savings Bonds	813.6
National Savings stamps and gift tokens outstanding	8.7
Other securities on the National Savings stock register	651.9
Total	15 735.8

[1] TSB savings accounts
[2] TSB investment and current accounts

Source: *Monthly Digest of Statistics*, Central Statistical Office

(*a*) **National Savings Certificates**
These were first issued in 1916 and there have been several subsequent issues, the current being the eighteenth. Each unit or certificate costs £10 and they may be purchased by almost anyone, including a child under seven years of age: the maximum holding of the present issue is 150 units. Units increase in value with time: each unit of the present issue becomes worth £15 after five years, which is equal to a compound rate of interest of 8·45 per cent per year. Repayment of units can be effected at any time, but with the present issue units increase in value most during the fourth and fifth years after purchase. After five years they continue to increase in value, but more slowly. The interest, which is paid only when the certificates are cashed, is free of all United Kingdom income tax and capital gains tax.

A special issue of National Savings Certificates is currently available which may only be held by people over retirement age—sixty-five for men and sixty for women. This is known as the *Index-linked Retirement Issue* and is designed to protect the buying power of the savings of retired people. Certificates do not have a set growth rate but instead increase in value in proportion to the rise in prices: this is measured using the United Kingdom General Index of Retail Prices, comparing the change in the index between the month of purchase and the month of sale of the certificates. The certificates must have been held for at least one year before this calculation may be made, only the purchase price being repaid on certificates encashed during the first year. If the certificates are held to maturity—five years—the holder receives an additional fixed bonus equal to 4 per cent of their face value. Repayments are free of all United Kingdom income tax and capital gains tax. Each certificate costs £10 (the minimum purchase) and the maximum holding is currently 70 units, costing £700.

(b) British Savings Bonds

These bonds may be held by almost anyone, including children under seven years old. They are sold in units of £5 (the minimum holding) and the maximum holding is £10 000. Interest is paid in June and December each year, gross of tax. To earn any interest the bonds must be held for a minimum period of six months; if they are held for five years to maturity, they are repayable with a 4 per cent tax-free bonus. Bonds that have been held for six months or more may be cashed before maturity but will not qualify for the bonus. In all cases, one month's notice of withdrawal is required.

(c) Premium Savings Bonds

These provide a popular method of combining a form of 'saving' with the possibility of winning a large prize. They may be held only by individuals, not by clubs or societies, and may not be bought by children under sixteen years old, although they may be purchased on a child's behalf by a parent or guardian. Bonds may be bought in units of £1, the minimum purchase being £5, and the maximum holding by one person is 2 000 units. When it has been held for three clear calendar months each bond is eligible for inclusion in the draw for prizes. The prize fund is formed by calculating one month's interest at the rate of $5\frac{3}{4}$ per cent per year on the bonds eligible for the draw. Each month there is a top prize of £100 000, followed by one prize of £25 000 and further prizes of £5 000, £1 000, £500, £100, £50 and £25. Additionally, each week there is a draw for one prize of £75 000, one prize of £50 000 and twenty-five prizes of £1 000. The numbers of the winning bonds are selected by an electronic device nicknamed ERNIE ('Electronic Random Number Indicator Equipment') and each £1 unit can only win one prize in each draw for which it is eligible. If, by chance, more than one prize should be won by the same £1 unit, it will be allotted the highest prize for which it is drawn. All prizes are free of all United Kingdom income tax and capital gains tax and bondholders are notified by post of any winnings. Bonds are easy to encash, the funds being received within a few days of completion of an encashment form.

(d) The Save-As-You-Earn (SAYE) Scheme

The Department for National Savings scheme, which is available to anyone aged sixteen or over, operates in a similar way to that offered by the building societies (see Unit 6.4). Under the contract a person agrees to save a regular monthly amount for five years: the minimum amount is £4 a month and the maximum £20. Unlike the building society scheme, which carries a fixed return, the National Savings scheme is linked to changes in the United Kingdom General Index of Retail Prices provided that the five-year contract is completed.

If the saver stops payments within one year of the starting date, no interest is paid and the savings are returned; if payment ceases after the first year but before completion of the contract, interest is paid at 6 per cent per year with no index-linking. If the contract is completed, each monthly contribution is index-linked separately from the first day of the month following payment. The savings may be withdrawn after five years or may be left invested in the scheme for a further two years and, at the end of this time, repayment will be made in accordance with changes in the index, together with a tax-free bonus equal to two monthly contributions. All interest and bonuses are free of United Kingdom income tax and capital gains tax.

Both the 'Retirement Issue' National Savings Certificates and the SAYE scheme operated by the Department for National Savings offer a form of 'inflation proofing' for savings in that, provided the investor conforms to the terms of the issue, he will receive an amount of money at the end of the period that will generally buy as much in goods and services as when the money was first invested. This new concept in savings has proved popular during the last few years of high inflation in Britain, and restrictions have had to be placed on the maximum amounts that may be invested.

6.7   Government Stocks and Bonds

While a wide range of Government borrowing in the form of stocks and bonds is quoted on the Stock Exchange, some are also listed on the National Savings Stock Register and may be bought and sold through savings bank post offices without having to use a stockbroker. This makes them very easy to buy and sell and low rates of commission are charged. There are currently between forty and fifty different stocks and bonds in which transactions may be effected in this way: these range from $2\frac{1}{2}$ per cent Consols and $3\frac{1}{2}$ per cent War Stock, both with no fixed date for repayment, to $15\frac{1}{2}$ per cent Treasury Loan to be repaid between the years 2012 and 2015. All are bought and sold on the London Stock Exchange by the National Debt Commissioners at the price ruling at the time of the transaction. As with any other quoted stocks, the prices at which they are bought or sold are subject to fluctuation and they should, therefore, be regarded as a longer-term investment, to be held for at least one year.

To make a purchase, an investment application form is completed and sent with a cheque or other payment to cover the estimated cost to the Bonds and Stock Office of the Department for National Savings—and over-payment would be returned. Like other stocks and shares (see Unit 6.12), an investor receives a certificate showing the description and amount of the stock or bonds registered in his name. To sell, a sale application form is completed and sent with the certificate to the Bonds and Stock Office. Using this system it is possible to buy up to £5 000 cash value of any particular stock or bond on any one day, but there is no limit to the total amount that may be held, nor to the amount that may be sold on any one day. Interest is paid twice a year by the Bank of England, without deduction of income tax. Investors are also liable to capital gains tax where a gain, or profit, arises from the sale of British Government securities within twelve months of acquisition. Gains arising after twelve months are exempt from capital gains tax.

6.8 Local Authorities

For the saver who is prepared to deposit his money for a number of years, local authorities provide a safe investment at fixed rates of interest. In return for his deposit, the saver receives a bond issued by the authority. Rates of interest, which is usually paid twice a year, vary with the amount of money and the period of the deposit: generally, the larger the amount and the longer the period, the higher is the interest rate. The minimum amount accepted by most authorities is £100 (often more), and the time period ranges from one to ten years. As the money is deposited for a fixed period of time it is extremely difficult to withdraw it before the due date of repayment.

Most local authorities accept loans from members of the public and some advertise their rates and terms in newspapers. The Chartered Institute of Public Finance and Accountancy (CIPFA) operates a Loans Bureau which co-ordinates the borrowing requirement of local authorities. A weekly list is produced containing details of authorities wishing to borrow and the terms they offer.

Another form of local authority borrowing is carried out by the issue of one-year bonds, known as *yearlings*, which are quoted on the Stock Exchange and may be purchased by private individuals.

6.9 Life Assurance

Every life assurance salesman will tell you what a good form of saving for the future it is to take out one of his company's policies. While this is probably perfectly true, some assurance companies have a better record than others and it pays to compare the terms offered by several companies.

The idea behind most life assurance policies is to provide a long-term method of saving and also to give protection to dependent relatives—usually wife and children—from the payment of the first premium by promising to pay out a sum of money in the event of the death of the assured. (Notice the term *assurance*, implying that the event covered by the policy is certain or assured to happen: the life assured will either reach a certain age or die before reaching that age. Contrast this with *insurance*: the law requires us to take out certain insurance before we drive a car or ride a motor-cycle on the roads—we hope that we will never have to make a claim on the policy but we insure against the possibility.)

Life assurance policies are sold by insurance brokers and banks, who usually deal with a range of assurance companies and earn a commission on sales, and also by company agents who only deal with their own company's policies and are paid a salary plus commission on sales. In order to encourage this form of savings, the Government generally gives tax relief on the *premiums* (the regular payments made to the assurance company, usually by the person whose life is assured). For most people, the effect of this relief is to give a saving of $17\frac{1}{2}$ per cent of the premium. Premiums are paid net (that is, less tax relief) to the assurance company, usually monthly.

The main types of policy are endowment, whole-life and term assurance. With all policies the amount of the premium paid depends on the *term* of the policy (the time period before the 'assured' event happens), the age of the life assured, the state of his or her health, the sum assured and whether the policy is with or without profits (see below).

An endowment policy provides life assurance for an agreed term of years for a fixed amount of money, known as the *sum assured*, and pays out at the end of the term or on death, whichever occurs first. It provides an excellent way of saving for retirement while at the same time giving protection to dependent relatives in the event of the early death of the life assured. The term of assurance can be arranged to suit the needs of the individual. A young man of twenty considering such a policy would probably take one out for a forty-year term, to mature when he is sixty. This would give financial protection to any dependants he might have in the future and would provide him with a lump sum of money at or near retirement age. A policy with a shorter term—perhaps ten years—might be taken out by a middle-aged or older man.

Endowment policies can be used as a means of financing house purchase. A mortgage is obtained, and at the same time an endowment policy is taken out for a sum that will repay the amount of the mortgage. During the period of the mortgage, the borrower pays only the interest and none of the capital sum; at the same time he pays the premiums on the endowment policy. At the end of the period, the endowment policy matures and the capital sum of the mortgage is paid off with the proceeds. In the event of the assured's death before the end of the period, the proceeds of the policy would always be sufficient to repay the amount of the mortgage. This method is particularly beneficial from a tax point of view because tax relief may be claimed by the assured on both his assurance premiums and mortgage interest; it becomes even more beneficial when a 'with-profits' endowment policy (see below) is used.

Whole-life assurance differs from endowment assurance in that the assurance company pays the benefits only upon the death of the life assured, whenever it may occur. The premiums are usually paid for the whole of a person's life, although some policies specify that premiums shall only be paid up to a certain age, after which the policy will remain in force without payment of further premiums.

Term assurance is similar to a whole-life policy in that it pays the benefits on the death of the life assured, but differs in that they are paid during the term of the policy which is for a shorter period of time—perhaps ten years—than the whole of a person's life. Thus it is a form of short-term assurance which can be used to give protection to dependent relatives at a much lower cost than an endowment or whole-life policy. It is an attractive policy for a man with a wife and young children who wants to provide a substantial sum of money for them in the event of his early death. If the assured survives the term of the policy he receives no benefits. There are variations on this type of policy: one of these, instead of paying a lump sum on the death of the assured, provides regular payments to the assured's wife for a certain number of years.

All endowment and whole-life policies can be taken out *with profits* or *without profits*. By investing the premiums paid by policyholders in stocks, shares and other investments—investment funds totalled over £27 000 million at December 1975—the assurance company earns profits. The policyholders can share in these profits by taking out a 'with profits' policy—the premiums for this will be slightly higher than an equivalent 'without profits' policy. The share of the profits or *bonus* is added to the original sum assured and the increased amount is paid out either upon maturity of the policy or upon the death of the assured, depending on the type of policy. During inflationary times, it is sensible to take out a 'with profits' policy as the profits earned will help the sum assured to retain its purchasing power, although there is no guarantee that it will do so.

Many companies offer life assurance linked to the purchase of unit trusts. Under this type of scheme a percentage of the premiums paid by the assured is invested in a named unit trust, and the balance is used to provide term assurance. At the end of the agreed term the policyholder receives either the sale proceeds of the units purchased by him over the period or the units themselves, which may be held as long as he wishes; in the event of the life assured's death within the term, the dependants would receive either the value of the units bought up to the date of death or a guaranteed sum of money, whichever is the greater. The advantages of this scheme are that all premiums are eligible for tax relief and that if the value of the units rises during the term of the policy, there could be a substantial increase in the sum paid when it matures. The disadvantage is that the value of the units might fall, although some schemes guarantee a minimum payment upon maturity. Schemes of this type are offered by banks, building societies and unit trusts as well as by assurance companies; advertisements appear each week in most Sunday newspapers.

Besides being good methods of long-term saving, most endowment and whole-life policies may be used as security for a bank loan or overdraft (see Unit 17.6).

6.10 Annuities

There comes a time in most people's lives, usually at retirement, when they can no longer save and have to start using their accumulated savings to supplement any pension they may receive. The problem at this stage is to know how much of the savings can be used each year to see them through to the end of their lives: a person may live to a 'ripe old age' or may die within a few months, so that the savings may have to last over a considerable number of years or only for a little while. Assurance and certain specialist companies help to resolve this problem by selling *annuities* which, in return for a lump sum of a person's savings, will provide him with a guaranteed income until his death, the company taking over the 'risk' that he will live to a considerable age.

There are different annuity schemes including *reversionary annuities* where payment is made to a person during his lifetime, with continuance in full on his death to his widow until her death. Some annuities are *immediate*, starting to pay a regular income from the date of purchase; others are *deferred*, commencing at some future specified date, and offering an opportunity for a saver to prepare for retirement by paying regular premiums while he is still in work, up to the date of the start of the annuity. *Temporary annuities* can be arranged for a fixed period of time, such as five or ten years; upon payment of the lump sum of money, the annuity will be paid for the period.

Rates charged for annuities vary with the type required and with the age and health of the saver. The amount paid under an annuity may be quoted per £100 of capital invested; alternatively, the capital cost of a specified amount of income each year may be quoted by the company. For income tax purposes, payments under an annuity are regarded partly as capital and partly as income.

6.11 Pension Funds

Many large employers operate pension funds on behalf of their employees. In most schemes the employee contributes an amount of money each week or month and the firm also makes a contribution. Both of these represent saving: the employee is deferring some part of his present income until retirement, while the employer is similarly saving on behalf of the employee. Pension funds have considerable investment resources at the disposal of their trustees and are often managed by professional advisers such as insurance companies and specialist bank departments; their funds may be invested in stocks and shares, in property and sometimes even in works of art. When an employee reaches retirement age he starts to receive the benefits of the fund based on the contributions he has made to it.

Certain pension funds are approved by the Inland Revenue and contributions to such funds are allowable for tax relief. The funds are free from United Kingdom taxes provided that the benefits obtained from contributions do not exceed certain limits.

6.12 Stocks and Shares

A *stock exchange* is a market place for 'second-hand' stocks and shares issued by public limited companies, public bodies and governments: those who have stocks or shares to sell are put in touch with those who wish to buy. The stocks and shares are 'second-hand' because the company or institution issued them to the public when it wanted to raise funds and it receives no further benefit as they now change hands: the only effect is that one shareholder or stock-holder is substituted for another. *Stock* is always stated in terms of cash—for instance, £50 of $3\frac{1}{2}$ per cent War Stock—and is usually issued by the Govern-ment and other public bodies; *shares*, which are usually issued by limited companies, are stated by the number—for example, 20 shares in Midland Bank Ltd. (Shares and limited companies are considered more fully in Unit 12.6).

Purchasing units in a unit trust is a way of investing in stocks and shares indirectly; but many people like to invest directly on the Stock Exchange, buying and selling the shares of their choice. It is often thought that, to invest in stocks and shares, one must have a lot of money and know a stockbroker; neither is true. A hundred pounds or so can be invested just as easily as ten thousand and a bank will always buy or sell stocks and shares on the instructions of a customer, using its own broker. It should be said that a Stock Exchange investment is usually a long-term venture and is not the place for money that may be needed urgently, and also that, while shares can go up in value, some-times quite dramatically, they can fall in value equally dramatically. This is one of the best reasons for investing in a unit trust; a fall in the value of one or two investments will be evened out by the other shares making up the unit

'My God! Aren't they the managers of our investment portfolio?'

trust's *portfolio*, or selection, of shares. Unit trusts can be readily bought and sold in small quantities; for investors with a little more money, there are *investment trust* companies that operate in a similar way—they pool the resources of their investors and purchase a portfolio of stocks and shares. Investment trusts have their shares quoted on the Stock Exchange and so have to be bought or sold through a stockbroker.

The problem with both unit and investment trusts is that though the investor is able to ascertain the general aims of the trust managers, he has no personal say in the purchase or sale of specific shares. Many people prefer to make their own investment decisions and, while a basic understanding of the techniques and procedures is required, it is not difficult to find sources of information. The *Financial Times* is the leading daily financial newspaper, and most stockbrokers, professional advisers and some banks also subscribe to the highly specialized *Stock Exchange Daily List*. These two newspapers are usually somewhat complex for the private investor, who is better advised to read the financial pages of the Sunday newspapers where certain shares are 'tipped' by financial journalists. It is worth remembering that shares recommended in this way will be 'marked up' on the Stock Exchange when it opens for business because of the expected increase in demand, and will cost more than the price quoted in the paper. There are also *investors' letters* available on subscription that claim to make recommendations of shares to buy or sell, but because of their cost these letters are not appropriate for the small investor. Stockbrokers' *opinions* on particular shares can be obtained by clients: these are usually well written and worth taking note of, but they are time-consuming to produce and the stock market price of the share can alter during their preparation. It is also usually possible to obtain a brief brokers' opinion over the telephone. Banks do not give advice on individual shares but will always obtain an opinion from their broker on behalf of a customer.

When a person has decided which stock or share he wants to buy, he gives the necessary instructions to a stockbroker either directly, or indirectly through his bank. If he is buying shares, he states the number of shares he requires; if stock, the money amount of stock. Alternatively, he may ask the broker to invest a certain amount of money—that is, to buy as many shares or as much stock as the money will buy. If there are likely to be sudden fluctuations in the price of the stock or share he wants, he may give the broker a limit above which he may not purchase without reference back to the investor; any limit, however, should be fixed with care in order not to handicap the broker— the price of a share quoted in a newspaper may well be the *middle price*, which is a price midway between the buying price and the selling price (see Unit 6.13). Once instructions have been received from a client, the stockbroker contacts the jobbers at the Stock Exchange and attempts to buy the number of shares required. The *jobbers* are the 'stallholders' of the Stock Exchange, each specializing in the shares of certain types of company, such as banks and insurance, engineering, shipping or oil, and buying and selling shares of the sector in which they specialize. They sell shares at a higher price than that for which they bought them, the difference being their *turn* or profit. If demand for the shares of a particular company is strong then both the buying price and the selling price will be increased or marked-up; if sellers exceed buyers, the price will be marked down. The Stock Exchange has often been described as the nearest thing to a perfect market in that demand increases the price, while an excess of supply reduces it. The stockbroker or his agent at the Stock Exchange finds a jobber prepared to sell the required number of shares at a satisfactory price and the *bargain*, as Stock Exchange transactions are called, is completed.

The broker sends his client a *contract note* which advises him of the number of shares purchased, the price, details of commission and expenses and a *settlement date*. The Stock Exchange year is divided into a number of *accounts*, usually of two weeks' duration, and the settlement day, when all the transactions of the account are settled and payments between brokers are made and received, falls a few days after the end of each account. Contract notes should always be kept by investors because they are the evidence required by the tax authorities to determine whether there is any liability to capital gains tax if the shares are later sold at a profit.

The shares belong to the investor from the date of the contract note but it will be some time before he receives the share certificate. In any transaction there are two brokers involved, one selling and one buying. The selling broker asks his client, who is disposing of the shares, to sign a special form called a *stock transfer form* and to return this to him with the certificate for the shares that have been sold. The signed stock transfer form and this share certificate are passed to the buyer's broker who, after inserting the name and address of his client, sends them both to the registrar of the company whose shares have changed hands. The company registrar, using the stock transfer form, withdraws the old share certificate, deletes the name of the original holder from the records and issues a new certificate in the name of the purchaser, recording his name and address in the register of shareholders. The new owner of the shares will receive dividends at least once a year (commonly twice), as his share of the company's profits, will be sent the directors' report and accounts after the end of the company's financial year and is entitled to vote at the company's annual general meeting and certain other meetings of the shareholders. He is not entitled to participate in the day-to-day running of the company, this being the responsibility of the chairman and board of directors who are voted into office by the shareholders at the annual general meeting. The purchase or sale of shares in a company or of stock in a Government loan does not affect the total number of shares or the total amount of stock in issue; all that has happened is that one stockholder or shareholder is removed from the records and another one put in his place.

On a large stock exchange such as London, trading takes place in many thousands of different company shares and Government and other stocks; but the total of these is only increased by fresh companies coming 'to the market' or by new stocks and shares being issued. This happens when a private company has reached a large enough size to become a public limited company (see Unit 12.6) and makes arrangements with an issuing house (see Unit 5.3) for its shares to be placed before the public in the form of a *new issue*, a procedure that may be carried out in several different ways. Usually an advertisement or prospectus is placed in financial newspapers inviting the public and financial institutions such as insurance companies, unit trusts and investment trusts—the *institutional investors*—to subscribe to the capital of the company. By law, the prospectus must contain certain information about the issue and the company. If sufficient subscriptions are received permission will be sought from the Stock Exchange Council for the shares to be quoted and dealt in on the Stock Exchange, and once this permission has been granted trading in the shares of the company may begin.

The total of stocks and shares may also be increased when a company already quoted on the Stock Exchange wishes to raise extra money, perhaps to finance a new project. This is usually done by means of a *rights issue* which gives shareholders the 'right' to buy more shares, often at an especially good price, in proportion to their existing holdings. Sometimes a *scrip* or *bonus issue* is made to shareholders—this is a book-keeping entry that gives a shareholder a number of extra free shares in proportion to the number he already holds. This is done when profits have been retained in the business rather than being distributed to shareholders as extra dividends, and also where the assets of the company, particularly land, have increased in value over the years. It may then be felt appropriate to increase the share capital of the company to reflect this enhanced value and these benefits are passed on to the shareholders. It may seem like 'something for nothing' but the shareholders are unlikely to be much better off because when a bonus issue is made, the stock market price of each share usually falls in direct proportion to the number of extra shares issued. Unless the rate of dividend (see Unit 6.13) is increased the shareholder's income will not change, because the company's total dividend will remain the same, though it will be spread over a greater number of shares.

6.13 Understanding the Financial Press

Information in the *Financial Times* about stocks and shares is classified under broad headings, such as 'Banks and hire purchase', which relate to the specialities of the Stock Exchange jobbers. Table 6.2 shows how the newspaper presents the details of the shares of the 'big four' clearing banks: information about most other stocks and shares is set out similarly.

High and low. As the heading suggests, this column gives the highest and lowest prices, in pence, reached by the company's shares during the period in question—in this case from 1 January 1978 to 23 October 1978.

Stock. This gives the name of the company whose stocks or shares are quoted, together with the *nominal value*—the face value, as opposed to the market value—of the shares, £1 in each of the examples. As there is no indication otherwise, they are all 'ordinary' shares (see Unit 12.6(*b*)).

Table 6.2   The presentation of share prices

				+ or	Dividend		Yield	
High	Low	Stock	Price	—	net	Cover	gross	P/E
368	296	Barclays £1	340	− 4	13.28	5.7	5.8	5.3
297	242	Lloyds £1	260	− 2	9.23	4.8	5.3	5.9
390	330	Midland £1	348	− 2	14.97	4.3	6.4	5.5
298	250	Nat. West £1	270	− 2	11.66	4.2	6.4	5.6

Banks and hire purchase
1978
Tuesday, 24 October 1978

Source: *Financial Times*

Price. The price, quoted in pence, is the *middle price*—midway between the buying and selling price—at the time that the exchange closed on the previous day. This is not necessarily the price that will be found ruling when the exchange opens the next morning, for there may have been 'after hours trading' following the closing of the exchange. Even though the nominal values of the shares of the 'big four' banks are all £1, it does not follow that the different market prices reflect in any way the relative strength or weakness of a particular bank—many other factors are involved.

Sometimes 'xd' is marked against a company's shares to indicate that dealings take place *ex-dividend.* This means that the company is shortly to pay a dividend, so that buyers of shares cannot be recorded on the shareholders' register in time to receive the dividend, and it will therefore be paid to the seller who will be entitled to keep it. The opposite of this is 'cd' or *cum dividend,* where the buyer is entitled to receive the dividend; should he not be registered in time so that the payment is sent to the seller, the money has to be handed over to the buyer.

+ or −. This gives the change in the share price in pence from the previous closing price.

Dividend net. This indicates the percentage dividend paid to the shareholders in respect of the last financial year, based on the nominal value of the shares. For example, for each £1 ordinary share held in Barclays Bank, the holder would have received dividends totalling 13.28p (£0.1328) from the profits earned by the bank in the previous financial year. It is a net dividend and there is no further liability on the part of the shareholder for standard-rate taxation because of the special way in which companies pay tax on their profits as assessed by the Inland Revenue: this tax is known as *corporation tax.* If required, the *gross dividend* may be found by making the following calculation:

$$\text{Gross dividend} = \frac{£1}{£1 \text{ less standard rate tax}} \times \text{Dividend received}$$

Using the figures from Barclays Bank, and allowing for standard-rate taxation at 33p in the pound,

$$\text{Gross dividend} = \frac{£1}{£0.67} \times £0.1328 = £0.1982$$

For shares with a nominal value of £1, this is equal to a 19.82 per cent dividend. On the advice sent to the shareholder with the dividend warrant or cheque, it would be shown as 'dividend payable £0.1328, tax credit £0.0654'. The *tax credit* is payable by the company to the Inland Revenue and represents a part payment of corporation tax: shareholders who pay little or no tax may be able to claim relief or payment to them of the amount of the tax credit.

Most shareholders own more than one share in the company and they would, of course, receive only one dividend warrant for all their shares.

Cover. Cover states the number of times the net profit earned—the profit after payment of all expenses—for potential distribution to the ordinary shareholders covers the amount required for the gross dividend. Thus, while Barclays Bank paid a gross dividend of £0.1982 on each £1 ordinary share, this amount was covered 5.7 times by profits available for distribution. Cover therefore gives an indication of the profitability of the company and shows that profits are being retained to increase the value of the business: the bank may well pay higher dividends in the future.

Yield gross. This translates into terms of the share's market price the dividend that the company paid in the previous year: it shows the amount of gross income that can be expected if £100 is invested. Supposing that I ask my stockbroker to invest £100 in National Westminster Bank ordinary shares and he is able to obtain them at £2.70 each (see Table 6.2). I would become the owner of thirty-seven shares (£100 ÷ £2.70). If the bank paid the same dividend this year as last, the gross earnings of the shares would amount to £6.40, made up as follows:

Net dividend on 37 shares at £0·1166 each	£4.31	(paid to me)
Tax credit	£2.12	(paid to Inland Revenue by the company as a part of the corporation tax due)
Gross dividend [(£1 ÷ £0.67) × £4.31]	£6.43	

(The difference of 3p arises because of a rounding of figures.)

When investing £100 in shares with a nominal value of £1 the gross dividend is also the gross yield in percentage terms. However, it may be calculated for any shares as follows:

$$\text{Gross yield} = \frac{\text{Gross dividend} \times \text{Nominal value}}{\text{Market price}}$$

Gross yield enables the shares of one company to be compared with those of another and comparison can also be made with interest rates payable by other investments.

P/E. The price/earnings ratio, or P/E as it is usually called, denotes how many years' purchase of the latest net earnings per share is represented by the current share price: put simply, this is calculated by dividing the market price by the earnings per share. In Table 6.2, each ordinary Lloyds Bank share with a nominal value of £1 pays a net dividend of £0.0923, covered 4.8 times: thus earnings per share are £0.44 (£0.0923 × 4.8), although only a part of this is distributed to the shareholders. With a share price of £2.60 it will take 5.9 years for the anual earnings per share to equal the market prices:

$$\text{P/E ratio} = \frac{£2.60}{£0.44} = 5.9 \text{ years}$$

It follows that the lower the price/earnings ratio, the sooner the current market price of the shares will be 'purchased' by earnings; the higher the ratio, the longer this will take. Thus the P/E ratio provides an indicator of the 'earning power' of different shares and comparison may be made between companies in the same sector.

You will find it useful to have a look at the share prices in a newspaper such as the *Financial Times*, perhaps comparing the 'big four' banks with some of the other quoted banks and hire purchase companies. Look at the cover, gross yield and price/earnings ratios too, and contrast them with shares listed in other sections.

6.14 Choosing an Investment

The range of investments available to a saver is extensive and, to some, bewildering. The answers to the following questions should be considered before making an investment decision:

(i) How much money have I available for investment?
(ii) How long before I shall need the money?
(iii) Shall I need a part of the savings in an emergency?
(iv) Do I pay standard-rate income tax and will I continue to do so in the future?
(v) How safe will my savings be?

If the amount of money to be saved is fairly small—perhaps less than £500—the choice of investments is restricted, since certain facilities are only available for minimum amounts; for bank fixed-term deposits, for example, the minimum is £10 000 and building society term share accounts start at £100. Usually, the larger the sum to be invested, the higher is the rate of interest. The period of time for which the money can be left is very important: generally the longer the period, the higher are the rates, although the actual rates obtained will depend on the borrower's view of the likely long-term trends in interest rates. Similarly, the longer the period of notice of withdrawal, the higher are the rates. Where money is deposited for a long period of time, emergency withdrawal facilities are usually very restricted or even non-existent: this reflects the view that a borrower who pays high rates of interest should be entitled to the full use of the money for the whole period.

The present and future tax position of the saver needs to be considered: if there is no liability to standard-rate income tax the saver, for the sake of simplicity, would be better with an investment where the interest is paid gross of tax, such as Government stocks and bonds on the National Savings Stock Register or a Trustee or National Savings Bank investment account. In particular, a non-taxpayer should avoid putting his savings in a building society because interest is paid 'net' of tax and it is not possible to reclaim tax that has already been paid by the society (see Unit 6.4).

As far as security of savings is concerned, most large institutions are completely safe. There should be no worries about leaving money with the large banks and their associated finance companies, the Trustee and National Savings Banks, any of the National Savings securities and Government stocks and bonds, building societies, local authorities and large insurance companies. Care should be exercised with smaller financial concerns advertising attractive rates of interest with short notice of withdrawal, though these may simply be perfectly sound organizations that do not have the backing of a major institution. Before investing in one of these, it is wise to make inquiries, to see a copy of the balance sheet and to ask advice—from the bank manager!

Where an investment in stocks and shares is being considered, it is wise for a beginner to purchase units in a unit trust or shares in an investment trust: direct dealings in stocks and shares are for those with more financial expertise who are, if necessary, prepared to lose some of their money. A stock exchange investment, whether made directly or indirectly, should always be considered only on a long-term basis.

Table 6.3 compares the interest rates available at the time of writing from the major savings and investment institutions, with a column left blank for you to fill in the rates at the time of reading.

All savings and investment represent a part of the 'money-go-round': the banks pool the savings of their millions of account holders and lend to commercial and industrial firms as well as to agricultural and personal customers; the building societies attract savings and channel them towards helping people to buy houses by granting mortgages; the issue of shares channels investors' funds into meeting the long-term capital requirements of industry and the Stock Exchange provides a market in shares; the purchase of Government stocks and bonds and National Savings securities helps to finance a part

Table 6.3 Interest rates paid by the major savings institutions, February 1979 (the final column has been left blank for the reader to complete)

	Percentage return		Percentage return		
	Gross of tax	Net of tax at 33%	Gross of tax	Net of tax at	%
Clearing bank deposit account	11.00	7.37			
National Girobank	11.00[1]	7.37			
National Savings Bank:					
Ordinary account	5.00[2]	3.35			
Investment account	12.00	8.04			
Trustee Savings Bank:					
Ordinary account	4.00[2]	2.68			
Investment account	8.00	5.36			
National Savings Certificates					
(eighteenth issue)	12.61[3]	8.45[3]			
British Savings Bonds	9.5	6.37			
SAYE (third issue)	Index-linked				
Building societies:					
Ordinary share	11.94	8.00			
Deposit	11.57	7.75			
SAYE Scheme (second issue):					
5 years	12.39	8.30			
7 years	12.87	8.62			
Finance houses	Various				

[1] Bonus of 1 per cent per annum paid on minimum balance over six months
[2] At present the first £70 of interest is free of all United Kingdom income tax
[3] Assumes NSCs are held for five years to maturity

of central Government debt, and investments in local authorities help to assist their financing. Assurance and insurance companies are also a part of this 'money-go-round': they pool the premiums and annuities paid to them and invest this in many different ways until some part of the pool is needed to pay a claim on a policy; principally they put their investment funds into shares and Government stocks. So the savings of many millions of individuals, when combined or pooled, help to keep the industry of a country turning by indirectly providing the finance that is essential to keep businesses up to date with new machinery and processes.

6.15 Questions

1. What savings and investment facilities do the clearing banks offer to the personal saver?

2. Describe the savings facilities offered by the Department of National Savings.

3. What are the main functions of a stock exchange? Of what benefits are these functions to Government and industry?

(The Institute of Bankers)

4. Distinguish between endowment, whole-life and term assurance policies.

5. Mrs. Brown, a customer of the bank where you work, is aged sixty and has recently been widowed. She has £15 000 available from her late husband's estate and asks your advice as to suitable investments for this money. Advise her.

6. Describe the administration and operation of a unit trust. Outline the attractions of this type of investment to small savers.

(The Institute of Bankers)

The London Money Market

7.1 What is the London Money Market?

As its name suggests, the London money market brings together those who wish to lend money and those who wish to borrow. Other markets, such as the London Stock Exchange, have a fixed 'market place' where business is transacted; but the London money market is not centred in any one building. It operates by means of the telephone and personal meeting of those who deal in money.

Until the mid-1950s there was only one type of money market in London, the *discount market*; this remains the major or primary money market in Britain and its activities are fairly closely controlled by the Bank of England. During the late 1950s and 1960s a number of specialized parallel or secondary markets developed, five dealing in sterling and two in other currencies (Fig. 7.1); these are not controlled by the Bank of England. The participants in the markets are those institutions that deal in money; they include the banks, discount houses, finance houses, building societies, insurance companies, investment and unit trusts, pension funds, large companies, local authorities and a few private individuals.

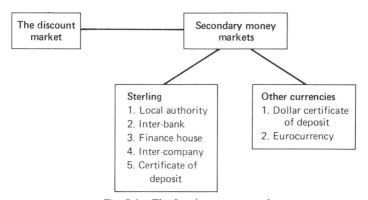

Fig. 7.1   The London money market

7.2   Development of the Discount Market

This part of the money market consists of the eleven discount houses which form the London Discount Market Association, together with certain firms carrying on a similar type of business known as *discount brokers.* The origins of the market go back to bill broking in the late eighteenth and early nineteenth centuries: in those days the cheque had not come into general use, and debts between traders in Britain were often settled by means of a *bill of exchange* (see Unit 10). A trader taking an accepted bill from another trader would have to hold the bill until the due date for payment, often three months ahead. If he needed the money sooner, he could sell the bill to a bill broker at face value, less an amount of discount. At first the bill brokers only acted as intermediaries and re-sold or re-discounted these bills to the many small banks then in existence, who had surplus funds available for short-term investment. During the 1820s and 1830s the bill brokers began to act on their own account by holding some of the bills they had discounted, using as finance their own capital and funds borrowed from the banks on a short-term basis—hence the name *discount houses.* A major reason for this development was the building up of larger banking groups with branch networks; if certain branches accumulated surplus cash, this was employed by transferring it to branches that were short of funds, rather than by purchasing bills from brokers. These larger banks instead preferred to lend to the developing discount houses and soon found that they could lend spare funds to the houses for very short periods of time— often overnight. They could call in this money very quickly when they needed it and thus were able to keep a smaller proportion of their deposits in the form of cash, which paid no interest. The banks liked this arrangement because they could put their liquid funds to better use; the discount houses were pleased because they could use the short-term loans to develop their business.

During the second half of the nineteenth century the importance of the inland bill as a means of settlement between traders declined as the use of the cheque increased. At the same time Britain was developing rapidly as a trading nation and a bill of exchange was the accepted method of settling international trading debts, with London as the major centre for much of world trade. The discount houses began to involve themselves in discounting these foreign bills also. Nowadays the practice established in the nineteenth century continues; these houses still take the surplus short-term funds of the banking system and convert them into longer-term money that can be used not only by traders but also by the Government and industry.

7.3   Liabilities and Assets of the Discount Market

Table 7.1 shows the sources of borrowed funds—the *liabilities* of the market. It shows that most funds are obtained from United Kingdom banks. Much of it is lent on a very short-term basis—on 17 January, £3 594 million, or 95 per cent of the sterling funds, was borrowed overnight—and the discount houses have to bear in mind that much of this money could quickly be recalled. When money is in short supply and the banks start to call in the funds lent to the discount market, there could be difficulties for the eleven discount houses were it not that the Bank of England acts as their lender of last resort.

Table 7.1   The discount market: sources of borrowed funds (17 January 1979)

	£ million	£ million
Sterling		
Bank of England	—	
Other UK banking sector	3 245	
Other UK	488	
Overseas	51	3 784
Other currencies		
UK banking sector	74	
Other UK	9	
Overseas	37	120
Total		3 904

Source: *Bank of England Quarterly Bulletin*

The Bank can help the market in two ways. Firstly, it can force the discount houses, if they have searched elsewhere for funds unsuccessfully, 'into the Bank'. This means that they have to borrow from the Bank at minimum lending rate, which is for them a penal rate of interest. Security for the loan would be provided by Treasury bills and 'parcels' of eligible bank bills (see below) made up into convenient bundles of £50 000 each. Such assistance, while enabling the discount houses to balance their books, means that they make a loss on the business covered by the advance from the Bank—they must pay higher rates of interest on the advance than they can receive on their assets. As discount houses work on narrow margins between borrowing and lending rates, a small increase in their borrowing rates can mean the difference between profit and loss on a transaction. Thus they will only borrow from the Bank if no other financial institution has funds to lend and, because of the importance of the market in affecting other short-term interest rates, the effect of borrowing from the Bank at minimum lending rate is to increase general market rates.

Secondly, if the Bank does not wish to see interest rates rising, it helps the market through its agent in the market, the discount house of Seccombe, Marshall and Campion, known as the *special buyer*. The Bank will instruct this house to purchase Treasury bills from the other houses and when these are paid for, money will be put into the market without forcing up interest rates.

Table 7.2 shows the *assets* of the market, the major items being United Kingdom and Northern Ireland Treasury bills, other bills (mainly commercial bills), local authority securities, certificates of deposit, and British Government stocks.

Table 7.2   The discount market: assets (17 January 1979)

	£ million	£ million
Sterling		
UK and Northern Ireland		
Treasury bills	611	
Other bills	1 998	
Certificates of deposit	327	
Other funds lent	332	
British Government Stocks	393	
Local authority investments	290	
Other investments	26	3 977
Other currencies		
Certificates of deposit	105	
Bills	12	
Other	8	125
Total		4 102

Source: *Bank of England Quarterly Bulletin*

Treasury bills are issued weekly to cover Government short-term debt and to 'tune' the money supply by taking up any surplus funds (see Unit 4.4). They are issued either as *tender* or as *tap bills*, the latter being made available direct to Government departments and certain overseas monetary authorities with surplus funds to invest, while the tender issue is bought mainly by the discount houses, discount brokers and banks. The amount of bills offered each week varies with Government borrowing requirements and the constraints to be placed on the growth of the money supply by the Authorities, but at the time of writing typical amounts are between £300 million and £500 million. Since the introduction of *Competition and Credit Control* in 1971, the members of the London Discount Market Association have agreed to underwrite the Treasury bill issue on a collective but competitive basis. Thus the Government knows that the full amount of the issue will always be taken up; in return, the Bank is always prepared to act as lender of last resort to the market. Treasury bills are issued with a life of ninety-one days after which they are repaid at face value. Each potential buyer tenders for an amount of bills—the minimum tender is £50 000—and as the bills carry no interest, offers to buy at a price below the nominal or face value; for example, an offer might be made at £98.50 for each £100 of face value, representing an annual rate of discount of approximately 6 per cent. The Bank issues the bills to those with the highest tenders, that is, with the smallest rate of discount.

Bills of exchange are still used in inland and international trade to settle indebtedness between businesses or as a means of short-term finance; most involve an element of credit, since they are repayable at some time in the future, commonly after three months. A trader holding a bill on which another trader promises to pay in the future may, if he wishes to receive his money before the maturity date, sell the bill at a discount to a discount house. In order to make a bill saleable at a finer (or smaller) rate of discount—that is, at a higher price—it may be *accepted* by an accepting house of a bank and then becomes known as a *bank bill* or *bank paper*. A commission is charged by the house or bank for this service of lending its 'good name' to the bill and guaranteeing payment of the bill to the holder. The quality of the bank acceptance leads to a distinction among bank bills—they can be either *eligible* or *non-eligible* for rediscount at the Bank of England. Eligible bills are those that bear the acceptance of a large British bank or a member of the Accepting Houses Committee; those that are non-eligible have been accepted by a smaller British bank or a foreign bank. This distinction becomes important when the discount houses wish to borrow from the Bank of England—parcels of eligible bank bills are acceptable as security, but other bills are not.

Since the 1960s there has been a considerable revival in the use of the bill of exchange in Britain, less as a means of settling inter-firm indebtedness than as a way of providing businesses with temporary finance. Finance houses and merchant banks, in particular, lend money to companies against the security of a bill of exchange under which the firm agrees to repay at a named future date. *Bill finance*, as this is called, charges interest rates that are usually competitive with other short-term rates, particularly with those paid on overdrafts, and in the 1960s provided a way of getting round the restrictions imposed on the growth of bank lending. Such bills come into the hands of the discount market and form a part of their assets.

The *local authority securities* held by the discount market consist of stocks, bonds and bills issued by British local authorities to finance their expenditure. The distinction between the three lies in the time period to maturity: *stocks* are usually the longest-dated and are issued only by larger authorities; negotiable *bonds* are issued by more authorities, having periods to maturity ranging from a few days to one year; while some local authorities have the legal powers to borrow by issuing *revenue bills* which are similar to Treasury bills and normally have a life of ninety-one days. Revenue bills are sought after by the discount houses because they, like certain bank bills, are eligible for rediscount at the Bank of England. This involvement in local authority securities has helped to give the discount houses an involvement in the local authority money market (see Unit 7.7).

The discount market also holds a proportion of its assets in the form of *certificates of deposit*, most of which are in sterling. Dollar certificates of deposit were first issued in Britain in 1966 although they had previously been issued in America; sterling certificates were first issued in 1968. A certificate of deposit is simply a certificate issued by a bank acknowledging that a sum of money has been deposited with it for a fixed period of time; the minimum amount accepted for sterling certificates is £50 000, larger sums being accepted in multiples of £10 000, with a normal maximum of £500 000. The certificates are negotiable and payable to bearer which means that the title to them can pass freely from one person to another by *delivery* of the certificate, and thus are ideal for the discount houses to trade in or to hold as an asset. Being negotiable, both sterling certificates of deposit and their dollar equivalent (see Unit 7.13) have to be kept with authorized depositaries—commonly banks—to comply with the United Kingdom exchange control regulations. This is to ensure that funds are not transferred to holders who are not United Kingdom residents without the required Bank of England permission. The rate of interest is fixed for the time period until maturity and certificates are usually issued for stated periods between three months and five years. Interest on certificates issued for a period of one year or less is paid on maturity with the capital sum; interest on certificates issued for longer periods is payable annually. The advantage to a bank of the certificate of deposit system is that it has the use of the money for the fixed time period and only has to repay on maturity of the certificate; this helps it to plan its future medium-term lending as it knows what funds are available and when they are due for repayment. For the depositor there are two advantages: firstly, the fixed rate of interest payable for the time period of the deposit and, secondly, that should the funds be needed urgently, the certificate can be sold on the certificate of deposit market (see Unit 7.11). Thus, from the depositor's point of view, the certificate is more flexible than a term deposit with a bank which the bank is not obliged to repay before the due date. Like the market in local authority securities, the certificate of deposit market has provided a new area of development in which the discount houses act as buyers and sellers.

British Government stocks—the longer-term debt of the Government—are also held as assets by the discount market. Most Government stocks have a maturity date (see Unit 6.7) and the discount market usually holds those that will mature within five years.

7.4 *Competition and Credit Control* and the Discount Market

In 1971, when the *Competition and Credit Control* document was first published, the Bank of England put certain proposals to members of the London Discount Market Association. The Bank asked the members to continue to apply for an amount of Treasury bills sufficient to cover the amount of bills offered at the weekly tender and stated that, in return for their agreement, it was prepared to continue to act as a lender of last resort to the members. Additionally funds lent by a bank at call to the market were allowed to count, without limit, towards its eligible reserve assets (see Unit 8.5), thus firmly establishing the discount houses at the centre of the *Competition and Credit Control* arrangements.

At the same time the Bank asked the members to agree to hold at least 50 per cent of their funds in public sector debt, mainly Treasury bills and short-term local authority and public sector bills. This agreement was designed to prevent the discount market investing too much of its funds in the private sector, and made it possible for the Authorities to maintain a better control over assets which could be used as eligible reserve assets by the banks. In practice, the 50 per cent requirement proved to be more constrictive than necessary and in July 1973 the public sector lending percentage was replaced by a new control. The discount houses were allowed to invest their funds as they wished, subject to the restriction of each individual house's holdings of certain assets—mainly in the private sector—to 20 times its capital and reserves. At 17 January 1979 these *undefined assets*, as the Bank of England calls them, totalled £2 668 million, being 16.3 times the capital and reserves of the market. Since July 1973 the houses have been free to invest their funds without further direction in the following public sector assets, the *defined assets*:

Balances at the Bank of England
United Kingdom and Northern Ireland Treasury bills
British Government stocks and stocks of nationalized } with not more
  industries guaranteed by HM Government } than five years
Local authority stocks } to final maturity
Local authority and other public boards' bills
  eligible at the Bank
Local authority negotiable bonds
Bank bills drawn by nationalized industries
  under specific Government guarantee

At the same time, similar arrangements were made with members of the market outside the London Discount Market Association. These changes give the market greater flexibility, but in practice it continues to invest large proportions of its funds in public sector assets because it is mainly these, together with eligible bank bills, that are acceptable to the Bank as security when it acts as lender of last resort to the market.

7.5 The Role of the Discount Houses

No other major financial centre has discount houses. What, then, is their importance in the London money market?

(i) The discount houses are very useful to the Bank of England because it knows that the weekly Treasury bill tender will always be covered by the market, thus ensuring that the Government short-term borrowing requirement will be taken up. Treasury bills also provide a way for the Bank to exercise fine tuning over the total amount of the money supply: by increasing or decreasing the amount of the tender, money can be taken out of the banking system or put into it, through the intermediary of the discount houses.

(ii) The rate of discount at the weekly Treasury bill tender is a good indicator of other short-term interest rates and it is of assistance to the Authorities in setting the Bank of England's minimum lending rate.

(iii) The market is also useful to the Bank in that it makes good use of the short-term funds of the banking system and invests these funds in substantial amounts of public debt that would otherwise have to be financed less conveniently and more expensively.

(iv) To the banks that lend to the market, it is a useful place for short-term funds to earn a satisfactory rate of interest instead of lying idle.

(v) In addition, as mentioned earlier, the discount houses provide a useful source of short-term funds to the company sector by holding commercial bills.

In 1959 the Government Report of the Committee on the Working of the Monetary System (the Radcliffe Committee) commented on the work of discount houses:

> It would not be beyond human ingenuity to replace the work of the discount houses; but they are there, they are doing the work effectively, and they are doing it at a trifling cost in terms of labour and other resources.

7.6   Secondary Money Markets

The last twenty years have seen the development of a range of new markets complementing the traditional discount market. These new markets—known as *parallel* or *secondary markets*—deal in either sterling or other currencies: like the discount market they consist of specialists who bring together those who wish to borrow funds and those who have funds to lend. Unlike the discount market there is no lender of last resort and transactions on these markets are largely outside the guidance and control of the Authorities.

Dealings on these markets are carried through in one of two ways: either directly between the banks, financial institutions and companies involved in the market, or indirectly using money brokers who bring lenders and borrowers together and charge a commission for their services. In the rest of this Unit we shall consider the different secondary money markets and the various functions they perform.

7.7   Local Authority Money Market

This was the first of the sterling secondary markets to come into existence, being established in 1955. As its name suggests, it is a market which brings together local authorities seeking short-term finance and institutions—not necessarily themselves local authorities—that have funds to lend. Until 1955 local authorities borrowed from the central Government almost entirely through its agency the Public Works Loan Board. During 1955, in an attempt to reduce the borrowing of local authorities, the Government limited the amount of funds that could be obtained through the Board. To get round the restrictions, local authorities borrowed increasing amounts from banks, other financial institutions and companies in the private sector and thus the market in short-term local authority finance was established. When funds are borrowed on this market a deposit receipt is issued; normally loans are repayable at either two or seven days' notice, although some are for longer periods such as three months. The smallest amount lent on this market is usually £25 000.

7.8 Sterling Inter-bank Market

This market was formed in the late 1950s, soon after the local authority market, and is a market in sterling funds in which the banks are the main participants, either lending to other banks or borrowing from them. We saw in Unit 7.3 that the banks lend part of their surplus short-term funds to the discount market; following the formation of the local authority market, the banks found that they had an alternative 'home' for short-term funds. Soon the idea of a further alternative money market came into being, and some of the non-clearing banks started to lend and borrow among themselves instead of going through the discount market; this was the beginning of the inter-bank market. Prior to the *Competition and Credit Control* measures of 1971, the clearing banks did not directly participate in the market because of the reserve ratios that they alone had to maintain at that time (see Unit 4.11(*a*)); they found it more advantageous to use the discount market and other traditional categories of short-term assets. Instead, they used their money market subsidiaries to deal in this market, as these subsidiaries were not subject to requirements concerning reserve ratios and therefore could use more of their funds for lending purposes. Since 1971 all banks have been subject to the same reserve asset requirements and the clearing banks have joined in the market.

It is a short-term market with most funds being lent on an overnight basis but, exceptionally, loans may go up to five years. The loans are large with a minimum of about £250 000 and lending is normally unsecured; the bank making the loan relies on the good name of the borrower, but in practice banks usually limit the maximum amount that may be lent to an individual borrower. The rates of interest on this market for money repayable at call are usually higher than those on the discount market: this is because the rates offered by the discount houses reflect the lower yields on the assets in which they invest. Despite this rate advantage of the inter-bank market, the banks still place a substantial proportion of their surplus funds with the discount market because money at call with the London money market counts as a part of a bank's eligible reserve assets.

Interest rates charged to company customers of the banks are increasingly being related to the rates on the inter-bank market; rates are now often linked to LIBOR (the London Inter-Bank Offered Rate) rather than to the bank's base rate. The reason for changing the starting point in calculating overdraft rates for company customers is that LIBOR is a more accurate indicator of the cost of money to the banks, because of the way in which interest rates on the inter-bank market are determined by the balance between supply and demand. For example, when demand for advances is rising strongly and the banks are under pressure, the competition for scarce funds between them will will drive up rates on the inter-bank market. Large loans are usually charged at a rate above LIBOR because a bank which needs funds in excess of its customers' deposits has to pay LIBOR to obtain them. The margin added to LIBOR by a bank when quoting a rate to its customers is needed to cover the cost of holding the reserve assets required by the Bank of England (see Unit 8.5), together with the cost of the bank's operating expenses and its profit element.

7.9   Finance House Market

This is a small secondary market in which the borrowers are finance houses and hire purchase companies. The lenders are banks, other financial institutions, companies and a few private individuals. Since the recognition by the Bank of England of most of the larger finance houses as banks the market has contracted considerably, and much of its business now passes through the inter-bank market.

7.10   Inter-company Market

The origins of this market arose from the tight restrictions imposed by the Authorities on the growth of bank lending in 1968 and 1969. Quantitative and severely restrictive directives were in vogue at that time (these have not formally been issued since the introduction of the *Competition and Credit Control* arrangements in 1971); the directive issued by the Bank of England to the clearing banks in January 1969, for example, limited all but priority lending to a total of 98 per cent of the November 1967 level. The banks being thus unable to increase lending to their customers, particularly their company customers, they were unwilling to pay high rates of interest for deposits. The development of the inter-company market was a way round the restrictions which suited both borrower and lender: the borrower was able to obtain finance that the clearing banks could not provide; the lender was able to obtain higher rates of interest than those being offered by the clearing banks. Following the relaxation of the credit 'squeeze', the market has continued to operate—the borrowers being companies and the lenders being companies and financial institutions.

Business is transacted by brokers and normally loans are only made to the top five hundred companies. The minimum loan involved is £50 000, with sums of £250 000 or larger being dealt in. Loans are generally made for any period from three months to five years and a broker will agree the terms for each individual loan to suit both the borrower and the lender. The market makes substantial use of bank guarantees in an attempt to overcome the difficulties encountered with regard to the status and creditworthiness of borrowers.

7.11   Sterling Certificate of Deposit Market

A certificate of deposit is a document issued by a bank certifying that a deposit has been made with that bank for a period of time at a fixed rate of interest (see Unit 7.3). Certificates, being negotiable, are an ideal way for banks and other financial institutions, companies and individuals to invest large sums of surplus money. If the funds should be required the certificate may be sold on the secondary certificate of deposit market. This market consists of the discount houses, banks and money brokers who buy certificates from existing holders and sell to new holders. The discount houses and the banks may choose to hold certificates purchased as investments until maturity; the money brokers, by contrast, buy and sell only for clients.

7.12   How the Sterling Secondary Markets Intermesh

The sterling secondary markets do not work in isolation from each other—lenders to each market are often the same and an example transaction will give an idea of how the markets intermesh.

(i) Worldwide Chemicals, a large industrial company with surplus funds available, lends £250 000 to National Barllands Bank for six months, and the bank issues a sterling certificate of deposit.

(ii) The bank, considering what it may do with the funds, looks at the local authority market but decides that the rates are too low; instead, it lends the money for seven days on the inter-bank market to a bank that is short of funds.

(iii) Seven days later the loan is repaid by the bank and National Barllands looks around again: by now rates on the local authority market have improved and the money is lent to a local authority.

(iv) In the meantime, Worldwide Chemicals has brought forward an investment project and needs money quickly. It makes use of the certificate of deposit market, and sells the certificate of deposit issued by the bank to a discount house.

(v) The discount house may either hold the certificate of deposit to maturity or sell it to another holder on the market.

(vi) Upon maturity of the certificate, the holder, whether the discount house or some subsequent holder, presents it at National Barllands Bank to receive the proceeds.

7.13   Dollar Certificate of Deposit Market

This is one of the two secondary money markets operating in London designated in currencies other than sterling; the other, the *Eurocurrency market*, is considered in Unit 7.14.

Dollar certificates of deposit were first issued in the United States during the early 1960s, and were introduced to the London market by the American banks in 1966. Since then most other banks have started to make their own issues and the American banks now account for only about half of the total amount outstanding. Like a sterling certificate of deposit, a dollar certificate is an acknowledgment by a bank of a deposit placed for an agreed period of time at a fixed rate of interest, but the currency of the deposit is dollars; again like their sterling counterparts, dollar certificates are negotiable. The dollar certificate of deposit market has developed as a secondary market where these securities may be bought and sold. The main participants in the market are discount houses, American banks and several United States and Canadian securities houses.

7.14   Eurocurrency Market

This is an international market in short- and medium-term money, of which London has become a leading world centre. The prefix *Euro-* often causes confusion as it seems to suggest that the market is confined to Europe, but this is misleading; while most of the market's business is transacted in Europe, there are other centres and it has now become worldwide. For currency to become 'Euro-', it must be owned by a person resident outside the country where it was issued and lent to another non-resident; that is, the money circulates outside its country of origin but is still designated in the original currency. Thus Eurodollars are deposits of United States dollars by people who are not resident in the United States with banks that are also situated outside that country; Eurosterling is the deposit of pounds sterling by non-residents of Britain with banks outside Britain.

Any currency can become 'Euro-', but the market in Eurodollars was the first and remains the most important. It originated in the early 1950s when a number of eastern European banks wished to disguise their ownership of dollar deposits and placed them with correspondent banks, particularly in Britain and France. The correspondent banks began to make use of these and other dollar deposits by offering dollar loans at lower rates of interest than those ruling in the United States. Further impetus was given to the development of the market as a result of an American banking control, 'Regulation Q', which held down deposit rates in the United States but which did not apply to dollars accepted from non-residents by American banks operating outside the States. This led to the development of a series of overseas branches by American banks, particularly in London, to obtain a share of this business;

European banks soon began to compete for these deposits as well. The 1958 relaxation of exchange controls in west European countries, which gave banks and businesses greater freedom of capital financing, contributed to creating the right conditions for the establishment of London as the major centre of the market. Besides the dollar, the other principal Eurocurrencies are sterling, Deutschemarks, Swiss francs, Dutch guilders and Canadian dollars.

A Eurocurrency transaction involves a bank outside the country of origin of a currency attracting a deposit or granting a loan in that currency. The Eurocurrency market involves bringing together those who have currencies to lend and those who wish to borrow in those currencies; it is essentially a 'wholesale' market dealing with large sums of money on a short-term basis—most borrowing is for six months or less, although there is also a medium-term element in the market where borrowing can go up to five years. The market is inter-bank (or 'bank-to-bank'): a company with Eurocurrency funds cannot directly place them on the market but must deposit them with a bank, and equally a company wishing to borrow must go through a bank. The lending between banks is unsecured and, as in the sterling inter-bank market, limits are set on the maximum amount to be lent to any one bank.

The market has expanded enormously since its origins in the 1950s, partly because it is free from national restrictions on the transfer of funds and from differences in interest rate structures between countries, and partly because it meets so well the needs of multi-national corporations, nationalized industries and governments who need large-scale, worldwide finance at reasonable cost. As the amounts borrowed and lent are large—on the Eurodollar market the minimum transaction is usually $1 million—the market can operate on smaller margins between the borrowing and lending rate than is possible in domestic banking. Since the market is free from control by national governments there are no reserve requirements and therefore funds do not have to be tied up in low-yielding reserve assets; a greater proportion of each deposit can thus be 'lent on'. Moreover, since funds are deposited for a fixed time, lending can be matched to the maturity of deposits and so the banks operating in the market can work with very small reserves. Because of its international nature it is difficult to estimate its size, but in March 1977 the world market was thought to be in excess of $300 billion.

While the Eurocurrency market is concerned with the provision of short- and medium-term loans, a market has developed in the provision of longer-term international finance—the *Eurobond market*. Loans in this market are issued by consortium banks (see Unit 5.6) and issuing houses in Europe, and are designated in dollars, Deutschemarks and other continental currencies. The borrowers on this market are governments, nationalized industries, municipal authorities and multi-national corporations. The method of issue is for banks in the consortium handling the loan to place the bonds with their customers and other banks in their own country. When the issue has been successfully placed, an advertisement is put in various newspapers announcing it, as required by law: this describes the issue and lists the names of the participating banks. Eurobonds can be traded in a limited secondary market that has developed in

London and Luxembourg, which is run by a small group of banks and stockbrokers.

7.15   Questions

1. Describe the markets that make-up the London money market.

2. What are the sources and uses of funds of the discount houses?

3. What functions are performed by the discount houses?

4. Few major financial centres have discount houses. Why has London?

5. Explain the inter-relationships between the Bank of England, the discount houses and the commercial banks.

A Bank's Balance Sheet

8.1 Introduction

It is important for you to be familiar with the make-up of a balance sheet, and you will find it helpful to study the annual Report and Accounts of one of the major clearing banks; these are generally readily available from branches and head office from about late March onwards each year, and cover the preceding financial year which usually runs from 1 January to 31 December. As an example of a bank's balance sheet, that of Lloyds Bank Limited at 31 December 1978 is given in Fig. 8.1. In this Unit we shall examine the items which appear there one by one, and discuss the information that can be derived from the figures it presents.

'Well, we haven't made any profit, but the report may win an Arts Council award'

8.2 Liabilities of a Bank

(a) Issued share capital

This is represented by a large number of shares held by individuals, institutional investors and companies. Most shares issued by banks are *ordinary shares*, with a nominal value of £1 each, but some have also issued *preference shares* (see Unit 12.6(*b*)).

(b) Reserves

These represent the profits earned over the years that have not been distributed to shareholders and that have been set aside to meet possible future requirements: reserves such as these are known as *revenue reserves. Capital reserves* come about when assets of the bank or company are revalued, as when branch bank premises that were purchased some years ago are revalued to bring them into line with current property valuations: the premises would be shown at the increased value on the assets side of the balance sheet, while on the liabilities side the amount of the increase would be placed into a capital reserve account called *revaluation reserve.* Another type of capital reserve arises when shares are issued to the public at a higher price than the nominal value: the amount of the issue price in excess of the nominal value is placed to a *share premium account.* The important distinction between a revenue reserve and a capital reserve is that the former can be distributed to the shareholders as a dividend (subject to the business having sufficient cash to pay the dividend) whereas the latter can never be distributed.

Although there is no legal requirement to publish full details of the make-up of the reserves figure, most banks do give the information in full, as a note appended to the accounts. But for many years banks were permitted to make transfers to hidden reserves which were not disclosed in the published balance sheet. The fact that banks were known to have substantial hidden reserves may have led to increased confidence in the British banking system. During the 1960s, however, there was pressure from the press and public for a disclosure of true profits, and matters came to a head in 1968, when the Monopolies Commission report into the merger of Barclays, Lloyds and Martins banks (see Unit 3.6) criticized the veil of secrecy drawn around bank profits and urged disclosure of the true figure. The banks finally agreed to this commencing with their financial year ending 31 December 1969.

(c) Loan capital

Most of the major clearing banks have loan capital of different types in issue. Like most Government stocks, the loan capital (or stocks) issued by banks has a date for repayment, the funds being lent to the bank for a limited period only. Some banks have made bond issues on the overseas capital markets; the Report and Accounts will give full details, of loan capital in issue, usually as a note. It will often be found that the loan stock or capital is described as *subordinated*: this is a type of stock rarely issued by companies other than banks.

Lloyds Bank Limited

Balance Sheet at 31 December 1978

	£'000		£'000
Issued share capital	166 371	*Current Assets*	
Reserves	659 388	Cash and short-term funds	770 119
Loan capital	100 293	Cheques in course of	
		collection	281 386
		Special deposit with the	
Current liabilities		Bank of England	68 460
Current, deposit and		Investments	418 879
other accounts	5 568 295	Advances and	
Balances with subsidiaries	6 544	other accounts	3 898 970
Taxation (deferred)	5 518	Balance with subsidiaries	462 935
Proposed final dividend	9 173		
		Fixed assets	
		Investments in	
		subsidiaries	213 484
		Trade investments	51 508
		Premises and equipment	349 841
	6 515 582		6 515 582

Fig. 8.1   A bank's balance sheet

In the event of the bank's winding up, the holders of this stock would be paid only after the depositors had been repaid in full; in a company winding up, on the other hand, the normal loan-stock holders would be paid in full before the general creditors. A bank's depositors are in fact its creditors, although they are a special class of creditors needing increased rights.

(d) Current, deposit and other accounts

These form the largest liability on a bank's balance sheet. They are a liability because the customers—personal and business customers as well as other banks—have paid money into their accounts and the bank is liable to repay that money; the depositors, whatever type of account they have, are creditors of the bank and thus have credit balances. In modern banking, deposits may take the form of several different types of account (see Unit 13) besides the traditional current and deposit accounts, although these still form the 'bread and butter' of any bank's balance sheet. The growth of deposits since

Competition and Credit Control has been considerable, even allowing for inflation. You will remember that, as a result of the operation of the credit-creation multiplier, every loan creates a deposit elsewhere in the banking system (see Unit 2.10) and the increase can be said to have occurred in part as a result of the increased amounts that the banks have lent since 1971.

(*e*) **Other liabilities**

This section includes any amounts due to subsidiary companies, provisions for taxation on profits due to the Inland Revenue, proposed dividends to shareholders, and other general creditors of the bank to whom amounts are owing at the balance sheet date.

8.3   Assets of a Bank

When listing the assets on a balance sheet, most companies commence with those assets that would take the longest time to turn into cash (usually factory premises), followed by those that would take the next longest time, and so on until the very last asset, cash itself. The idea behind this used to be to impress upon a person looking at the balance sheet the strength of the company in its *fixed assets*, as the first items on the assets side of the balance sheet are called—normally factory premises, machinery, motor vehicles and so on. A bank, on the other hand, prefers to show the readers of its balance sheet its liquid position, that is, that it holds sufficient cash and other liquid assets to be able to repay its depositors. Ever since the days of the country banks, therefore, bank balance sheets have always listed their assets starting with cash, followed by other liquid assets and finishing with fixed assets.

(*a*) **Cash**

This is the amount of notes and coin held by bank branches and head office to meet demand for withdrawals from customers. Prior to the 1971 *Competition and Credit Control* arrangements, the Bank of England required the clearing banks to hold a minimum of 8 per cent of total deposits in the form of cash. Under the 1971 scheme cash is excluded from the list of eligible reserve assets (see Unit 8.5) and the banks now maintain only sufficient notes and coins to meet demand. On 17 January 1979 the cash held by the London clearing banks amounted to 2.6 per cent of their total sterling deposits.

(*b*) **Cheques in course of collection**

Any cheques paid into a bank that are drawn on other banks and branches need to be 'cleared' through the clearing system, which takes three to four days (see Unit 10.9); a cheque paid in at the branch on which it is drawn is debited to the drawer's account on the same business day. Most cheques, however, have to be cleared, and the asset on a bank's balance sheet represents the claim that the bank has on other banks for items in course of collection. On the balance sheet of Lloyds Bank Limited in Fig. 8.1 this item is £281 million and is the total of all cheques drawn on other banks that have been paid into Lloyds Bank branches for the credit of accounts and which still remain in the clearing system. During the few days following the date of the balance sheet, these items would pass through the London Bankers' Clearing House and payment would be received by Lloyds from the banks on which they were drawn. As cheques are constantly being paid into accounts at banks other than that on which they are drawn, at any moment there are always cheques in course of collection.

(c) Money at call and short notice

This asset consists of funds lent mainly to the discount houses; they are secured by the deposit of Treasury bills, certain commercial bills and short-dated Government stocks. It is either lent *at call*—that is, it can be called in immediately—or at short notice for periods of up to fourteen days. The rates of interest earned by the banks on this asset vary with the length of the loan and availability of funds in the market. An overnight loan usually earns a lower rate of interest than one for a week; when funds are in plentiful supply on the money markets the rates are lower than when there is a shortage.

After cash, this is the most liquid asset on a bank's balance sheet, and would be called in if the bank was short of funds.

(d) Treasury bills

These provide a safe short-term investment for part of a bank's assets and also earn a reasonable return (see Unit 7.3). Being issued weekly and having a life of ninety-one days they give a 'quick turn-round' from cash back to cash again and can normally be bought and sold through the discount market at any stage in their life.

(e) Other bills

These are bank bills, trade or commercial bills and local authority bills which the bank has either discounted for its customers or purchased in the market to hold as assets until maturity. Bank bills are bills of exchange that bear the acceptance of a bank and, depending upon the quality of the acceptance, these may be either eligible or non-eligible for re-discount at the Bank of England (see Unit 7.3). Trade or commercial bills are those that have been accepted by a business; local authority bills are issued, of course, by certain local authorities as a means of short-term finance. The return on this asset varies depending upon the type of bill held: 'eligible' bank bills, often known as 'fine' bank bills, are considered undoubted and command the 'finest' rates, giving the lowest return; other bank bills, local authority bills and trade or commercial bills bearing the acceptance of a first-class company follow at somewhat higher rates; other trade and commercial bills have the largest rates of discounts and therefore the highest return, but they will carry the greatest risk of non-payment.

(f) Other market loans

The banks, besides lending substantially to the discount market, also make other loans on the secondary money markets such as the inter-bank, local authority and inter-company markets. Such loans are for differing time periods; most are short-term, but some may be for up to five years.

(g) Certificates of deposit

These are issued by banks to customers who are prepared to deposit funds for a fixed period of time at fixed interest rates (see Units 7.3, 7.11 and 7.13). Certificates issued by banks in exchange for a deposit received would form a part of the liabilities on the balance sheet in the 'other accounts' section. However, banks also hold certificates issued by other banks as investments and these feature on the assets side of the balance sheet. The rates of interest earned on certificates held vary according to the period remaining to maturity: for those approaching repayment date, rates are close to bank base rates; for those with longer periods to run, rates are higher.

(h) Special and supplementary special deposits

These are sums of money that all banks are required to deposit with the Bank of England (see Unit 4.9(b)). While these are held by the Bank of England they cannot be used by the banks, so that they have the effect of reducing the amount that can be lent to customers. Interest is usually paid on these deposits at rates that are linked to the weekly Treasury bill rate, but at certain times when the Bank wishes to penalize the banking system severely, no interest is paid at all.

(i) Investments (other than trade investments)

A study of the notes forming part of the annual Report and Accounts of a bank will show the make-up of these assets. The majority of investments are either British Government stocks or stocks guaranteed by the Government— 'gilt-edged' securities. Most of these have fixed repayment dates and a bank's investments will aim to give a good spread of repayments over the next five or six years. From the security point of view, they are first-class assets to hold, as the British Government, whatever we may think of it, is unlikely to default on its debts. Interest earned is well above the bank's base rate, particularly that on the medium-dated stocks, and if these investments have to be realized, they can be readily sold on the Stock Exchange.

(j) Advances to customers

This is the largest asset on a bank's balance sheet and includes all forms of bank lending; as we saw in Unit 1.1, a basic function of any bank is to lend the surplus funds deposited with it. The balance sheet of Lloyds in Fig. 8.1 shows that its advances and other accounts were at that date £3 899 million, or 70 per cent of current, deposit and other accounts of £5 568 million. All loans and overdrafts are technically repayable on demand, except for amounts lent for a specific period of time, such as medium-term and personal loans. In practice few advances could be repaid immediately and some lending is 'solid', showing little, if any, reduction from year to year. Thus advances, although shown in the current assets section of the balance sheet, are the most illiquid of these assets. The rates of interest charged on loans and overdrafts reflect this illiquidity and also the greater risk of bad debts. Rates (except for those charged to very large companies, which are now often linked directly to money market rates) are generally linked to a bank's base rate: big company operators whose rates are linked to base rate will probably pay lower effective rates (say 1 or 2 per cent above base rate) than small businesses and private customers, who will often pay 3 or 4 per cent above base rate; the difference could reflect a different degree of risk and/or a lesser degree of lending priority. Most interest on advances is calculated on the daily balance outstanding on the account, but that charged on certain types of accounts, particularly personal loans (see Unit 13.6), is calculated on the amount of the original loan for the period of the loan even though regular repayments are reducing the original amount. This mean that the 'true' rate of interest is higher than the 'nominal' rate.

Table 8.1 shows the amounts lent by the London clearing banks at 15 November 1978 to different categories of borrowers. These amounts will vary somewhat with the time of year; advances to agriculture, for instance, reduce in the autumn as payments are received for crops and increase in the spring when the farmers' expenses often exceed their income. Similarly Bank of England qualitative directives which tell the banks which customers are to receive priority (see Unit 4.9(a)) vary the amounts lent to different categories of borrower; thus the Bank can discover whether its directives are being carried out by inspecting the regular classifications of advances that it calls for from the other banks.

(k) **Investments in subsidiaries and associates**
These are the investments in subsidiary and associated companies and trade investments that the bank has made in order to diversify its activities: a note in the annual Report and Accounts will give a list of these. *Subsidiaries* are companies that are directly controlled by the parent bank; they may include such companies as the bank's finance company, merchant bank, Scottish and/ or Northern Ireland bank, insurance services company and so forth. *Associated companies* are those in which the bank does not have a controlling interest, but holds at least 20 per cent of the share capital on a long-term basis, and participates in the management. There are some associated companies in which all the major clearing banks participate, such as Bankers' Automated Clearing Services Ltd. (formed to process computer tapes which contain the details of bankers' orders and direct debits) and The Joint Credit Card Company Ltd. (which operates the 'Access' card scheme on behalf of Lloyds, Midland and National Westminster banks). There are also the major banks' associated companies such as their consortium and overseas banking interests. *Trade investments* are those in which the bank has a smaller holding than 20 per cent of the share capital, and are used to give a bank access to specialist companies or to provide an opening overseas for a British bank. For example, all the clearing banks have a share in the Bankers' Clearing House Ltd., each of the 'big four' banks holding 17 per cent of the share capital and the rest being

Table 8.1 London clearing banks: Analysis of advances in sterling and foreign currencies to UK residents at 15 November 1978. (*Figures are rounded to the nearest million by the Bank of England, so individual totals and sub-totals do not always add up.*)

	£ million	£ million
Financial		
Hire purchase finance houses	140	
Property companies	788	
Other financial	1 128	
	——	2 056
Services		
Transport and communications	410	
Utilities and national government	704	
Local government	66	
Retail distribution	1 113	
Other distribution	954	
Professional, scientific and miscellaneous	1 882	
	——	5 129
Manufacturing		
Food, drink and tobacco	713	
Chemicals and allied industries	531	
Metal manufacture	276	
Electrical engineering	401	
Other engineering and metal goods	1 051	
Shipbuilding	402	
Vehicles	204	
Textiles, leather and clothing	418	
Other manufacturing	789	
	——	4 784
Other production		
Agriculture, forestry and fishing	1 401	
Mining and quarrying	153	
Construction	1 022	
	——	2 577
Personal		
For house purchase	1 234	
Other	2 681	
	——	3 915
Total advances		18 461
of which:		
Sterling	16 889	
Foreign currencies	1 572	
	——	
	18 461	

Source: *Monthly Digest of Statistics*, Central Statistical Office

held by the other clearing banks. Most banks also have a holding in Finance for Industry Ltd. (which provides finance for industrial firms that, for various reasons, cannot obtain funds direct from their own banks) and The Agricultural Mortgage Corporation Ltd. (which provides specialist long-term mortgages for the purchase of farms—the type of lending that, because of the time period, would not be acceptable to a commercial bank).

(*l*) Premises and equipment
This represents the investment made by the bank in branch and other premises, and in assets such as vehicles, accounting machines and other equipment.

8.4   Liquidity versus Profitability

Many a small private country bank in the mid-nineteenth century went out of business as a result of difficult trading conditions in the district in which it operated. If a rumour began that a bank was having difficulty in making repayments to its customers, no matter how ill-founded it might be, there would soon be a queue of people wanting to withdraw their deposits. This could escalate into a 'run on the bank', which would most probably result in the bank having to close its doors and go out of business. Even in the 1970s, there have been banks in Britain unable to meet repayments: in late 1973 and early 1974 several secondary banks faced financial difficulties after becoming over-involved in lending to property speculators, and had to be helped out by means of a rescue operation, known as the 'lifeboat', organized by the Bank of England and largely financed by the clearing banks. It is still therefore important for banks to maintain sufficient cash and liquid funds that could be used to repay depositors: the Bank of England requires that all banks operating in Britain should maintain at least $12\frac{1}{2}$ per cent of their eligible liabilities in the form of *eligible reserve assets* (see Unit 8.5). The list of eligible reserve assets does not include cash and, as all banks obviously need adequate supplies of notes and coin, a further 3 or 4 per cent of deposits must be kept in this form. The problem of maintaining assets in the form of cash or eligible reserve assets is that the quicker an asset can be turned into cash, the lower the rate of interest it earns. Assets that take longer to turn into cash command higher rates of interest, and the highest rates are charged for the most illiquid of a bank's current assets, advances to customers. Thus a bank has to strike a balance between good liquidity and its reducing effect on profits, and high profitability with the consequent worsening of the liquidity position. Fig. 8.2 highlights the problems of liquidity versus profitability.

8.5   Eligible Liabilities and Reserve Asset Ratio

With the introduction of the *Competition and Credit Control* measures in 1971, all banks operating in Britain were required to maintain a minimum of $12\frac{1}{2}$ per

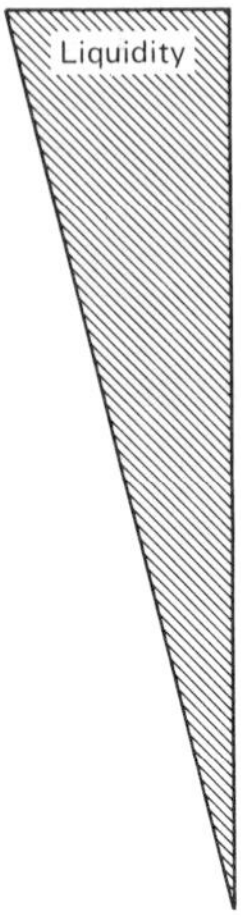

Asset	Period of loan	Borrower	Approx. per cent yield[†]
Cash	—	—	Nil
Money at call and short notice	1–14 days	Mainly discount houses	9–13
Bills discounted	Average about 1½ months (some mature regularly)	Government, businesses, local authorities	12½ (Treasury bills) 12½–13½ (other bills)
Other market loans	Up to 12 months or longer on exceptions	Banks, local authorities	12½–14
Investments	Up to 5–6 years (spread of repayments)	Government and local authorities	10–15½
Advances	Technically most are repayable on demand (but see Unit 8.3)	Private persons and industry	15–18

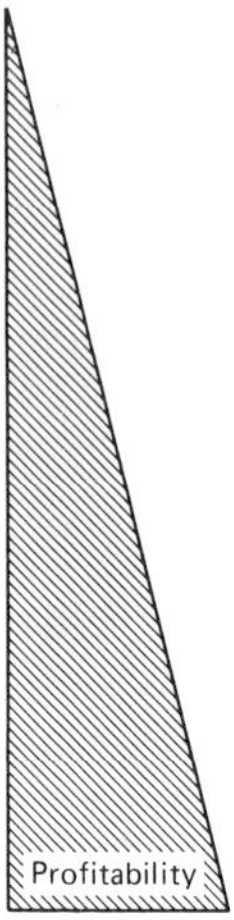

[†]Approximate rates at February 1979 (minimum lending rate 14 per cent)

Fig. 8.2   Liquidity versus profitability

cent of eligible liabilities in the form of eligible reserve assets. For finance houses the percentage was 10 per cent.

(a) Eligible liabilities
A bank's eligible liabilities comprise:

(i) sterling deposits, of an original maturity of two years or under, from United Kingdom residents (other than banks) and from overseas residents (other than overseas offices), and all funds due to customers or third parties which are temporarily held on suspense accounts (other than credits in course of transmission);

(ii) all sterling deposits—of whatever term—from banks in the United Kingdom, less any sterling claims on such banks;

(iii) all sterling certificates of deposit issued—of whatever term—less any holdings of such certificates;

(iv) the bank's net deposit liability, if any, in sterling to its overseas offices;

(v) the bank's net liability, if any, in currencies other than sterling;
less

(vi) 60 per cent of the net value of transit items in the bank's balance sheet.

Put more simply, eligible liabilities consist of all the sterling deposits of the banking system that are repayable within two years—current and deposit accounts and so forth, plus the net balances of deposits from other banks (whenever they are repayable), plus the net amount deposited in respect of certificates of deposit, plus net deposits in foreign currencies. Deducted from this total is 60 per cent of net transit items to allow for credits in course of transmission (a liability) and cheques in course of collection (an asset). The 60 per cent figure applies because 'transit' items affect overdrawn or loan accounts as well as credit accounts and this is thought to be a fair estimate of the proportion concerning credit accounts.

(b) Reserve assets
The reserve assets of a bank comprise:

(i) balances at the head office or branches of the Bank of England (other than special deposits);

(ii) British Government and Northern Ireland Government Treasury bills;

(iii) money at call with the London money market;

(iv) British Government stocks and nationalized industries' stocks guaranteed by HM Government, with one year or less to final maturity;

(v) local authority bills eligible for re-discount at the Bank of England;

(vi) commercial bills eligible for re-discount at the Bank of England, up to a maximum of 2 per cent of eligible liabilities.

8.6   Calculation of the Reserve Asset Ratio

The Bank of England requires that a bank's eligible reserve assets must be at least $12\frac{1}{2}$ per cent of its eligible liabilities, there being no restrictions (other than the limitation on commercial bill holdings mentioned above) on the distribution of funds between the different categories of assets. The London clearing banks agreed with the Bank to hold $1\frac{1}{2}$ per cent of their eligible liabilities in balances at the Bank of England to ensure that there are always sufficient funds to enable the bankers' clearing system to operate satisfactorily.

Table 8.2 shows the assets and liabilities of the London clearing banks at 17 January 1979. Eligible liabilities are £26 115 million and eligible reserve assets are £3 378 million, giving a reserve asset ratio of 12.9 per cent.

8.7   Sterling and Other Currency Deposits

In Unit 5 we discussed the wide range of banks operating in Britain today, from the London and other clearing banks to overseas banks from most countries of the world. In this Unit we have looked particularly at a clearing bank's balance sheet, but the other banks also have comparable assets and liabilities. The main difference between the banks lies in the proportions in which they hold their assets and liabilities. Among liabilities, for example, Table 8.2 shows that the sterling deposits of the London clearing banks at 17 January, 1979 were £31 122 million while their foreign currency deposits were £6 325 million; thus sterling dominates the deposits of these banks. At the same date the sterling and other currency deposits of the American banks operating in Britain were £6 400 million and £46 272 million respectively; currencies other than sterling thus dominate their deposits. On the assets side of their balance sheets, a similar position emerges when the figures for advances are compared.

Table 8.2   London clearing banks: assets and liabilities at 17 January 1979.
(*Figures are rounded to the nearest million by the Bank of England, so individual totals and sub-totals do not always add up.*)

	£ million	£ million		£ million	£ million
Liabilities			**Assets**		
Sterling deposits			*Sterling assets*		
UK banking sector	2 010		Notes and coin		810
Other UK	26 337		Reserve assets:		
Overseas	1 688		Balance with Bank		
Certificates of deposit	1 086		of England	380	
		31 122	Money at call	1 519	
			UK and NI		
Other currency deposits			Treasury bills	343	
UK banking sector	1 309		Other bills	643	
Other UK	648		British Government		
Overseas	4 051		stocks up to 1 year	493	
Certificates of deposit	318				3 378
		6 325			
Capital and other			Special and supplemen-		
liabilities		7 357	tary special deposits		571
Note:			Market loans (other		
Eligible liabilities included			than reserve assets)		
in above total £26 115 million.			Banks in UK and		
			discount market	3 807	
			Certificates of		
			deposit	186	
			UK local authorities	385	
			Other	61	
					4 439
			Bills (other than		
			reserve assets)		138
			Advances:		
			UK	17 749	
			Overseas	3 073	
					20 822
			Investments:		
			British Government		
			stocks over 1 year		
			and undated	1 424	
			Other	1 291	
					2 715

Table 8.2 cont.

	£ million	£ million		£ million	£ million
			Other currency assets		6 667
			Sterling and other currencies		
			Miscellaneous assets		5 263
		44 804			44 804

Source: *Bank of England Quarterly Bulletin*

Table 8.3   Banks in the United Kingdom: assets and liabilities at 17 January 1979

	£ million		£ million	£ million
Liabilities		**Assets**		
		Sterling assets		
Sterling deposits	63 962	Notes and coin	1 318	
Currency deposits	140 075	Reserve assets	6 138	
Notes outstanding	443	Special and supplementary special deposits	1 101	
Items in suspense and transmission	3 032	Market loans (other than reserve assets)	19 783	
Capital and other funds	11 668	Bills (other than reserve assets)	378	
		Advances	36 537	
		Investments	4 367	
		Miscellaneous	7 142	
				76 763
		Foreign currency assets		
		Market loans	102 069	
		Advances	37 575	
		Bills	425	
		Investments	1 734	
		Miscellaneous	614	
				142 417
	219 179			219 179

Source: *Bank of England Quarterly Bulletin*

Table 8.3 shows the assets and liabilities of all banks operating in the United Kingdom. (For statistical purposes 'all banks' are those observing the $12\frac{1}{2}$ per cent reserve ratio, excluding the Banking Department of the Bank of England and certain other institutions.) The surprising fact to emerge is that foreign currency deposits exceed sterling deposits by more than two to one; foreign currency advances exceed sterling advances by nearly £1 000 million. A very high proportion of foreign currency assets are in the form of market loans and reflect the importance of London as a major centre in the Eurocurrency market. Fig. 8.3 illustrates the relative importance of sterling and foreign currency deposits to the different types of banks.

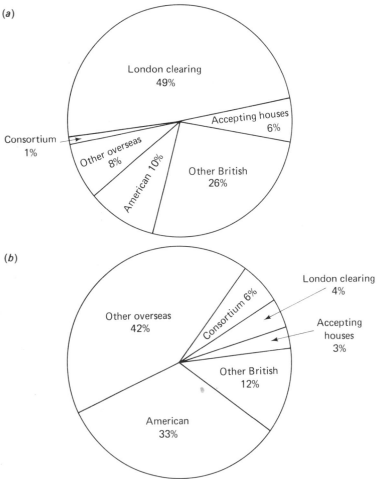

Fig. 8.3   Banks in the United Kingdom (a) sterling deposits and (b) other currency deposits 17 January 1979 (from data given in the Bank of England Quarterly Bulletin)

8.8   Questions

1. Describe the main assets that appear in a commercial bank's balance sheet, indicating their special characteristics and their relationships to banking business.

    (*The Institute of Bankers*)

2. Why does a bank need liquidity? How does a bank provide for liquidity in the use it makes of the deposits entrusted to it?

    (*The Institute of Bankers*)

3. Describe the eligible liabilities and eligible reserve assets of banks operating in Britain. What ratio of one to the other do they have to maintain?

4. Using the balance sheet and information given below, list the bank's eligible reserve assets and calculate the bank's reserve asset ratio:

Worcester Bank Ltd.

	£ million		£ million
Capital	60	Cash in tills	70
Reserves	90	Balance at Bank of England	40
Current accounts	900	Treasury bills	60
Deposit accounts	800	Commercial bills	80
		British Government Securities (of which £30m have less than	
(Note: eligible liabilities are £1 500m.)		one year to maturity)	250
		Money at call with London money market	80
		Other call money	95
		Advances	1 000
		Investments in subsidiaries	60
		Special deposits	45
		Premises	70
	1 850		1 850

5. The whole business of banking depends upon maintaining the confidence of depositors. What steps does a banker take to safeguard depositors' interests?

    (*The Institute of Bankers*)

6. Draw up a typical commercial bank's balance sheet, illustrating the main classes of liabilities and assets and indicating any appropriate relationships between them.

    (*The Institute of Bankers*)

Unit Nine

Organizational Structure of a London Clearing Bank

9.1 Head Office and Regional Offices

All the major London clearing banks have broadly similar organizational structures, with a head office in the City of London and regional offices situated in various parts of the country, each controlling a number of branches. Fig. 9.1 indicates, in simplified form, the type of structure adopted by the banks with specialist services—foreign, executor and trustee, corporate finance and so on—available to head office, regional offices and branches. With a total of some 12 000 branches and 200 000 staff between them, the organizational structure of the major clearing banks is, of necessity, somewhat complex.

Fig. 9.2 shows the management structure, again simplified, of a major clearing bank. The *shareholders* are the owners of the bank and their elected representatives, the *chairman* and *board of directors*, control general policy and approve certain very large applications for loan and overdraft facilities. Most members of the board of directors do not work full-time for the bank; they usually come from families that have had connections with the bank for many years, and are often people who have distinguished careers in industry, the civil service or the armed forces. The *chief general manager*, the highest position a full-time employee can reach, is usually a member of the board of directors as is one or more of his deputies, the *assistant general managers*. After the

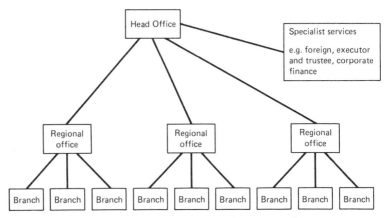

Fig. 9.1   Structure of a London clearing bank

chief general manager and his deputies come the *general managers*, each of whom normally has a responsibility for a specific function in the bank. A group of general managers has responsibility for domestic banking (that is, banking in Britain), and a smaller number may be responsible for overseas banking. Individual general managers take charge of such areas as corporate services (covering all aspects of services for company customers; see Unit 15), executor and trustee department (dealing with wills and trusts; see Unit 14.12) and those areas concerned with the efficient running of the bank such as staff, training, administration and management services.

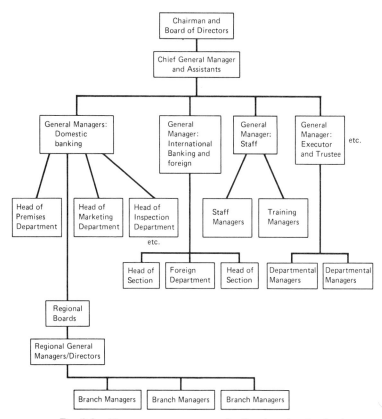

Fig. 9.2   Management structure of a London clearing bank

The organization continues 'down the line' from the general managers. Domestic banking, for example, delegates authority to regional offices and it is here that the management structure of the regions differs from bank to bank. To consider one instance: Midland has its twenty-four regional head offices under the control of a *regional director*, supported by assistants. Lloyds, on the other hand, has fifteen regional boards each with a chairman and up to six or seven regional directors who, like members of the main board of directors, are not usually full-time employees of the bank but are people who have distinguished careers in fields other than banking and who are well known locally; each regional board also has a full-time *regional general manager*. The other banks also have developed regional structures; this decentralization establishes a local identity for the bank and to some extent helps to dispel the idea that all decisions are taken at a large impersonal head office in London. The regional offices exercise considerable power over the branches in their areas: most applications for loan and overdraft facilities, or for their renewal, that are too large for a branch manager to approve on his own can be sanctioned by the regional office without reference to head office; only requests for very large advances will be above the limit of the regional office and require the approval of head office and possibly the main board of directors. Regional offices are also able to report to head office about the state of local industry and commerce, and each has a responsibility to ensure that Bank of England directives are adhered to in their area. After the regional directors and managers come the *branch managers*—the highest-ranking member of the bank's staff that most customers will meet; Unit 9.2 considers the people involved in the organization of a 'typical' branch. Besides domestic banking, other divisions of the bank are often also organized on a regional basis: a specialist foreign branch and an office of the executor and trustee department often serve each region.

The more specialist divisions of the bank which do not warrant regional representation, such as corporate services, have a structure that ranges downward from the general manager responsible for the service, involving specialist managers or heads of departments. The services of these divisions are available to both regional offices and branches to enable them to provide specialist advice to customers, and are fully discussed in Units 14 and 15. Additionally, every major clearing bank includes departments that provide specialist services to assist in the smooth running of its organization or to promote its image and services generally. We will discuss these one by one.

(a) Staff department
This is concerned with recruitment, transfer from branch to branch of staff to ensure that they gain a variety of experience at branches of different sizes, training, welfare and the consideration of suitable staff for promotion. Members of this department regularly interview staff so that career prospects, problems and difficulties can be identified.

(b) Training department
Working closely with the staff department, the training department is responsible for running the training courses on which every member of the bank's staff will go. The first course is designed as an induction course for new entrants and will cover the basic book-keeping routines of branch operations. As a member of staff progresses in the bank he will go on further

training courses to learn how to be a terminal operator (using the computer terminals installed in branches through which accounting information is fed into the central computer), a cashier, a foreign clerk and a security clerk (the duties of these staff members are discussed in Unit 9.2). With some 50 000 to 60 000 staff employed by each major clearing bank, the training department is a very large operation and will involve running either several regional training centres or a large central training branch. More advanced courses for staff being considered for appointment to branch accountant, and management development courses for branch accountants, assistant managers and managers are usually run at regular intervals at large country houses that have been bought by each bank and converted into management training centres.

(c) Inspection department

With so many branches involved, it is essential to ensure that each carries out the day-to-day banking operations in a uniform manner in accordance with the instructions from head office. It is the job of the inspection department to 'visit' branches and check on their work and make recommendations to the manager of any shortcomings at his branch. They are also available to managers in any emergency which needs the attention of bank investigators from outside the branch, such as a large discrepancy of cash.

'I had a touch of sciatica last night. That usually means the inspectors are coming'

(d) **Marketing department**

Nowadays the banks are increasingly using marketing techniques to sell their services. Marketing involves undertaking research to find out what services the customer wants, planning new services and advertising in all its forms—in newspapers and magazines, on television, with posters and through leaflets displayed in the branches and mailed to customers. The department is also concerned with training managers and staff to sell new services—this is particularly important because unless staff fully understand a new (or existing) service and can point out its advantages to customers, the service will be undersold.

Working closely with the marketing department, and perhaps a part of it, are staff dealing with public relations, concerned with the 'public image' of the bank. This department is particularly involved with releases to the media—press, radio and television—concerning developments within the bank, and with commenting on banking topics in the news.

Other departments providing specialist services within the bank include the *premises department*, involved in all aspects of acquisition, maintenance and sale of bank premises, the *computer department*, which organizes computer operations, the *organization and methods department*, which studies the work of branches and makes recommendations as to methods of doing certain tasks that are more efficient or otherwise improved, and the bullion department, which arranges the distribution and collection of bank notes and coin throughout the branch network.

During the 1960s and 1970s, the major clearing banks in Britain acquired and formed companies providing highly specialized services. These subsidiaries, associated companies and trade investments, together with the parent bank, together make up the banking group and, although they may be separate in legal, management and name terms from the main bank, the services they provide are available to its customers. They are involved in areas such as hire purchase, factoring, insurance and merchant bank services, and are considered more fully in Units 14 and 15. The clearing banks differ from each other in the ways in which they fit these specialized areas into their structure, however: one bank may provide a service through the parent company, while another may provide the same service through a subsidiary or associated company. For example, Lloyds Bank has a division of the parent bank providing the executor and trustee services, while the same services in the Midland Bank are available through Midland Bank Trust Company Ltd. As far as the customer is concerned this difference does not matter, but it is of interest to the banking student as representing a different organizational structure.

An indication of the complexity of a large clearing bank can be obtained from Fig. 9.3, an advertisement for the National Westminster Bank Ltd. that shows the range of associated and subsidiary companies making up the group.

National Westminster Bank Ltd.

Over 3,000 banking branches in England, Wales and Scotland.
Representation of the International Banking Division in major cities of England
and Scotland, and in the leading financial centres of Australia,
Canada, France, Germany, Greece, Holland, Hong Kong, Italy, Japan, the
Middle East, Singapore, Spain, Switzerland, U.S.A. and U.S.S.R.

International Westminster Bank Ltd.

Head Office: London. Branches in Bahamas, Belgium, France and Germany.

The National Westminster Group also includes:

Centre-file Ltd.
Computer Services.

County Bank Ltd.
Merchant Banking.

Coutts & Co.
Personal and Commercial banking, and other financial services.

Credit Factoring International Ltd.
U.K. and International factoring service.

Eurocom Data (Holdings) Ltd.
Computer output to microfilm.

Isle of Man Bank Ltd.
Commercial banking in the Isle of Man.

Lombard North Central Ltd.
Banking, credit finance and leasing in Great Britain. Subsidiary companies in
Australia, New Zealand, Cyprus and Malta.

National Westminster Bank Finance (CI) Ltd.
Channel Islands based deposit-taking institution.

National Westminster Insurance Services Ltd.
Incorporated Insurance Brokers.

National Westminster Unit Trust Managers Ltd.
Unit Trusts.

Ulster Bank Ltd.
Commercial banking in Ireland.

Ulster Investment Bank Ltd.
Merchant banking in Ireland.

Global Bank A.G. & Handelsbank NW
West Germany.   Switzerland.

And you thought NatWest was just a bank.

↻ National Westminster Bank Group

*Fig. 9.3   Associated and subsidiary companies in the
National Westminster Bank Group*

9.2   Branch Organization and Staff

(a) The manager

In the eyes of the local community, the manager is the bank and it is his duty to sell the services and develop the business of his branch. In this task he has overall responsibility for his customers but can, as we have seen, call in specialists from the various divisions and departments of the bank and can always look to his regional director for advice and guidance. A manager will have spent many years in the bank, usually having started as a junior straight from school and worked his way up through the various different banking tasks—all good preparation for the day when he takes charge of his 'own' branch. While at present most managers are men, all bank jobs are open to women and there are increasing numbers of female managers, assistant managers and accountants. (However, for the sake of simplicity, we shall continue to refer to individual staff as 'he'.)

The manager does not spend all his time lending money; while many of his visitors wish to see him for this purpose, many call to seek advice on a wide range of financial and personal problems. It follows, therefore, that the ideal manager must be good at lending the bank's money (and getting it back safely!), well versed in all aspects of finance, a good listener and able to get on well with people from all walks of life. The manager doesn't spend all the time at his desk—part of his job is to get to know local people by visiting them in shops, factories and on the farm.

Depending on the size of the branch and his experience as a manager, he is given a limit up to which he can lend without reference to his regional office. This ensures that, for ordinary day-to-day lending, the manager can make up his mind quickly and not keep the customer waiting for days for a decision by somebody else further up the hierarchy, who doesn't personally know him. The lending limit usually applies to the maximum amount that the manager may lend to an individual customer and may be higher if the advance is secured; when requests are made for advances above his limit the manager must send full details of the request to his regional office for sanction. The regional office also has a lending limit, although a much higher one than that of most branch managers, and only requests for the very largest loans and overdrafts are required to be submitted to head office for the approval of the board of directors. All advances are approved for a fixed period which will not normally exceed twelve months, except in the case of medium-term loans (see Unit 15.2(b)). At the end of the period the manager reviews the advance with his customer, and where appropriate renews, or requests his regional office to renew, the facility for a further period. Thus much of the manager's time is spent in reviewing existing lending.

The manager has overall responsibility for the staff of his branch and for ensuring that it is run in accordance with head office instructions. In larger branches he has one or more *assistant managers* and *manager's assistants* to help him in certain areas of the work.

'I need the jacket to accommodate a pocket calculator, a pocket bleeper and a pocket dictating machine'

(b) The accountant

This is the person who is responsible for the day-to-day organization and administration of the branch so that the bank's business is run efficiently and correctly. Depending on which bank he works for, he may be called *sub-manager, chief clerk* or *accountant*. As the last title suggests, he is particularly concerned with the smooth running of the accounting side of the branch and handles inquiries from customers about their accounts and from people who wish to open new accounts. During the course of an average day he meets a good many customers at the inquiry counter, on a less formal basis than can the manager in his office. He is also usually involved in lending and often deals with requests for loans and overdrafts from personal rather than business customers. Besides these tasks his main responsibilities are to ensure the smooth and efficient running of the branch, that staff are trained within the branch in different aspects of the bank's work and that appropriate returns and other information are sent to head office at the right time and correctly completed. In his work he may be helped by one or more *assistant accountants*.

The accountant, like most staff, has usually worked for the bank since leaving school and has spent periods at several branches doing different tasks. During this time he will have attended appropriate courses at the bank's training branches. In his present job he will already be preparing for his next promotion —perhaps as manager of a small branch, or accountant or assistant manager at a larger branch—by deputizing for the manager or assistant manager during holiday or sickness periods.

The manager, assistant manager, manager's assistant, accountant and his assistants are often known as *appointed officers*; this indicates that they have reached a certain level of responsibility in their careers and are appointed by head office to run the branch at their different work levels.

(c) The security clerk

He is concerned to see that, when the manager accepts security for an advance (see Unit 17), the necessary formalities are carried out to ensure that the securities are held by the bank in a correct manner to cover the advance. He is also concerned with buying and selling stocks and shares and other investments for the bank's customers, with taking deeds, documents and other valuables into safe custody for those who wish to leave them in the bank's safe and with giving advice about a wide range of bank services.

Special training courses help to prepare for this job and promising young men and women who are making good progress in the Institute of Bankers examinations will be chosen to attend. A sound level of legal knowledge, banking practice and financial awareness are required to understand the implications of this job which, in smaller branches, may also incorporate the work of the foreign clerk. In very large branches the security clerk may be an 'appointed officer' and in many branches, because of his contact by letter with customers, solicitors and stockbrokers, the security clerk often has authority to sign 'for manager'.

The security clerk works closely with the manager in dealing with securities and in preparing the 'application for advance' forms that are needed when a customer wishes to borrow an amount above the manager's limit and reference has to be made to the regional office. Administratively, the security clerk is directly under the control of the accountant, and, in holiday and sickness periods, may 'move up' and deputize for him or for his assistant. This is all good training for his next promotion which may be as assistant accountant at a large branch or accountant at a small branch.

(d) The foreign clerk

Most larger bank branches employ a clerk who deals specifically with foreign work. During the peak holiday periods the foreign clerk spends a lot of his time making up *travel orders* consisting of travellers' cheques and foreign currency (see Unit 14.6) for customers going abroad, and handling unused foreign currency brought back to the bank after holidays are over. The foreign clerk must therefore be fully conversant with rates of exchange for currencies and with the United Kingdom exchange control regulations concerning taking funds out of the country.

Travel orders are only one part of a foreign clerk's duties, however: nearly every branch has at least one business customer who deals with either exporting or importing and the bank is almost always involved in settlements with his overseas customers. To handle this work requires a good working knowledge of the receipts and payment processes, the documents involved and how to deal with any discrepancies. Business customers also seek advice and information about exporting or importing and the foreign clerk is expected to know most of the answers. (Exporting and importing are dealt with fully in Unit 16.)

Like all bank clerks, the foreign clerk will have spent some years learning the basic routines of banking and then will have been specially selected and trained for his present job. He may choose to continue to specialize in foreign work and his next promotion might be transfer to a regional foreign branch; alternatively he may wish to remain in normal branch banking and seek promotion to assistant accountant at a large branch or accountant at a small one.

(e) The cashiers

These are the people who meet the bank's customers more than any other members of the staff. The branch is usually judged in its locality by the efficiency, pleasantness, helpfulness and courtesy given by the cashiers to customers. We all know the standards of courtesy that we expect when we go into shops or restaurants, but it is a different matter to have to maintain those standards for five hours each day as a cashier. The banks have realized the importance of the cashier as the main link with the customers and place great emphasis on this aspect in the training course for cashiers. Some banks have, in recent years, run special 'courtesy campaigns' within their branches for those members of staff who have most contact with customers.

In large branches the cashiers spend the whole of the day at the counter and deal with all aspects of paying in and drawing out by branch customers and total strangers. At the same time, besides being courteous and efficient, the cashier has to bear in mind many other things such as endorsements on cheques (when necessary), stopped cheques, lost or stolen cheque and credit cards, and the list of customers (one hopes, a short one) for whom cheques should not be cashed without reference to the manager or accountant. The bank's internal regulations, especially those concerning the control of cash, should also be adhered to, and at the end of the day the cashier must balance his till against the total cash he has received and paid out. In a smaller branch, besides counter duties, cashiers are involved in dealing with general inquiries, cheque books, statements, standing orders, travellers' cheques and foreign money, although in a large branch most of these matters are handled by an *inquiry clerk* who passes the customers on to the appropriate specialist staff.

It is not unusual for a cashier to be relatively new to the bank, perhaps having spent twelve months as a junior clerk and then going on a cashiers' course at the bank's training branch. During a period of counter duties, a cashier may have the opportunity of gaining further experience of the bank's procedures by spending time as the *first cashier*, responsible to the accountant for the counter. The ambitious cashier looks for opportunities to progress to security clerk and will spend his time working hard at the Institute of Bankers examinations (see Unit 19.3) and finding out as much as possible about work concerned with securities.

(*f*) **The accounting staff**

These are the people who carry out the accounting functions of the branch; they work directly under the supervision of the accountant. The *control clerk* is responsible for controlling and balancing the work of the branch each day and for making appropriate book-keeping entries. The *terminal operator* uses a terminal unit situated in the branch and connected, usually by telephone line, direct to the bank's computer centre, to feed in information concerning customers' accounts—credits received and cash, cheques and standing orders drawn on the account. He should also be looking out for irregularities on cheques such as 'stops' or cheques not signed in accordance with the mandate held by the bank. The *remittance* or *waste clerks* are concerned with credits paid to the cashiers: they sort credits and cheques paid in by customers into different banks and, at the end of the day, balance the totals of these with the total credits paid in. The credits that have been paid in for other branches and other banks, together with the cheques drawn on other branches and other banks, are then sent off to head office where they are handled by the bank's clearing department and those on other banks passed through the London Bankers' Clearing House (see Unit 10.9).

A young person joining the bank as a junior is likely to start as a remittance or waste clerk. In small branches the junior clerk is also expected to deal with outgoing post, answer the telephone, handle requests for statements and other inquiries at the inquiry counter and make coffee in the morning and tea in the afternoon!

In medium-sized or large branches there are also *secretaries* who make appointments for customers to see the manager and assistant manager, type outgoing correspondence from all departments of the bank and are concerned in keeping the non-accounting records of customers up to date. In smaller branches there may well be no typist and it is not unknown for managers to have to do their own typing.

In this Unit, the broad areas of staff work and responsibility have been discussed with reference to the ways in which they fit into the working of a branch. But of course different banks are organized in different ways, and there are often variations even between branches of the same bank. You should compare carefully the organization of the bank you know best with the description given above, and make notes of differences of which you are aware.

9.3   Questions

1. Describe the main divisions of responsibilities of the general managers of a major clearing bank, indicating the areas with which each is concerned.

2. Detail the organizational structure of the branch where you work. Who is responsible for the different aspects of the work of the branch?

3. Draw up a job specification for the person in charge of the securities department of a medium-sized branch.

Unit Ten

Bills of Exchange and Cheques

10.1 Introduction

Cheques are familiar to most people and are commonly used to settle debts. *Bills of exchange* are not so well known but are used extensively in the settlement of overseas trade: they may be payable on demand or may be worded so as to make the payment due at some future date, thus giving the purchaser of goods a period of credit. There are many similarities between bills of exchange and cheques, but as bills developed before cheques came into general use, they will be considered first.

10.2 Bills of Exchange: a Definition

The Bills of Exchange Act 1882, which remains an important piece of legislation for bankers, gives the definition as:

> an unconditional order in writing addressed by one person to another, signed by the person giving it, requiring the person to whom it is addressed to pay on demand, or at a fixed or determinable future time, a sum certain in money to or to the order of a specified person or bearer.

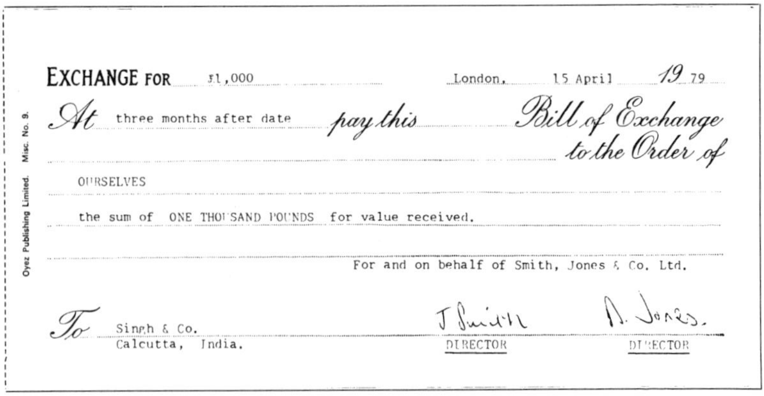
EXCHANGE FOR £1,000 London, 15 April 1979

At three months after date pay this Bill of Exchange to the Order of

OURSELVES

the sum of ONE THOUSAND POUNDS for value received.

For and on behalf of Smith, Jones & Co. Ltd.

To Singh & Co.
Calcutta, India.

DIRECTOR DIRECTOR

Oyez Publishing Limited. Misc. No. 9.

Fig. 10.1 A specimen bill of exchange

This definition sounds complex, but using the specimen bill of exchange shown in Fig. 10.1 we can examine its elements one by one, and see how it has been built up.

'An unconditional order.' There are no conditions stipulated that must be carried out before payment; the bill simply says 'pay'. A *conditional order* is a document ordering payment subject to the fulfilment of some condition, for example: 'Pay *AB* the sum of £100 on condition that the receipt below is duly signed and dated'.

'In writing.' The bill must be in writing, whether typewritten or in ink, print or pencil. The writing may be on paper, parchment or cardboard—in a famous case it was even on the side of a cow!

'Addressed by one person to another.' It is addressed by Smith, Jones & Co. Ltd. to Singh & Co.

'Signed by the person giving it.' It is signed by the directors on behalf of Smith, Jones & Co. Ltd.

'Requiring the person to whom it is addressed to pay.' It is addressed to Singh & Co. and they are the people required to pay.

'To pay on demand or at a fixed or determinable future time.' This bill is not payable on demand, nor is it payable at a fixed future time, since it does not say 'pay on 15 July 1979'; instead it is payable at a determinable future time—three months after date—and is therefore determined to be payable on 15 July 1979.

'A sum certain in money.' The exact money amount, £1 000, is clearly stated.

'To or to the order of a specified person or bearer.' This bill is not a bearer bill, which would say 'pay ... to the Order of Bearer'; instead it says 'pay ... to the Order of Ourselves', the 'ourselves' being Smith, Jones & Co. Ltd.; the words 'to the Order of Ourselves' allow Smith, Jones & Co. Ltd. to transfer their interest in the bill to another person by endorsement (see Unit 10.4).

'Value received'. These words are often added to the wording of a bill to establish 'valuable consideration' which is normally one of the essentials of a valid contract.

10.3 Parties to a Bill

There are initially three parties to a bill: drawer, drawee and payee. The *drawer* is the person who has drawn the bill; the *drawee* is the person on whom it is drawn and who has to make payment; the *payee* is the person to whom the money will be paid. On the bill shown in Fig. 10.1, the drawer is Smith, Jones & Co. Ltd., the drawee is Singh and Co. and the payee is also Smith,

Jones & Co. Ltd.: in this example, therefore, Smith, Jones & Co. Ltd. is both the drawer and payee. It sometimes happens that there are three different parties to a bill at the start: if Smith, Jones & Co. Ltd. owed £1 000 to W. Harris who was prepared to accept the money direct from Singh & Co., in settlement of the debt due to him, then the bill would be drawn to read 'three months after date pay to W. Harris or his order the sum of one thousand pounds', and Harris would be the payee.

Where a bill is payable at a time in the future it is known as a *term bill*—because it is drawn for a certain term—and must be sent to the drawee for *acceptance*. This is done by the drawee 'accepting' his liability by signing his name on the bill and agreeing to pay the bill at maturity. The bill shown in Fig. 10.1 would be sent to Singh & Co. for their acceptance and, when this was done, they would be known as the *acceptors*. If the bill had been payable at sight—a *sight bill*—there would be no need to obtain the acceptance of Singh & Co. because they would be expected to pay immediately on 'sight' of the bill; if the bill had been payable three months after sight, the bill would need to be presented for acceptance and the acceptance dated, in order to determine the date of payment.

There are two major types of acceptance: a general acceptance and a qualified acceptance. A *general acceptance* confirms that the drawee is in agreement with the terms of the bill as drawn. A *qualified acceptance*, however, has the effect of varying the terms of the bill as drawn; for example, there may be a partial acceptance of the amount: a bill drawn for £1 000 may be accepted for £900 only. If the holder takes a qualified acceptance he generally loses his right of recourse against previous parties to the bill (see Unit 10.5).

10.4 Endorsement of a Bill

The bill shown in Fig. 10.1 is an example of an *order bill* in that it contains the words 'pay to us or to our order'. This means that such a bill may be transferred to another person on the 'orders of' the payee by endorsement and delivery—handing over—of the bill to the other person: this transfer of title is called *negotiation*. More precisely, a bill is payable to order when:

(i) it is expressed to be payable to order, *or*

(ii) it is payable to the order of a particular person, *or*

(iii) it is payable to a particular person and does not contain words prohibiting transfer.

For example, a bill payable to 'J. Smith or order' is obviously an order bill; a bill payable to 'J. Smith' is also an order bill because it does not contain words prohibiting transfer; but a bill payable to 'J. Smith only' is not an order bill and may not be transferred to another person.

When an order bill is transferred to another person by endorsement and delivery, a number of different types of endorsement are possible, and these also apply to cheques.

(i) A *blank endorsement* specifies no endorsee (that is, no person in whose favour it is endorsed) and therefore the bill or cheque becomes payable to bearer. For the bill in Fig. 10.1 a blank endorsement would appear on the reverse as:

for and on behalf of Smith, Jones & Co. Ltd.,
J. Smith   A. Jones (signed)
Directors

(ii) A *special endorsement* specifies the endorsee:

Pay D. Williams or order
for and on behalf of Smith, Jones & Co. Ltd.,
J. Smith   A. Jones (signed)
Directors

Notice that the words 'or order' could be omitted and the bill would still be an order bill. A blank endorsement may be converted by any holder into a special endorsement by adding the words 'pay ....', naming the person to whom it is to be payable.

(iii) A *restrictive endorsement* prevents further endorsement of the bill:

Pay D. Williams only
for and on behalf of Smith, Jones & Co. Ltd.,
J. Smith   A. Jones (signed)
Directors

10.5 Negotiation of a Bill

Under the terms of the Bills of Exchange Act, every person who has signed a bill guarantees to a subsequent holder that it will be paid on the due date. Thus the holder of a bill that is not paid on the due date (see Unit 10.6) may sue any or all previous parties to the bill. Therefore a bill that carries the acceptance of a reputable person known to be of first-class financial standing is considered better than a bill carrying the acceptance of an unknown trader. This recalls the origins of the merchant banks among the wealthy merchants who, for a fee, began to lend their name to bills by accepting them for less well-known merchants (see Unit 5.3). They continue to accept bills on behalf of their customers—hence the name *acceptance houses* for the banks most involved in this business—and such bills command a finer rate of discount than trade bills.

A holder of an accepted bill of exchange can:

(i) sell the bill for face value less discount to his own bank or a discount house, *or*

(ii) negotiate the bill by asking his bank for a loan against the bill and request the bank to collect the proceeds upon maturity, *or*

(iii) hold the bill until maturity if he does not need the money urgently.

10.6   Discharge and Dishonour of a Bill

Normally a bill will be paid by the acceptor upon presentation on the due date; the legal obligations on the bill are then said to be *discharged*. There are other circumstances in which a bill may be discharged:

(i) where the acceptor of the bill is or becomes the holder of the bill at or after maturity—that is, he becomes the owner of the bill on which he is liable;

(ii) where material alteration has been made to the bill—such as a change of the date or the amount payable—without the assent of all parties liable on the bill, then all parties liable prior to the alteration will be discharged, but not those liable by negotiation after alteration;

(iii) where the holder renounces his rights and makes a written cancellation on the bill itself, that is, he makes it clear in writing that he will not make a claim on the acceptor for the amount of the bill;

(iv) where the bill becomes *statute-barred* under the provisions of the Limitation Acts; this means that no bill is enforceable in law after six years from the date when the cause of action first happened, subject to certain complex rules regarding the revival of a statute-barred debt.

Most bills are correctly accepted when presented for acceptance and paid when presented for payment. Sometimes acceptance is refused and the bill is then said to be *dishonoured by non-acceptance*; similarly a failure by the acceptor to pay on the due date leads to *dishonour by non-payment*. It is important for the person presenting a bill which is dishonoured to take the correct legal steps. For foreign bills (generally drawn in this country and payable abroad) these steps are known as *noting* and *protest*.

A bill is *noted* in order to secure official evidence that it has been dishonoured. The holder of the bill that is to be noted applies to a legal official called a *notary public* whose job it is to attest deeds and documents to confirm their authenticity. The notary public re-presents the bill for acceptance or payment, whichever is required, and if the drawee (or acceptor) still refuses to accept (or pay) the bill, the bill is noted. The noting is a minute made by the notary public which contains the date of presentment, the notary's charges, a reference to the notary's register and his initials. This noting is a preparatory step to a formal document called a *protest* which bears the seal of the notary public and attests that the bill has been dishonoured. A protest is accepted in the courts of most countries as evidence that the bill has been dishonoured.

Where a dishonoured bill has to be protested and no notary public is available at the place of dishonour, any householder or substantial resident may in the presence of two witnesses, give a certificate, signed by them, attesting the dishonour of the bill, and the certificate will operate as if it were a formal protest of the bill. This is known as a *householder's protest*.

These legal procedures are necessary to establish the liability of previous parties to the bill.

10.7   Definition and Development of Cheques

The Bills of Exchange Act defines a cheque as *a bill of exchange, drawn on a banker, payable on demand.*

The parties to a cheque are the same as for a bill: drawer, drawee, and payee. The *drawer* is the person who has signed the cheque, the *drawee* is the bank on which the cheque is drawn and the *payee* is the person to whom the cheque is payable and who is to receive the benefit. Normally the holder of a cheque has no rights against the drawee banker. A cheque does not need to be accepted prior to payment as it is payable on demand. Cheques differ from bills of exchange in that notice of dishonour by non-payment is rarely needed in order to claim against the drawer of a cheque. This is because non-payment is almost always due to lack of funds or because the cheque has been 'stopped' by the drawer: both of these are valid excuses for not giving notice to the drawer. Where the holder is concerned, mere return of the cheque is deemed to be sufficient notice of dishonour, but in practice an answer is always written on the cheque (see Unit 10.10). The steps known as noting and protest are not necessary in order to preserve the right of recourse against the drawer or endorser of an inland bill. Most cheques in Britain fit the definition of an inland bill—they are drawn and payable within the British Isles—and therefore these legal steps do not apply.

Cheques came into general use in Britain with the emergence of the joint-stock banks in the second quarter of the nineteenth century. The Bills of Exchange Act brought cheques within the general scope of all the provisions of the Act applicable to bills payable on demand. In particular the Act contains specific provisions relating to crossed cheques which give valuable protection against loss through theft and fraud (see Unit 10.8). Under section 60 of the Act, bankers are protected when they pay in good faith and in the ordinary course of business a cheque bearing a forged endorsement, and will not be liable to the customer for the amount, provided it is an order cheque payable on demand and drawn on the banker. The Act, with its protection for both bank and customer, also brought together—or *codified*—previous law relating to crossings on cheques, and gave banks considerable scope for developing current account business.

The other major legislation concerning cheques is the Cheques Act 1957, which removed the requirement that payees should endorse cheques before paying them in to their bank account, with the exception of a few specific cases. The Act also provides that an unendorsed cheque, if it appears to have been paid by the drawer's bank, should be evidence of receipt by the payee of the amount of the cheque. This explains why, when bills are paid by cheque, receipts are only issued on request; in the event of any dispute over payment, the paid cheque can be obtained from the drawer's bank as proof of payment.

10.8   Crossings on Cheques

Unlike a bill of exchange, a cheque may be *crossed* by drawing two parallel lines across its face.

This ensures that the cheque cannot be cashed at a bank but must be paid in for the credit of an account. Thus crossed cheques provide a safer means of payment than open cheques which can easily be cashed at the drawee bank. A thief who has stolen crossed cheques is forced to pass them through a bank account, most probably by asking shops or pubs to cash them for him and pass them through their accounts, and this may lead to him being traced by the police. The only exception to the rule on not cashing crossed cheques is, of course, when the account holder or 'his known agent'—his wife or his wages clerk, perhaps—wishes to draw cash. Most cheques issued by banks nowadays already carry a pre-printed crossing but under certain circumstances open cheques may be useful to a customer who wants another person to be able to draw cash from the bank on his behalf.

There are two main types of crossings: general and special. A *general crossing* is described by the Bills of Exchange Act as being two parallel lines across the face of a cheque, with or without the words 'and company' (or any abbreviation) and with or without the words 'not negotiable'. Fig. 10.2 shows some examples of general crossings as described in the Act.

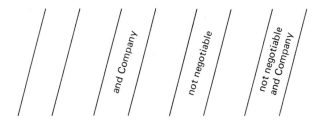

Fig. 10.2   Crossed cheques: general crossings

The effect of all these crossings is that the cheque must be paid into a bank account: the words 'and company' have no legal significance and date back to the days of private banks when it was usual for the payee of a cheque, when paying it in for the credit of his account, to add his bank's name which would end in 'and company'; thus the words were pre-printed on cheques as a service to payees. 'Not negotiable' as a crossing is considered below.

A cheque is *specially crossed* when, as well as a general crossing, it bears across its face the addition of a banker's name: the cheque is then said to be crossed specially to that banker—the words 'and company', 'not negotiable' and 'account payee' may also be included. Fig. 10.3 illustrates some examples of special crossings.

The effect of a special crossing is that the cheques can only be paid into

Fig. 10.3   Crossed cheques: special crossings

an account with the specified bank and, if indicated on the crossing, the specified branch. All banks cross cheques paid in by customers specially to themselves by means of a rubber stamp which bears the name and address of the branch, together with its sorting code number, so that if the cheques were lost in transit to the drawee bank, they would be useless to anyone and could not again be paid into a bank account. The identification of the collecting bank also helps when cheques are returned unpaid by the drawee bank (see Unit 10.10).

Cheques, unless they bear words prohibiting negotiation, are *negotiable instruments* (as are also bills of exchange, bank notes and certain other documents). The characterisitics of a negotiable instrument are:

(i) the document must be transferable by delivery, or by endorsement and delivery;

(ii) the legal title passes to the person who takes it in good faith and for the value and without notice of any defect in the title of the transferor;

(iii) the legal holder for the time being can sue in his own name;

(iv) notice of transfer need not be given to the party liable on the instrument; and

(v) the title passes free from equities or counterclaims between previous parties of which the transferee has no notice.

A bank note is payable to bearer and thus, unlike most cheques, needs no endorsement to transfer the title. How do you know that one of the bank notes in your wallet or handbag has not at some time been stolen? As bank notes are negotiable instruments and provided you acquire them 'in good faith and for value' (that means that you had no idea they had been stolen and you either earned them, received them as a present or were given them in change) you have no need to worry—your title to them is 'good'. Most cheques and bills of exchange are *payable to order*—take a look at one of your own cheques and you will see the words 'or order' already printed—and require endorsement and delivery to transfer the title: the exceptions to this rule are those that are *payable to bearer* when, like bank notes, the title passes by delivery.

As most cheques are negotiable instruments—unless they bear the words 'not negotiable'—it is possible to obtain a good title even though the transferor's title was faulty or non-existent. Suppose that a thief steals a cheque which has conveniently already been endorsed in blank by the payee, and negotiates the cheque to an innocent shopkeeper who agrees to cash it in exchange for goods. Under such circumstances, the transferee (the shopkeeper) has a right to the value represented by the cheque and all previous parties would be liable. Thus the drawer of a stolen cheque may still find himself liable for the amount of it even though he may have placed a 'stop' on it. The way to avoid such possible liability is to cross cheques 'not negotiable': this does not mean, as is often mistakenly thought, that the cheque cannot be transferred from one person to another, but that a person taking such a cheque shall not have and shall not be capable of giving a better title to the cheque than that of his transferor. This means that a break in the 'good title' remains broken and an innocent transferee cannot acquire any better rights than those of the person from whom he received it. To be absolutely certain that you will not be liable for the amount of your cheques in the event of their being stolen, you should always cross them 'not negotiable'. Nowadays most cheques are paid into the account of the payee without transfer and there is little risk; but where cheques are customarily passed from one person to another there is always the chance that a negotiable cheque could, after being stolen, be passed to an innocent person—known as a *holder in due course*—who could recover the value of the cheque from any previous party. A holder in due course—who could be our innocent shopkeeper, for instance—is a person who has taken a bill or cheque in good faith, complete and regular on the face of it (that is, with nothing apparently wrong with it), for value, before it is overdue, and without notice of any defect in the title of his predecessor or of the dishonouring of the bill.

The crossing 'account payee' has no statutory significance: it is not mentioned in the Bills of Exchange Act or the Cheques Act. However, by custom, when a cheque crossed in this way is paid in for the credit of an account, the bank accepting it—the *collecting bank*—looks to see if it is being credited to the account of the payee. If it is not, the collecting bank is *put on inquiry* and should take steps to find out why it is being paid into another account. If it does not obtain a satisfactory explanation, the collecting bank may be liable for *conversion* (allowing a cheque intended to be of benefit to one person to be converted to the benefit of another).

Sometimes when a person is buying goods by mail order, he does not know the exact cost of the purchase and sends a signed and dated cheque to the supplier requesting him to complete the amount in words and figures. The danger is that the signed cheque could be made out for a much larger amount than that intended, and one way around this is for the drawer to cross the cheque 'not to exceed £—'. While this crossing has no statutory significance, the paying banker will observe his customer's wishes when the cheque is presented for payment and will return it where the amount exceeds the limitation of the crossing. A signed cheque or bill of exchange made out in this way is known as an *inchoate (incomplete) instrument*.

Another crossing sometimes used is that of 'not transferable'. Every cheque is transferable unless it contains words prohibiting transfer or indicating an intention that it shall not be transferable. To prevent transfer the word 'only' should appear after the payee's name (for example: 'pay J. Brown only'), the words 'order' or 'bearer' should be deleted—this alteration being initialled by the drawer—and the words 'not transferable' written across the face of the cheque. The collecting bank would then make inquiries if the cheque appeared to have been transferred.

10.9   The Clearing System

This is the means whereby banks exchange cheques drawn on each other. During the course of a day's business a bank has many cheques paid in by its customers that are drawn on other branches and banks and the total of those on other banks appears on the bank's balance sheet as an asset (see Unit 8.3). Most of these have to pass through the London Bankers' Clearing House where they are exchanged so that each bank receives the cheques drawn on its own branches. To settle differences in amounts, one bank will pay another by drawing a cheque on its account at the Bank of England. Prior to the establishment of the clearing house clerks used to go round the banks, handing over cheques and receiving payments. To ease their task, the clearing house was started in 1773 in a London coffee house where the clerks would meet to exchange cheques and reach a settlement (and, of course, have a cup of coffee). From simple beginnings, the business of the clearing house, which is jointly owned and managed by the London clearing banks, has expanded enormously and in 1977 the average value of cheques cleared each working day was £9 998 million, represented by some five million cheques.

How a cheque is cleared

The process of clearing a cheque is perhaps most easily studied by monitoring the route followed by an imaginary example.

(i) On Monday morning Smith, a customer of Midland Bank, Worcester, pays into his account a cheque for £10, drawn on the account of Williams at Lloyds Bank, Gloucester. The remittance clerk at Midland, Worcester lists the cheque and includes it in the daily total of cheques drawn on Lloyds Bank. It is sent off to Midland's head office at the end of the day along with all the other cheques drawn on branches and banks other than Midland, Worcester.

(ii) On Tuesday morning the cheques from the Worcester branch are received at Midland's clearing department at head office along with cheques from all the other Midland branches. All the cheques drawn on Lloyds are placed together and a summary is made to arrive at the total amount. Cheques drawn on the other clearing banks are dealt with in the same way.

(iii) Clerks from Midland take the cheques and listings to the clearing house where they are handed over to representatives of each of the other clearing banks, who also have cheques to hand over.

(iv) The clerks of the various banks, now with bundles of their own cheques, return to their head offices. Thus the £10 cheque arrives at the clearing department of Lloyds Bank along with the others received in the exchange that day. All the cheques are sorted according to the different Lloyds branches on which they are drawn, and their details fed into the bank's computer so that the customers' accounts can be debited next day. The cheques themselves are then posted off to the various branches, the one for £10 being included in the bundle destined for Gloucester branch.

(v) On Wednesday morning, Gloucester branch receives the cheque clearing from head office. Cheques that are in order are automatically debited to the drawers' accounts, including the £10 on Williams' account, by the bank's computer.

The above, which is illustrated in Fig. 10.4, is a simplification of the clearing

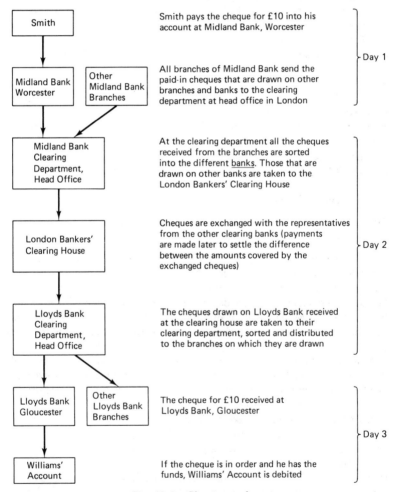

Smith	Smith pays the cheque for £10 into his account at Midland Bank, Worcester
Midland Bank Worcester / **Other Midland Bank Branches**	All branches of Midland Bank send the paid-in cheques that are drawn on other branches and banks to the clearing department at head office in London

⎱ Day 1

Midland Bank Clearing Department, Head Office	At the clearing department all the cheques received from the branches are sorted into the different <u>banks</u>. Those that are drawn on other banks are taken to the London Bankers' Clearing House
London Bankers' Clearing House	Cheques are exchanged with the representatives from the other clearing banks (payments are made later to settle the difference between the amounts covered by the exchanged cheques)

⎱ Day 2

Lloyds Bank Clearing Department, Head Office	The cheques drawn on Lloyds Bank received at the clearing house are taken to their clearing department, sorted and distributed to the branches on which they are drawn
Lloyds Bank Gloucester / **Other Lloyds Bank Branches**	The cheque for £10 received at Lloyds Bank, Gloucester
Williams' Account	If the cheque is in order and he has the funds, Williams' Account is debited

⎱ Day 3

Fig. 10.4   Clearing a cheque

procedures: a high degree of automation has been introduced, involving cheque-sorting and listing equipment and the banks' computer systems. In the example, clearing has taken three days; this assumes that there have been no delays and normally represents the fastest time in which a cheque can be cleared. Not all cheques pass through the clearing house: in particular, those that are paid in at other branches of the bank on which they are drawn (such as a cheque drawn on Midland Bank, Gloucester being paid in for the credit of an account at Midland Bank, Worcester) only travel as far as the bank's head office, where they are sorted into branch order and dispatched to the branches on which they are drawn: this is known as the *inter-branch* clearing.

Four different types of clearing pass through the London Bankers' Clearing House: general clearing, town clearing, credit clearing and computer clearing.

General clearing. Most of the cheques handled by the clearing house pass through the general clearing by the procedures as outlined above.

Town clearing. A fast clearing service operates for bank branches in the City of London that are within walking distance of the clearing house in Lombard Street; such branches can easily be identified because the cheques they issue have the letter 'T' after the national sorting code number, which is printed in the top right-hand corner of the cheque. The Town clearing operates for cheques of £5 000 and over that are drawn on and have been paid into one of the branches participating in the clearing: all other cheques pass through either the general clearing or the inter-branch clearing. The clearing is also used for bills of exchange accepted payable by or on a Town clearing branch, bankers' payments and bankers' drafts.

The Town clearing exists to serve the banks, insurance companies, shipping companies, the Stock Exchange and other financial institutions operating in the City of London. As these concerns continually deal in large amounts of money they need a speedy system for clearing cheques and this is what the Town clearing offers: a cheque can be paid in for the credit of an account just before the banks close for business in the afternoon, and it is possible to find out later that day if it is cleared. You will appreciate the benefits of this special clearing for large cheques when you realize that if a company has an overdraft of £1 million or more on which it is charged 10 per cent per annum, and pays in a cheque for the credit of its account of £1 million, it can save interest of £821.92 by passing the cheque through the Town clearing rather than through the general clearing procedure. (For cheques which are not eligible for the Town clearing alternative fast clearing arrangements can be made, which are discussed later in this Unit).

The volume of cheques handled by the Town clearing is considerably less than that of the general clearing, but because the amounts are larger, the value of the clearing is much greater.

Credit clearing. Since 1960 a clearing system similar to the general clearing has operated for credit transfers—or bank giro credits—for the credit of accounts at branches and banks other than the one at which they are paid in. Like cheques, credits may be inter-branch or inter-bank, and both kinds are sent to the clearing department at head office by each branch of the bank. There they are sorted, and inter-branch items are dispatched to the different branches; the inter-bank items are amalgamated and taken to the clearing house where, like cheques, they are handed over to the representatives of the other banks.

Computer clearing. With the increasing use of computers in banking, a special clearing system has been developed to make possible the transfer of funds from one bank account to another by putting details of transfers to be made on to magnetic tapes that can be 'read' by a computer. To facilitate the use of this system and in an attempt to cut down the volume of paperwork required daily to effect transfers, the banks have formed a special section of the clearing house called Bankers' Automated Clearing Services Ltd. (BACS), which has its computer centre at Edgware in Middlesex. The system is used by the banks and some of their large customers who prepare magnetic tapes containing details of transactions to be made. The tapes are then passed to BACS where they are read by a computer and the entries are electronically sorted into the various banks and branches for which they are intended. The entries are then transferred to other magnetic tapes, one for each bank, which are then passed to the appropriate bank. The tapes are then run into each bank's own computer system and the transfers involved are effected automatically, each branch receiving a print-out of the details of the transfers concerning its own accounts. This clearing system can be used for both bank giro credits and direct debits (see Units 11.3 and 11.4).

The daily settlement. This is the means by which the exchanges of cheques and credits between banks is balanced. It is effected at the end of each working day and includes details of that day's Town clearing, and the general, credit and BACS clearing of the previous day. Each clearing bank prepares a summary of the balances due to be received from other banks and due to be paid to other banks as a result of the various credit and debit items that have passed through the clearing house. The summary is totalled and a balance worked out which is the net amount due to be received (or paid) in respect of the transactions. This balance is settled either by making a payment out of, or receiving a credit into, that bank's account at the Bank of England. Each clearing bank follows the same procedure, so that, mathematics permitting, the total settlement cheques received by the clearing house equal the total settlement payment that it makes.

Other clearings. We have already mentioned the *inter-branch clearing* which does not pass through the clearing house but is dealt with at the clearing department of each bank. A large number of banks are not members of the London Bankers' Clearing House: some of these have an agency arrangement whereby one of the clearing banks allows their cheques to be cleared through them. Other

'Our branch is beautifully situated—two hundred miles from the head office computer'

cheques drawn on merchant banks, Government departments and the Post Office do not pass through the clearing house but, instead, are dealt with by the *walks clearing*. This operates by branches sending such cheques to their clearing department at head office where they are sorted into the different banks and payment offices. The cheques are then taken by messenger—'walked'—to the banks and offices where they are payable and exchanged for a banker's payment or a cheque drawn on a clearing bank.

There are special arrangements for cheques drawn on Scottish and Northern Ireland banks that are paid into branches of the London clearing banks: these are cleared either by sending them to the London office of these banks or by sending them direct to the head office, and payment is received in return. Cheques drawn on banks in Eire are either sent direct to the Southern Irish Clearing House in Dublin or passed to an agent bank represented in Eire. These clearing arrangements take considerably longer than the three working days minimum that is normal for the general clearing.

In 1978 a *dollar clearing* was established enabling cheques drawn in dollars on a London bank and paid into an account at another London bank to be cleared in London. (Previously such items had to be cleared through New York with all the resultant costs of money transmission, delay and commission paid to New York banks.) The American and other banks participating in this clearing do so through a clearing bank acting as their agent.

If a customer wishes to know quickly if a cheque has been cleared in circumstances in which the Town clearing arrangements do not apply, he can ask his bank to arrange a *special presentation*: his bank then sends the cheque direct to the drawee bank and telephones next day to find out if it is cleared. A fee is normally charged for this service, but it does enable a customer to discover the fate of a cheque within twenty-four hours, instead of waiting for it to pass through the clearing system.

10.10   Payment of Cheques

Every day, each branch bank receives from its head office an in-clearing of cheques drawn on that branch which have been paid in for the credit of accounts at other banks and branches. Its task now is to ensure that each cheque is technically correct and that the branch has the authority to debit the customer's account. It must ensure that the customer has not countermanded or 'stopped' payment of the cheque, that the customer has sufficient funds in his account to meet the cheque or that sufficient overdraft facilities have been arranged, that the cheque is signed and the drawer's signature is genuine, agreeing with the specimen held by the branch, and that the cheque is signed in accordance with the bank's authority (for example, a joint account with husband and wife may require the bank to pay only cheques bearing both signatures). Even if all these are in order, the following technical errors might still cause non-payment:

(i) the value of the cheque given in words is different from that stated in figures;

(ii) the cheque is out of date (usually this means it is dated to suggest that it was written six months or more ago);

(iii) the cheque is *postdated*, that is, dated at some time in the future;

(iv) no payee's name is entered on the cheque;

(v) alterations made to the cheque have not been initialled or signed by the drawer of the cheque as being correct;

(vi) the cheque has been mutilated in some way, perhaps torn completely in half, and there is no banker's confirmation that the mutilation was accidental;

(vii) an endorsement (required on certain cheques as a receipt) is omitted or incorrect.

The death of a customer cancels a bank's authority to pay his cheques, as do certain other legal circumstances such as notice of his mental incapacity or bankruptcy. Cheques that are not to be paid are returned on the day of receipt by the drawee bank direct to the collecting bank—this is where the special crossing applied by rubber stamp to all cheques paid in helps to identify the bank and branch to which a cheque must be returned. A special form for unpaid cheques is used to adjust the book-keeping entries between the two banks. When an unpaid cheque is received back at the collecting bank, the customer—the payee—will be debited and the cheque posted back to him. It is then up to the payee to contact the drawer of the cheque and, if it has been returned because of technical errors, to ask him to correct them. If the cheque has been returned because the drawer has insufficient funds on his account, the payee will certainly have questions to ask.

It is particularly important that a collecting bank receiving back an unpaid cheque, forwarded for collection on behalf of the customer, must give the customer notice of dishonour. As we have said, this is usually done by returning the cheque to the customer with a covering letter. Sometimes the bank will re-present the cheque for payment—for instance, where the bank confirms an irregular endorsement—but must nevertheless send notice of dishonour to the customer. Failure to do so could mean that in the event of the cheque being dishonoured a second time, perhaps for a different reason, the customer could refuse to have his account debited on the grounds that he did not receive notice of dishonour the first time and assumed the cheque was paid. From the point of view of both the collecting bank and the paying bank, therefore, the procedure for non-payment is important in order to retain the liability of the customer for the cheque.

10.11   Questions

1. Define a bill of exchange. How may a bill be used in settlement of a debt?

2. What was the significance of the Bills of Exchange Act 1882 on the development of banking in Britain?

3. What are the characterisitcs of a negotiable instrument? Explain by reference to cheques the terms 'negotiable' and 'not negotiable'.

4. You have just opened a current account for Mrs. Williams; she asks if she should use crossed or open cheques. Advise her.

5. *A*, the drawer of a crossed order cheque, sends it through the post to *B*, the payee, who also has a bank account. Trace the course of the cheque until it is finally paid.

   (*The Institute of Bankers*)

6. What is the significance of a crossing on an order cheque? Is this affected in any way if the words 'not negotiable' are included?

   (*The Institute of Bankers*)

7. (*a*) What is the practical effect of crossing a cheque? (*b*) Define the types of crossing on a cheque provided for in the Bills of Exchange Act 1882. (*c*) What is the effect if the words 'account payee' are added?

   (*The Institute of Bankers*)

Methods of Payment through the Banking System

11.1 Introduction

There are various ways of making a payment through the banking system and those appropriate for inland payments within Britain differ from those used for overseas payments. In this Unit we shall consider the following:

Inland:
cheques;
bank giro credits and standing orders;
direct debits;
credit cards;
bankers' drafts.
Overseas:
cheques and credit cards;
telegraphic and mail transfers;
bankers' drafts;
international money orders;
bills of exchange and letters of credit.

11.2 Inland Payments: Cheques

Cheques are well known to most people and represent a convenient method of making payments—although, of course, they are not legal tender and creditors may refuse to accept them (see Unit 2.11). A specimen cheque is shown in Fig. 11.1.

When writing out a cheque, care should always be exercised to ensure that all details are completed: the date, name of payee, amount in words and figures and the drawer's signature. Cheques should always be written in ink and no room should be left for fraudulent additions, any blank spaces being ruled through. Where an open cheque book is in use, cheques should be crossed, preferably 'not negotiable', whenever they are to be sent through the post (see Unit 10.8). If any corrections or changes are made to the cheque by the drawer he should, besides signing the cheque in the normal way, also place his signature against the alterations. Naturally, sufficient funds should be available in the drawer's account to meet cheques when they are presented for payment and cheques drawn should be technically correct.

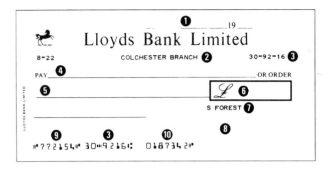

(1) Date
(2) Name of the account-holding branch
(3) The sorting code number of Lloyds Bank, Colchester
(4) Payee's name—the person to whom the cheque is payable
(5) The amount in words
(6) The amount in figures
(7) The name of the account
(8) Signature
(9) The cheque number
(10) The account number
      The numbers along the bottom of the cheque are written in specially designed characters ('E13B') that can be read by cheque-sorting and listing machines.

Fig. 11.1   A specimen cheque: (a) blank, (b) completed

    In order to increase the acceptability of cheques, the clearing banks issue *cheque cards* to suitable customers. This plastic 'card' acts as a guarantee that the drawer's cheque will be paid up to a maximum (at the time of writing) of £50 in any one transaction (see also Unit 14.2) and have been particularly useful in persuading retailers to accept cheques from strangers in payment for goods. A cheque card can also be used with a cheque book to draw cash at any branch of the major British and Irish banks.

11.3   Inland Payments: Bank Giro Credits

Bank giro credits—or *credit transfers*, as they are often called—enable a person to pay money into someone else's bank account, whether he has an account of his own or not. For example, if Smith owes Jones £10 and Jones has an account with National Barllands Bank, Worcester, Smith can go into that bank and make out a credit for Jones's account and pay the £10 in cash; alternatively he can go into any other bank branch and pay the cash in, together with a credit made out in the favour of Jones's account at National Barllands, Worcester. In the second case the credit would be passed through the credit clearing system to arrive at Jones's bank three days after being paid in, subject to any delays. Equally, Jones can use a bank giro credit when he wishes to pay money into his own account at National Barllands Bank, Worcester at another branch of National Barllands or at some other bank. Fig. 11.2 shows a specimen bank giro credit slip.

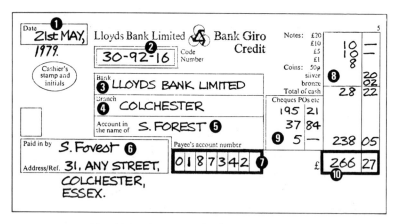

Fig. 11.2   A specimen bank giro credit slip

(1) Date
(2) Sorting code number of the account-holding branch
(3) Name of the account-holding bank
(4) Name of the account-holding branch
(5) The name of the account
(6) Signature of person paying money in
(7) Account number of payee
(8) Breakdown of cash paid in
(9) Amounts of cheques paid in
(10) Total of the credit to the account (cash and cheques)

The bank giro credit system is particularly useful for paying accounts such as gas, electricity, telephone and rates, and often the bills for these services have a credit form pre-printed on them. Hire purchase companies, home shopping clubs and building societies often issue their customers with books of bank giro credit forms. Employers can use the system for paying wages and salaries: a credit slip is made out for each employee with the details of the name and number of the account to be credited, the bank and branch where it is maintained and the money amount, and these slips, together with a summary slip detailing all the payments, are handed to the bank with one cheque payable to the bank for the total amount. This method of making wage and salary payments has the obvious advantage of not requiring large quantities of cash to be withdrawn on pay day, with the attendant security problems, but the system cannot operate unless each employee has a bank account and agrees to be paid in this way. Some large companies, instead of making out a voucher for each payment, prepare computer tapes containing details of all the payments to be made and these are passed through BACS (see Unit 10.9).

The banks use the system themselves for making *standing order* or *bankers' order* payments. If a customer has regular payments to make for fixed amounts—for a mortgage, for instance, or for insurance premiums or club subscriptions—he can give the bank instructions to make payments on his behalf. The bank will automatically do this by debiting his account and sending a credit to the bank and branch of the beneficiary, either by using a bank giro credit voucher and the credit clearing system or by putting the payment details on a computer tape and passing this through BACS.

11.4   Inland Payments: Direct Debits

Standing orders, just mentioned, are a convenient method of making regular payments for fixed amounts. Direct debits are also used for regular payments but they differ from standing orders in two ways. Firstly, they can be used for either fixed or variable amounts and/or where the time intervals between payments vary. Secondly, it is the beneficiary of the payment who prepares the voucher or computer tape that acts as a debit to the payer's account and is passed through the clearing system in the same way as a cheque; this contrasts with the standing order system where the payer's bank prepares a credit which is passed through the credit clearing system to the bank and branch of the beneficiary. Under the direct debit system there are safeguards to prevent irregular use of the system:

(i) only organizations approved by the banks are allowed to operate it;
(ii) direct debits must be made strictly within the terms of the instructions signed by the customer;

(iii) where the bank customer's instructions permit the payment of variable amounts (*variable amount direct debits*, often abbreviated to VADD), the organization concerned has to inform the customer in advance of the amount and date of the payment; and

(iv) each organization operating the system has to give the banks an indemnity in case of mistakes: the banks will reimburse a customer if a debit which does not conform to the instructions held is charged to his account.

The system is particularly useful for insurance companies, building societies, hire purchase companies and indeed for any organization which receives large numbers of payments. It operates rather like the bank giro credit system for wages and salaries in reverse: the beneficiary prepares the direct debit forms or computer tape and takes them to his bank together with a credit for the total amount. The debits are distributed through the clearing system to the banks and branches to which they are addressed and the payers' accounts are debited; in the meantime, the credit is applied to the account of the beneficiary. The great savings for the beneficiary are in administration: checking large numbers of standing order payments received into the account is much more laborious than initiating direct debits, and the payments are made without the delays involved in waiting to receive credits through the clearing system. Moreover, any direct debits which cannot be paid are returned quickly and the follow-up steps can be instituted promptly.

11.5　Inland Payments: Credit Cards

Credit cards (see also Unit 14.4) provide a means of obtaining goods and services immediately but paying for them later. Each cardholder is given a credit limit on his credit card account, which is entirely separate from his normal bank account and is maintained at his bank's credit card department. Payment for goods and services can only be made by this method at premises having the special machine for preparing sales vouchers to record the transaction, and retail outlets usually display the signs of the credit cards they are prepared to accept.

To pay for goods, the card is handed to the retailer, who places it in the special machine together with a sales voucher: when the machine is operated the embossed characters on the card, which detail the name and number of the account, are recorded on the sales voucher, together with the retailer's name and address. The details and amount of the sale are entered on the voucher and signed for by the purchaser; after comparing this signature with that on the card and being satisfied with its authenticity, the retailer gives a copy of the voucher to the purchaser and hands back the card. The retailer sends his part of the sales voucher to the credit card department of the bank concerned, through the local branch bank, and receives payment accordingly.

Each month a cardholder is sent a statement detailing his purchases and he has the option of either paying the full balance of the account or paying a certain minimum amount and carrying forward the remaining balance to

'Pick a card—any card!'

next month. Cardholders are charged interest on outstanding balances and retailers are required to allow the credit card company a rate of discount on all card sales—this varies from one trade to another, and is between 1 and 5 per cent. The card can also be used to draw cash at bank branches and correspondent banks displaying the relevant credit card sign.

The present extensive use of credit cards means that the Government must control their use at times when it wishes to restrict credit, as it does with hire purchase facilities: it imposes minimum monthly repayment amounts and restricts the use of the card's cash withdrawal facilities.

11.6   Inland Payments: Bankers' Drafts

A bankers' draft is a cheque drawn by a branch bank on its head office: it is issued on request to a customer who has to make a guaranteed payment, that is, in circumstances where the payee wishes to be absolutely certain that the cheque will be paid upon presentation. After cash, the next best thing is a bankers' draft, which avoids the necessity of having to carry sums of money to effect a payment. A common use of a bankers' draft is in buying a house, when the seller's solicitors want to be certain of payment—they cannot afford the risk of a 'bouncing' cheque—and they will usually only hand over the deeds of the property against receipt of a draft.

Naturally, before issuing a draft the bank checks to see that the customer has sufficient funds on his account to pay for it, his account is then debited and a credit passed to head office to meet the draft when it is presented for payment.

11.7   Overseas Payments: Cheques and Credit Cards

It is not a satisfactory payment method to use a normal cheque when buying goods abroad or to settle with an overseas supplier for goods imported. One of the problems concerns the United Kingdom exchange control regulations, since a cheque used in this way must be officially stamped to confirm that exchange control approval for the payment has been granted. Also, the cheque would normally have to be drawn in sterling and this might not suit the overseas supplier who would have to ask the bank to collect the proceeds on his behalf—this would cost money in bank charges and he would have to wait some time before receiving the proceeds.

Both cheque and credit cards can be used abroad to obtain cash from banks. The cheque card, however, cannot be used as a guarantee for a cheque to pay for goods and services. The credit card can be used as a means of payment at overseas outlets of the card company and its associated companies.

11.8   Overseas Payments: Telegraphic and Mail Transfers

A customer may instruct his bank to use one of these transfer methods to make a payment to a person abroad. The differences between them lie in their speed and cost, a telegraphic transfer being quicker but more expensive. The customer has his account debited in sterling and the beneficiary receives the sterling equivalent in his own currency, either paid in cash or credited to his bank account. All charges are normally debited to the sender's account but can, if required, be deducted from the amount received by the beneficiary. As with all overseas payments, the United Kingdom exchange control regulations must be observed, but there are normally no difficulties in obtaining approval for trading and similar transactions.

The actual transfer of funds is effected by the bank of Britain contacting a convenient bank in the overseas country. All the major banks have their *correspondent banks* overseas with whom they maintain currency accounts, and similarly the correspondent banks maintain sterling accounts in this country. These accounts are known as *nostro* and *vostro accounts*—the Latin words for 'our' and 'your' respectively. A United Kingdom bank's nostro accounts are those which are maintained in its name in the books of banks overseas, such as an account maintained with an American bank in New York in US dollars; its vostro accounts are those maintained with it in sterling in the United Kingdom by overseas banks.

The method of transferring funds is simple. If a customer of a United Kingdom bank wishes to remit sterling to an overseas beneficiary in, for example, Toronto, the procedure is as follows:

(i) the customer completes a bank application form stating the beneficiary and the method of remittance to be used—telegraphic or mail transfer, or banker's draft (see Unit 11.9);

(ii) the necessary exchange control evidence is produced by the customer and checked by the bank;

(iii) the bank debits the customer with the amount and credits the (sterling) vostro account of the Toronto correspondent bank it proposes to use;

(iv) the remittance is then made and the beneficiary receives or is credited with the Canadian dollar equivalent of the sterling amount;

(v) to complete the book-keeping, the Toronto bank debits with the sterling amount an account it maintains in its books which mirrors its sterling account in London.

If a customer of a United Kingdom bank wishes to pay a currency (rather than sterling) amount to a beneficiary in, for example, New York the procedure is as follows:

(i) the application form and exchange control evidence are completed as before;

(ii) the bank debits its customer with the sterling equivalent of the dollars;

(iii) the United Kingdom bank credits the mirror account in its books of its dollar account maintained in New York;

(iv) the remittance is then made and the New York bank debits the United Kingdom bank's nostro account and credits the beneficiary with the dollar amount.

Some 500 of the largest European and North American banks have recently joined together to form an international communications network to speed up the transfer of international payments and other messages between themselves. This network is called SWIFT (the Society for Worldwide Interbank Financial Telecommunication) and uses the computer systems of participating banks. Thus when a customer wishes to make an international payment by mail transfer his bank, if a participant in SWIFT, sends a 'SWIFT message'; transfers and messages previously sent by telegraph or cable will become 'urgent SWIFT messages'. As a safeguard, wherever funds are sent by urgent SWIFT message or telegraphic transfer, some form of coding is included which is checked by the recipient bank to prove the authenticity of the instruction.

11.9 Overseas Payments: Bankers' Drafts

A draft used to pay an overseas debt is a bankers' cheque similar to the draft used as an inland payment method, but instead of being drawn by a branch bank on head office, it is drawn by the overseas department of a British bank on one of its correspondent bank accounts. An overseas draft is usually available either in sterling or foreign currency amounts. A customer requesting a draft has his account debited in sterling and, within a few minutes, is handed the draft to send direct to the beneficiary. The transfer of funds from bank to bank is effected in the same way as described in Unit 11.8.

11.10 Overseas Payments: International Money Orders

Barclays bank has recently introduced a simple method of sending relatively small amounts of money abroad called the Barclays International Money Order. It is a cheque drawn on Barclays Bank International which can be obtained by customers and non-customers from most branches of Barclays for amounts not exceeding £500 or US $1 000 at the time of writing. The purchaser then mails the money order direct to the beneficiary abroad; it will be accepted by major banks worldwide either for the credit of an account or to be cashed. It is not a suitable method of payment where the sender wishes the beneficiary to receive an exact sum of money in a currency other than US dollars or sterling; it is, however, ideal for use in sending gifts of money to friends and relatives overseas.

11.11 Overseas Payments: Bills of Exchange and Letters of Credit

Both these methods of payment are used extensively by firms in Britain making payments for imports and arranging to receive money from abroad for exports supplied. They are considered fully in Unit 16.

11.12 Questions

1. List the various methods of making payments within the United Kingdom through the banking system. Describe the main features of two of the methods listed which are most likely to be used for the payment of insurance premiums.

(The Institute of Bankers)

2. Compare and contrast direct debits and standing orders as methods of payment.

3. You live in Britain and are planning to go on holiday to France and rent a cottage. The owner of the cottage, who lives in France, requires a deposit of 250 French francs. What method of payment, using the banking system, would be the most suitable? Why would the other methods be inappropriate?

Who are the Customers?

12.1 Legal Relationships

The customers of the clearing banks consist of millions of private individuals, hundreds of thousands of small businesses—some formed as private limited companies, the majority being sole traders or partnerships—thousands of public limited companies, some with shares quoted on a stock exchange, and a few giant multi-national companies. In this Unit we shall consider the larger groups of different customers and, where these operate within a specialist legal framework, briefly consider this from the bank's point of view.

Legally speaking, the relationships that can exist between the banker and his customer are:

> debtor and creditor (or vice versa);
> principal and agent;
> bailor and bailee;
> mortgagor and mortgagee;
> relationships defined by the rules of banking practice.

The basic legal relationship is that of *debtor and creditor* respectively, although the roles are sometimes reversed when the customer is overdrawn. In the case of *Joachimson* v. *Swiss Bank Corporation* (1921), it was laid down that the banker undertakes to receive money for his customer's account, and that money so received is not held in trust for the customer but borrowed from him with a promise to repay it or any part of it during banking hours at the branch of the bank at which the account is kept, against the customer's written order addressed to the bank at that branch. Thus the general rules of the law of contract apply, in that both bank and customer are required to carry out certain courses of action and a failure to do so may result in a breach of contract and could result in a legal action by one party against the other.

The relationship between the two parties is that of *principal and agent* when a bank is acting as its customer's agent by collecting cheques for him.

The *bailor/bailee* relationship is established when a banker takes charge of his customer's valuables for safe custody; he is then bound to take reasonable care of his customer's property (see Unit 14.9). The *mortgagor/mortgagee* relationship applies when a bank takes a mortgage over securities when granting an advance to a customer (see Unit 17.4).

The *rules of banking practice* that have developed over the years are generally enforced by courts of law; for instance, a bank that failed to follow the practice of taking references when opening a current account would be held to be negligent (see Unit 12.2).

12.2   Personal Customers

These form by far the largest group of customers in terms of numbers. Most receive wages or a salary at the end of each week or month which is often paid direct into the bank account by the employer; others are retired, receiving a State pension and perhaps a pension from a former employer; another group are students who may be in receipt of a grant cheque each term. The formalities required for an individual to open an account in his own name are minimal and while each bank has its own regulations, all require the same basic information: the person's name, address and occupation and a specimen signature. Where a current account (see Unit 13.2) is being opened, the names and addresses of two *referees* are usually required although often a reference from the current employer is satisfactory. A reference may also be required when a deposit account (see Unit 13.3) is opened with a cheque.

The question of taking references when opening an account is a very important one. Firstly, the bank wishes to confirm that the new customer is reputable; secondly, the taking up of a reference is one very necessary step for the bank to acquire protection from liability for conversion in respect of any stolen cheques paid in by the new customer, on the grounds of negligence. Where a person who is not the true owner of a cheque uses it to open an account, the bank can be sued for conversion. Under such circumstances the defence a bank could employ is that its staff acted in good faith and without negligence in accordance with section 4 of the Cheques Act 1957. In a past case, negligence has been attributed to a collecting bank where it has failed to attend to all the necessary formalities in opening an account for a customer who, later, converts cheques and uses the bank to collect the proceeds. Negligence has been held to include, among other things, failure to obtain references or to follow up references when opening an account, and failure to obtain the name of a customer's employer. Thus the procedures for opening accounts should be strictly adhered to: legal cases on this subject include *E. B. Savory & Co.* v. *Lloyds Bank Ltd.* (1932) and *Marfani & Co. Ltd.* v. *Midland Bank Ltd.* (1968).

Nowadays a husband and wife often open a *joint account*. The details required are the same as for an account in a sole name but the bank also needs to know who is going to sign cheques and other withdrawals from the account. The customers are asked to complete a *joint account mandate* which usually gives the bank the authority to pay on the signature of either account holder. If required, the mandate can be worded so that the signatures of both account holders are required. The mandate also establishes *joint and several liability* for any monies owing to the bank: this means that the parties are jointly liable for indebtedness and are also liable for the full amount as individuals. For example, suppose that Mr. and Mrs. Brown have a joint account with an overdraft of £1 000. Should the bank need to take legal action to recover this amount, it can proceed against both of them jointly *and* as individuals. Thus Mrs. Brown cannot, by paying £500, discharge her liability because it is joint and several, and if her husband fails to pay anything her liability is £1 000.

'I want to make this withdrawal from my husband's half of our joint account'

12.3 Business Customers: Sole Traders

Sole traders are people who are in business on their own: they run shops, small factories, farms, garages and so forth. The businesses are generally small because the owner, being in business by himself, usually has limited funds—or capital—with which to start and profits are often small and, after the owner has taken his share as drawings, are ploughed back into the business.

Why do people set up in business of their own? There are several reasons:

(i) The owner has independence—he can run the business as he thinks fit without consulting anyone else.

(ii) In a small business with few, if any, employees, personal service and supervision by the owner are available at all times—the customers are not dealing with a large, impersonal organization and receive good service; employees can be personally supervised and there is generally little wastage of resources in the business.

(iii) The business is easy to establish legally. If it is to operate under the owner's name, no formal procedures are required; if it is to use a trading name, such as 'Southtown Grocers', this must be registered by filling in a simple form and depositing it with the Registrar of Business Names under the Registration of Business Names Act 1916. A bank would record such an account in its records as 'J. Smith, trading as Southtown Grocers'.

The disadvantages of a sole-trader business are:

(i) The owner has unlimited liability for the debts of the business. This means that if the firm should become insolvent, the owner's personal assets may be used to pay its creditors.

(ii) Expansion is limited because it can only be achieved by the owner ploughing back profits to increase his stake in the business or by borrowing, usually from a bank.

(iii) The owner usually has to work long hours and it may be difficult for him to find time to take holidays. If he should go sick the work of the business will at best slow down, and at worst stop altogether.

Opening a bank account for a sole-trader business follows the same procedures as for a private individual. If the business is using a trading name, the bank will wish to see the certificate issued by the Registrar of Business Names before accepting for the account any cheques payable to that name.

The bank is often the only source of finance used by sole-trader businesses, and a lot of the branch manager's time is spent in attending to the needs of this category of customer. Some businesses, such as farmers or toy manufacturers, need finance or extra finance at certain times of the year because their trade has a seasonal nature; others, like grocers and garage proprietors, have a steady all-the-year-round trade and may require finance throughout the year. While there is no legal requirement for a sole trader to produce a set of accounts at the end of his financial year, it is usual for these to be prepared in order that the profit (or loss) shown by the accounts may be used by the Inland Revenue to assess liability to tax. If the bank is lending, the manager will wish to see these year-end accounts and balance sheet so that he can tell how profitable the business has been and can assess any risk to the bank advance.

12.4   Business Customers: Partnerships

A partnership is defined by the Partnership Act 1890 as *the relation which subsists between persons carrying on a business in common with a view of profit.*

The partnership is in many respects very similar to the sole trader as a business unit, but is often larger because, as there is more than one owner, there is likely to be more capital. A partnership may be formed to set up a new business or it may be the logical growth of a sole trader firm taking in partners to increase the capital. Besides the types of business mentioned in Unit 12.3 for sole traders, partnerships are often formed by professional people such as doctors, dentists, accountants and solicitors.

Why form a partnership?

(i) There is the possibility of increased capital because there are more owners to subscribe capital and also (it is to be hoped) larger profits to plough back into the business.

(ii) Individual partners may be able to specialize in areas of work that interest them.

(iii) With more people running the business, there is cover for sickness and holidays.

There may, however, be problems:

(i) As there is more than one owner, decisions may take longer because each partner may need to be consulted.

(ii) There may be disagreements among the partners.

(iii) The death of one partner may adversely affect the business because his capital may need to be withdrawn to pay the beneficiaries of his estate.

As with the sole trader, if the names used by the business do not accurately describe all the partners, a trading name must be registered. Also, like the sole trader, each partner is fully liable for the debts of the firm. Legally, a partnership may be created orally, by conduct or in writing; however, it is sensible for partners to draw up a written deed of partnership which sets out their rights and duties. If there is no deed of partnership, the Partnership Act applies; among other things, this Act states that profits are to be shared equally among the partners and that they are to contribute equally to losses, even where one partner has contributed a greater proportion of capital. The Act also restricts the number of partners: the minimum is (obviously) two and the normal maximum is twenty, although this may be exceeded by partnerships of certain professional people.

From the banking point of view, the usual formalities for opening an account are followed. Instructions are needed as to who is to sign cheques and standing order and direct debit authorities on the account and a mandate is taken to determine this, which is signed by all partners and which establishes the joint and several liability of each partner for any monies lent to the partnership. If a trading name is being used by the partnership, the registration certificate needs to be seen before cheques can be accepted in that name. A problem could arise when the partnership wishes to arrange a loan or overdraft, in that any one partner is presumed in law to have authority to enter into contracts on behalf of the partnership in the ordinary course of its business—any one partner in a firm of builders, for instance, could arrange to obtain building supplies on credit and the business would be liable to pay. A bank advance, however, is likely to be outside the ordinary course of business and therefore would need the authorization of all partners. As a partnership may have up to twenty (or sometimes more) partners, it might prove impracticable to get them all to come to the bank; therefore the banks usually insert a clause in the mandate which says that an act carried out by any partner in connection with the bank account is deemed to be for carrying out the ordinary course of business. This means that one partner can arrange an advance for which all partners will be jointly and severally liable.

12.5   Business Customers: Private Limited Companies

The logical step for a partnership growing in size is the formation of a *limited company*. There are two major types of limited company: private (of which there are some 600 000 in Britain) and public (of which there are about 20 000). The important advantage that both types of companies have over sole traders and partnerships is that of *limited liability*. This means that the owners of a limited company—the shareholders—are liable only for the amount of their share capital: this is their 'limit' and their personal assets cannot be taken to pay the debts of the company. The limited company has a separate legal entity and anyone taking legal action would normally take it against the company and not the individual shareholders; this contrasts with sole traders and partnerships where legal action would be taken against the individual or partners forming the business. All limited companies are controlled specifically by a number of Acts of Parliament—the principal current ones are the Companies Acts of 1948, 1967 and 1976. Under the terms of these, all companies are required to file their annual accounts and directors' report with the Registrar of Companies, where they are available for public inspection.

Private limited companies differ from public companies in that they are not permitted to advertise their shares for sale to the public: thus they are considerably smaller than most public companies. They are often formed by partnerships seeking limited liability or by a group of friends pooling their savings to provide a service or manufacture a product for which they think there is a demand. Private companies are restricted in the number of their share-holders: there must be a minimum of two, and normally a maximum of fifty; restrictions are also placed on the transfer of shares, and they must often be offered to existing shareholders first. The private limited companies' scope for capital raising, although restricted by their inability to advertise shares for sale, is considerably greater than that of sole traders and partnerships. The share-holders in a limited company have no right to a say in the day-to-day affairs of the business but instead elect a board of directors for this purpose; where a partnership has been converted into a private limited company, it is likely that all the general partners of the former partnership (those who took an active part in running it) will form the board of directors and will, therefore, continue to have a say in the affairs of the company.

12.6   Business Customers: Public Limited Companies

A public limited company is normally the largest form of business unit in the private sector; its shares are often quoted on a stock exchange. Most present-day public companies were once private, having at some stage 'gone public' with the aid of a merchant bank. The big advantage of forming a public company is that advertisements may be placed in financial newspapers inviting the public to apply for shares: a *prospectus*, as this advertisement is called, gives details of the company's past trading record and estimates of future earnings, together with other information required by law. Prospectuses can be seen from time to time in newspapers; sometimes a clearing bank is involved in the issue and copies of the prospectus are then sent to branches to be made available to interested customers.

A public company has no upper limit on the numbers of its shareholders, but at present it must have a minimum of seven; there are no restrictions on the transfer of its shares. Not all public companies are quoted on the Stock Exchange: if a company wishes its shares to be quoted, it must apply to the Stock Exchange Council and then undergo a thorough investigation to ensure that it fulfils the Council's strict requirements. If the company is found to be satisfactory, the Council will agree to grant a quotation of its shares.

(a) Forming a limited company

As a limited company has a separate legal personality, there are a number of steps that must be taken in its formation. The bank where the company wishes to open an account will be particularly interested in seeing copies of the two major controlling documents: the Memorandum of Association and the Articles of Association.

The *Memorandum of Association* is a document signed by the first members of the company setting out the company's constitution and its powers. It governs the relationship of the company with the outside world and contains six main clauses:

(i) the name of the company with, in the case of a company limited by shares or by guarantee, the word 'limited' or 'cyfyngedig' (Welsh for 'limited') as the last word;

(ii) a statement as to whether the registered office of the company is to be in England, Wales or Scotland;

(iii) a description of the objects of the company, i.e. the purposes which the company is to pursue;

(iv) a statement as to whether or not the liability of the members is limited (there are a few unlimited companies in existence; see Unit 12.6(*c*));

(v) details of the capital structure of the company;

(vi) the *association clause*, which is an undertaking signed by the founder members of the company that they wish to form a company and agree to purchase the number of shares stated against their name.

The *Articles of Association* are regulations for the internal management of the company. They define the method of appointment and duties of the directors and secretary, the directors' borrowing powers, the provisions as to notice of general meetings and procedure to be followed at such meetings, details of

'I changed my name by deed poll to "Bank"'

the issue, transfer and forfeiture of shares, voting rights of shareholders, and provision as to audits, accounts and so on.

Registration of a company is effected by depositing the Memorandum and Articles of Association with the Registrar of Companies. A 'model' set of articles is contained in the Companies Act 1948, and if a company does not deposit a set of articles with the Registrar, these model articles apply. There are certain other legal formalities to be observed before the Registrar will issue a *Certificate of Incorporation*—a document that has been described as the company's 'birth certificate'. A private company may commence trading upon the granting of the Certificate of Incorporation, but a public company has to raise its capital from the public and observe certain other legal formalities before the Registrar will issue a *Trading Certificate* enabling it to start in business.

(b) Types of shares issued by limited companies

Paragraph (*a*) above mentioned that one clause of the Memorandum of Association states the proposed share capital of the company and its division into shares of fixed amount. This is known as the *authorized share capital*, and contrasts with the amount that the company has issued. You will recognize the distinction between the two if you study a company balance sheet, which normally shows both the authorized and issued capital; for instance, the authorized share capital of Lloyds Bank Ltd. at 31 December 1978 was 200 million shares of £1 each, of which just over 166 million had been issued and were fully paid. The issued capital can never exceed the authorized: if a company which has issued the full extent of its authorized capital wishes to make an increase it must first pass the appropriate resolution at a meeting of the shareholders.

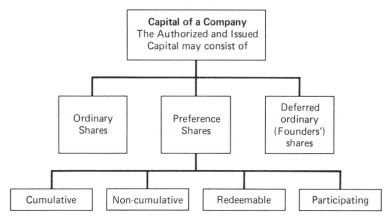

Fig. 12.1   Types of share

The authorized and issued share capitals are divided into a number of classes or types of share which usually includes ordinary shares, perhaps preference shares and, more rarely, certain other classes (Fig. 12.1). Each share has a *nominal* or *face value* which is entered in the accounts and is commonly £1, although shares may be issued with nominal values of 5p, 10p, 25p or 50p. Thus a company with an authorized capital of £100 000 might state in its Memorandum of Association that this is divided up into

100 000 ordinary shares of 50p each	£50 000
50 000 seven per cent preference shares of £1 each	£50 000
	£100 000

The nominal value of the shares often bears little relationship to their true value. The way to assess the value of shares in a public limited company is to look at their price in the *Financial Times* or *Stock Exchange Daily List*. As shares of a private company are not quoted on a stock exchange and, moreover, are subject to restrictions on their transfer, it is more difficult to value them. One way is to obtain a copy of the company's latest balance sheet and then calculate the value of net assets (assets less liabilities) belonging to each share, based on the 'book' values shown in the balance sheet; an alternative way is to calculate the value of net assets if the company had to be sold—the 'break-up' basis. Other methods exist, but like these two are at best only estimates. However, if shares have changed hands recently the company secretary could be asked the price that was charged at the time.

Ordinary or *equity shares* are the most commonly issued class of share, and they take a share of the profits available for distribution after allowance has been made for all expenses of the business, including loan interest and corporation tax. When the company makes good profits, it will be able to pay high dividends to the ordinary shareholders (subject to any Government restrictions); when poor profits or losses are made, these shareholders will receive a small or no dividend. Companies rarely pay out all their profits in the form of dividends, however; most retain some in the form of reserves. These can be used to enable a dividend to be paid in a year when the company makes little or no profit, always assuming that the company has sufficient cash to make the payment. In the event of a company winding up (going out of business), the ordinary shareholders will be the last to receive any repayment of capital on their shares. They therefore carry the main risks of the company; but the concept of limited liability nevertheless means that the maximum a shareholder can lose on fully paid shares is the amount he paid for them.

Preference shares have a fixed rate of dividend—7 per cent, for example—which, as their name suggests, is paid in preference to the ordinary shareholders; but it is only paid if the company makes profits. In the event of winding up the company, the preference will usually also extend to the repayment of capital before the ordinary shareholders. There are two classes of preference shares: *non-cumulative* and *cumulative*. If insufficient profits are made during a certain year to pay the preference dividend and the shares are designated as non-cumulative, then there is no provision for payment of 'lost' dividends in future years. This contrasts with cumulative shares (all preference shares are cumulative unless otherwise stated); if the dividend on these is not paid in one year, it accumulates so that past dividends will always be paid provided that the company makes sufficient profits in the future. A *participating preference share* is a further variation. With this class of share, the fixed rate of dividend is paid first and then, if the ordinary shareholders are paid more than a specified percentage, extra dividends are paid; thus in a profitable year when large dividends are paid to ordinary shareholders, the preference shareholders will also participate in the company's increased prosperity.

Deferred ordinary shares or *founders' shares* are now very rare but are sometimes issued to the original founders or promoters of the company. These shares usually receive their dividend only after the ordinary shareholders have been paid up to a certain maximum; any remaining profits are then distributed to the owners of the deferred ordinary shares. In a highly profitable company the holders of these shares could earn the highest rates of dividend.

The Companies Acts specifically state that a company may not redeem any shares it has issued. This is an important protection for creditors for a dishonest company heading for liquidation might otherwise decide to pay off the shareholders while funds were still available, so that by the time the company was wound up the creditors would only have the remaining 'crumbs' to collect. As a result of the protection of the Acts it is the shareholders who must be left with the 'crumbs'. It was realized, however, that many companies were often in need of temporary capital and were not too happy about issuing shares that could not be redeemed when the need for additional capital had passed. To meet this situation, therefore, the Companies Acts permit companies to issue *redeemable preference shares*—shares which the company can redeem at a later date—provided that, when the shares are paid off, the amount so paid is replaced by a new issue of shares, either ordinary or preference. The creditors are thus still protected by the shareholder's stake in the business, because any cash going out of the company to repay the redeemable preference shareholders is immediately replaced by the receipts from the new issue of shares.

An alternative procedure is allowed by the Acts: the company may capitalize some of the distributable profits (the balance on profit and loss account or general reserve)—in other words, 'freeze' some of the distributable profits and make sure they can never be distributed to shareholders. This is done by taking part of the profit and loss account balance or general reserve and transferring it to a capital reserve account (which cannot be used to pay dividends; see Unit 8.2(*b*)); the Acts insist that this be called a *Capital Redemption Reserve Fund*. This protects the creditors because, while the company has not received any cash, it ensures that a certain amount of the existing or future cash balance will never be paid to shareholders and has therefore conserved cash that might otherwise have been paid out. It is also possible for a company to repay its redeemable preference shares partly from the proceeds of a new issue of shares and partly by a transfer of distributable profits to the Capital Redemption Reserve Fund. The main thing is that each of these methods of redemption prevents the company from repaying such shares to the detriment of its creditors.

In addition to money provided by shareholders, who are the owners of the company, further funds can be obtained by borrowing in the form of *debentures*. These are a form of loan capital earning interest that must be paid whether the company makes profits or not, just like other business expenses. (Debenture-holders may be contrasted with shareholders who receive dividends appropriated from profits and who, in a bad year, might not receive anything.) Some public company debentures are quoted on the Stock Exchange and these usually represent a good safe investment particularly as, in the event of the winding up of the company, debenture-holders would be repaid before the shareholders. Debentures are either 'secured' or 'naked': *secured debentures* are backed by assets such as deeds of property that, in the event of winding up, could be sold and used to repay the debenture-holders before the other creditors; *naked* debentures do not have this backing.

(*c*) **Other types of company**
So far, we have been concerned with companies limited by shares, this being the most usual form of company operating in Britain. There are two other types of company for which a bank may be asked to open an account, however: companies limited by guarantee and unlimited companies, both of which may be either private or public.

Companies limited by guarantee are usually non-profit-making organizations such as professional societies, educational bodies or the larger sports clubs and societies. Each member of such a company guarantees to contribute an amount of money in the event of winding up, but no more. The name of such a company will end with the words 'limited by guarantee'.

Unlimited companies are those in which the liability of members to pay the company's debts is unlimited. As you can imagine, such companies are rare in the business world, where one of the benefits of forming a company is to limit liability. A slight advantage for an unlimited company is that, if it can meet certain conditions, it need not file accounts and directors' reports with the Registrar of Companies. Such companies are usually formed only for charitable non-profit-making purposes.

(d) The bank and the limited company customer

When a bank opens an account for a limited company customer, it needs to see the Certificate of Incorporation and, in the case of a public company, the Trading Certificate. The bank usually asks to have copies of the Memorandum and Articles of Association as well, together with a copy of the resolution passed by the company authorizing the opening of the bank account. The bank also needs a mandate giving specimens of the signatures of those who will sign the company's cheques.

As a company is a separate legal entity, any loans are made to the company and not to the shareholders. All trading companies have an implied authority to borrow money and to give security, subject to any limitation imposed in the Memorandum of Association. One of the dangers of lending to a company is that the amount lent may exceed this limit. All lending beyond this amount would be known as *ultra vires*—beyond the powers of the company—and this phrase is used to describe any act not permitted by a company's Memorandum. Where there is an *ultra vires* loan to a company the lender, if he is aware that the loan is outside the powers of the company, may only:

(i) enforce any collateral guarantee given;
(ii) obtain a 'tracing order' to follow the money through into assets;
(iii) take the place of any creditor who may have been paid using the *ultra vires* loan.

Thus there is the danger that a bank could lose money if it makes an *ultra vires* loan to a company. However a lender, such as a bank, acting in good faith and unaware that a loan is outside the company's powers, is protected by section 9, sub-section 1 of the European Communities Act 1972, and would be able to recover the amount of the advance. This can place a bank in a difficult position because it very often has a copy of the Memorandum of Association in its files and therefore is deemed in law to be aware of any limitations on the company's borrowing. This problem, which has yet to be resolved in a court decision, can be alleviated to some extent by requesting a certificate from the company secretary stating that the proposed advance is within the powers of the company (and also within the powers of the directors, although this latter point is not so serious).

The separate legal personality of a company causes a problem when a bank wishes to take security. As the company cannot sign the bank's charge forms (see Unit 17), an equivalent process has to be carried out by affixing the seal of the company to the documents, or *under hand* where officials of the company are authorized to sign on its behalf. In either case, any charge that has been created must be registered with the Registrar of Companies within twenty-one days of its creation. The bank's internal regulations will detail the procedure for registering such a charge.

The directors must present to the company's shareholders the annual accounts and directors' report within a stipulated period of time after the end of the financial year. The Companies Acts require that, for all types of company, these should be audited by independent auditors, who must be members of certain accountancy bodies, and that certain minimum information should be contained in the accounts. The bank should each year obtain copies of the reports and accounts of companies to which it is lending.

12.7 Other Customers

So far in this Unit we have considered the most common types of personal and business accounts; a few specialist accounts should also be mentioned.

(a) Clubs and societies
Most branches have accounts of small clubs and societies such as social clubs, sports clubs or church societies. These accounts usually deal with small sums of money, the income comprising mainly subscriptions and the expenditure being outgoings in connection with running the club or society. The bank account will be opened in the name of the club and a mandate will be taken giving details of who is to sign, with their specimen signatures. The mandate usually includes a clause confirming that a resolution to open an account has been approved by a committee meeting. Unincorporated clubs and societies cannot be sued for a debt, nor can any member of the committee; if the bank is to lend on the account, therefore, it is usual for someone connected with the society to assume personal responsibility for the overdraft. This is customarily done by the bank taking a guarantee from that person (see Unit 17.8) to secure the account.

(b) Executors and administrators
Most branches have a few accounts of executors or administrators. When someone dies, his will should appoint certain persons to deal with his estate by collecting all monies due to the estate and making distributions to the beneficiaries of the will: these people are called *executors*. Where no will is left—that is, the person dies *intestate*—or where the executors named in a will are unwilling or unable to act, friends or relatives are appointed as *administrators* to deal with the estate. There are certain distinctions between executors and administrators in the way in which they handle the estate of the deceased; but both may need to borrow money to pay capital transfer tax. This tax is

based on the value of a person's estate at death and also takes into account certain transfers of money and assets made by the deceased during his lifetime. Some transfers, both on a person's death and during his lifetime, are exempt from the tax and, generally speaking, on death an estate with a value of less than £25 000 (at the time of writing) pays no tax. If capital transfer tax is payable, this must be attended to before the executors or administrators can obtain a legal document called a *Grant of Probate* which is their authority to deal with the assets of the deceased.

(c) **Trustees**

Executors or administrators hold their appointments for the relatively short time it takes to collect together the assets of a deceased person, pay any tax that may be due and distribute the estate to the beneficiaries. A person who looks after another person's property for a long period of time is known as a *trustee*, and most branches have trustee accounts. A common example of a trust is where a sum of money is left in a parent's will to be invested and held 'in trust' for the children until they reach a certain age, often eighteen years: here the trustee's responsibilities are to invest the funds (the choice of investments is often limited by law to those having 'trustee' status—that is, the authorized investments to which trustees are confined by the Trustee Act 1925 and the Trustee Investments Act 1961), to receive interest and to pay the money to the children in accordance with the terms of the trust. Another type of trustee takes charge when a person goes bankrupt; he has the task of selling the assets of the bankrupt and then using the money to settle his debts.

(d) **Liquidators and receivers**

We saw in Unit 12.6(a) that the Certificate of Incorporation can be regarded as a company's birth certificate. When a company 'dies' or is wound up, the final formalities are carried out by a *liquidator*. The liquidator is appointed by the Court in a compulsory winding up, or by the members of the company in a voluntary winding up where a declaration of solvency of the company is made, and by the creditors in a creditors' winding up where a declaration of solvency cannot be made. The task of a liquidator, as the name suggests, is to gather together all the assets of the company, realize them and distribute the proceeds among those entitled to receive a share.

The work of a *receiver* is often associated with that of a liquidator, and in a company liquidation they may be the same person. A receiver is frequently appointed by the Court to manage the business of the company until such time as it may be liquidated; this is because a business will often sell for more if it can be kept working normally until a buyer is found who will take it as a going concern, rather than if it ceases trading and all the assets are sold at an auction. A receiver carries out other duties: he may be appointed by the Court to attend to the assets of a mentally disordered person, to deal with the dissolution of a partnership, to receive rents and profits of property in the administration of an estate or to act as an interim receiver of a debtor's estate.

(*e*) **Solicitors**

Most bank branches have a solicitor as a customer, and for their business solicitors usually maintain at least two accounts. One of these is always designated *clients' account*, and this contains funds received by the solicitor on his clients' behalf that will be paid to them at a later date; this account should never be overdrawn. The other account is usually designated *office account* and is concerned with the day-to-day expenses of running the business.

(*f*) **Local authorities**

The main income flowing into local authority bank accounts comes from Government grants, rates, council house rents and trading activities such as swimming pools and car parks; the main expenditure consists of wage and other payments for services provided by the authority. Local authorities finance most of their longer-term activities in other ways than from a bank (see Unit 7.7) and usually only temporary bank borrowing is required to cover the period before a loan is raised or revenues are received.

12.8   A Banker's Duty of Secrecy

The one duty that all customers expect from their banks is that of secrecy and any breach of this duty gives a customer a claim to damages which will be awarded by the Court in proportion to the damage done to his financial reputation. Care should be exercised in all dealings with customers' statements, requests from other banks for status reports and references, and when returning cheques for lack of funds on the account. In particular, telephone inquiries concerning the balance of an account should be handled cautiously: each bank has its own regulations but, generally speaking, the balance should be disclosed only upon the positive identification of the customer. This is difficult over the telephone but the caller could be asked to state the amounts of recent standing orders or items paid in during the past week or so, or to estimate the balance of the account. It is not very sensible to ask for the account number or for details of recent cheques; if it is a thief with your customer's cheque book at the other end of the phone, he will be able to give you this information and you will then innocently give him the balance of the account so that he knows just how much to draw out on a forged cheque!

Under certain circumstances, information about a customer's account can be disclosed. These circumstances are:

(i) under compulsion by law (for example, under the Bankers' Books Evidence Act 1879);

(ii) under a public duty;

(iii) where required by the interests of the bank;

(iv) where made by the express or implied consent of the customer.

'Granted open-plan banking lacks a certain privacy, Mr. Wilkins, but there are advantages in the communications field'

12.9 Questions

1. What are the advantages and disadvantages of being in business as a sole trader?

2. Distinguish between private and public limited companies.

3. Compare and contrast ordinary shares, preference shares, deferred ordinary shares and debentures.

4. Bankers wish to give good service to customers but must also be mindful of their duty of secrecy. How would you reconcile those two principles in the case of a telephone call from a person who says that he is your customer Albert Brown and wishes to be told, over the telephone, the balance on his current account?

(The Institute of Bankers)

5. J. Smith & Co. Ltd., a public company, has an issued share capital made up as follows:

50 000 eight per cent cumulative preference shares of £1 each	£50 000
50 000 ten per cent non-cumulative preference shares of £1 each	£50 000
200 000 ordinary shares of 50p each	£100 000
	£200 000

The company also has in issue £100 000 of seven per cent debentures. Net profit, before payment of debenture interest, is as follows:

Year 1	£26 000
Year 2	£9 000
Year 3	£18 000
Year 4	£35 000

Company policy is to distribute all available profits as dividends. Calculate the dividend or interest payable on each class of shares and debentures for each year: ignore taxation.

(Answers at the end of the book.)

Bank Accounts

13.1 Types of Account

There are two main types of account offered by all the major clearing banks: *current accounts* and *deposit accounts*. Other accounts offered include savings, loans and personal loans, budget and revolving credit accounts. A customer may have two or more different types of account and more than one account of each kind; a company customer, for example, may require several current accounts for various purposes. This Unit highlights the main features of each of these accounts and indicates any restrictions on the use of other bank services that may be placed on the account holder.

13.2 Current Accounts

This is the most popular kind of account. Funds are paid in by the customer, who may also ask his employer to pay his wages or salary direct into the account by means of a bank giro credit. The customer is usually issued with a cheque book although some customers use their accounts solely for the payment of standing orders or direct debits. Funds may be withdrawn on demand either by drawing cash by cheque at the branch where the account is maintained or by writing cheques in favour of another person. Current accounts should always be maintained in credit unless overdraft arrangements have been previously made: these arrangements will include an agreed 'limit' on the account beyond which the customer should not draw. Interest is calculated on the amount of the overdraft on a daily basis and charged to the account half-yearly, at a rate based on a percentage over the bank's base rate. Where facilities for an overdraft are granted the bank may also make a special charge for arranging them and committing the bank's money, whether the facilities are used or not. Security might be required to back an overdrawn account (see Unit 17).

Interest is not paid by banks when a current account is in credit, although the idea is under consideration at the time of writing. Instead, charges are made on the basis of the number of transactions passing through the account. If any charges are to be made they are debited either quarterly or half-yearly and are shown on the bank statements which are regularly sent to all current account customers to show the transactions on their account. Most banks do not charge for payments into the accounts but operate an item charge for debits such as cheques paid, standing orders and direct debits. The cost of these items is calculated quarterly or half-yearly by the bank's computer and against this is set off a 'notional' rate of interest on the customer's average credit balance during the period. Where the notional interest exceeds the cost of the debit items no charge is made, although no interest is credited to the account. Most banks make no charge at all if the credit balance on the account does not fall below a certain figure (which varies from one bank to another) and nowadays all the major banks either publish their scale of charges or will explain them to a customer or potential customer on request.

Current account holders are entitled to make use of most services of the bank.

13.3 Deposit Accounts

These, together with savings accounts, represent the simplest form of bank account: the customer deposits funds and withdraws them as required. No cheque book is issued on this type of account and therefore the formalities of opening an account are simple: often there is no need for a reference (although this may be required if the account is opened with a cheque), the customer's name, address and occupation, together with a specimen signature and an initial deposit being all that are needed.

Payments into a deposit account, which can consist of cash, cheques, postal orders and so on, may be paid in at the branch where the account is maintained or at any other branch of the bank. Funds may be withdrawn to the amount of the credit balance on the account normally only at the branch where it is maintained, although some banks do permit limited withdrawals at other branches. Withdrawals are subject to the required period of notice—often seven days—but in practice prior notice is not always insisted upon, provided that the amounts required are not too large. No overdrafts are permitted and a customer may generally not draw cheques on a deposit account. Where a deposit account customer has a large bill to pay and does not wish to carry cash, the bank can issue a cheque drawn on an account maintained especially for this purpose: the customer's deposit account is debited, the special account credited and a cheque issued to the customer for the amount required. Where a customer maintains both a deposit and a current account at the same branch, funds can be transferred from one to the other freely, so that if deposit account funds are required to pay a bill, the appropriate sum may be switched to the current account and a cheque issued.

Interest is calculated on a daily basis on the cleared balance of the account. This means that, if a cheque is paid in to the account, the sum deposited does not start to earn interest until the cheque is cleared; nor are withdrawals permitted against the cheque until then. The current rate of interest allowed is displayed in all branches and changes usually follow the trend of the bank's base rate. Interest is paid gross of tax on most accounts and account holders should declare on their tax returns the full amount of interest paid to them during the year. The customer may receive a passbook recording debits, credits and the balance on the account or, more likely, will be sent a statement of the account at regular intervals.

A deposit account is a convenient place for funds that are surplus to immediate requirements; the attractions are that it is simple and convenient both to pay in and to make withdrawals and that the money is absolutely safe. The rate of interest paid is, after tax, normally less than that paid by other investment agencies (see Table 6.3), but reflects the degree of safety and ease of withdrawal of funds.

Most advisory services of the bank are available to deposit account holders but a range of current account services, particularly standing orders, direct debits and cheques, are not normally available. It follows that cheque cards and cash cards are also unavailable to deposit account holders, although credit cards (see Unit 14.4) are not restricted to current account holders only.

In addition to the more straightforward deposit accounts, most banks accept larger sums of money for fixed terms at fixed rates of interest. Each deposit—generally the minimum is £10 000—is regarded as a separate contract and cannot be withdrawn before the end of the term. For customers with larger amounts to invest—a minimum of £50 000—and particularly for companies, most banks will issue a certificate of deposit (see Units 7.3 and 7.11).

13.4   Savings Accounts

Some banks still operate these accounts as well as offering a deposit account service; others have withdrawn them and converted them to deposit accounts. The original idea of the savings account was to appeal to the 'small saver', and to this end 'home safes' or savings boxes were issued to customers. These were locked by the bank and the customer took the box home, put his regular savings into it and then brought it to the bank for it to be opened and the proceeds placed to the credit of his account. The trend nowadays is to withdraw the locked boxes, which used to cause chaos at busy counters ten minutes before closing time on a Friday afternoon, and instead to issue boxes that can be opened at home so that the savings can be changed into larger-denomination notes and coins for paying into the bank in the normal way.

Interest rates on savings accounts are very close to those offered on deposits. Some banks allow a lower rate on savings account balances up to a certain figure and deposit rate on balances in excess. With some banks, the savings account permits withdrawals up to a limited figure at branches other than that at which the account is maintained; to help with identification, a passbook is issued which contains the customer's signature. In other respects the methods of operating savings accounts are very similar to deposits, although in some banks only cash and not cheques can be paid in. As with deposit accounts, usual current account services are unavailable to the savings account holder.

13.5   Loan Accounts

An overdraft on a current account represents one way of lending money to a customer; the loan account represents another way. Where this is used, a separate loan account is opened and debited with the amount of the loan, which is credited to the customer's current account. Repayments of the loan are made, usually monthly, by debiting the customer's current account and crediting the loan account. Interest is calculated on the daily balance of the loan account at a given percentage over the bank's base rate and this, together with any other charges for the loan, will be debited quarterly or half-yearly either to the loan account or to the current account. Thus the customer has two accounts: his normal current account—which, in the absence of any other borrowing arrangement, must remain in credit—and a loan account, on which the only transactions will be the amount of the original loan, repayments and, if they are to be applied to this account, interest and charges. It is not possible for a customer without a current account to borrow money by way of a loan.

A loan account, as opposed to an overdraft, is especially appropriate where a customer, particularly a business customer, wishes to buy some vehicles or plant and machinery and the bank manager wishes to see regular repayments being made. Should the manager find that the current account becomes overdrawn because of the loan account repayments, he might conclude that the cash flow benefits from purchasing the new assets were not being received; thus the danger signals would be perceived early on, and the matter taken up with the customer. Normally, security is needed to 'back' a loan account (see Unit 17).

A loan granted for more than a year or two—between three and seven years, for instance—is a medium-term loan available mainly to business customers. These facilities are considered in Unit 15.2(*b*).

13.6   Personal Loans

Most banks operate personal loan schemes which are similar to loan accounts except that they are designed for personal customers only and that the regular (usually monthly) repayments incorporate the interest charges. Under a personal loan scheme, a customer borrows a sum of money for an agreed period of time and makes monthly repayments, which include interest, fixed so as to exactly extinguish the debt at the end of the time.

Personal loans are commonly used as finance for the purchase of consumer durables such as motor vehicles, furniture, carpets or television sets, and are sometimes thought of as being the same as hire purchase. There is, however, an important legal distinction between the two: under a hire purchase agreement the goods remain the property of the finance company until the last payment is made, whereas under a personal loan scheme the goods belong to the bank customer as though he had paid cash for them. Indeed, there is no need for the seller of the goods even to know that the purchaser has arranged a personal loan to raise the finance: once the bank has agreed the loan, the amount of money is transferred to the credit of the customer's current account and debited to a personal loan account, and so the bank customer pays for the goods by cheque.

The rate of interest charged on a personal loan is invariably fixed for the period of the loan, and is based on the capital sum (the amount originally borrowed), rather than on the amount of the loan outstanding on a daily basis. This means that the true rate of interest is considerably higher than the nominal rate. For example, on a loan of £200 over two years at a nominal rate of 8 per cent per annum the total interest payable is £32: this, because repayments reduce the balance outstanding, works out at a true rate of nearly 16 per cent per annum. The Consumer Credit Act 1974 requires both nominal and actual rates of interest to be advised to all borrowers under personal loan schemes.

No security is required for personal loans but they are normally only granted to holders of a current account and the manager will check to ensure that the past conduct of this has been satisfactory before granting the loan. Most bank personal loan schemes incorporate a form of life assurance so that in the event of the borrower's death during the period of the loan, the debt would be extinguished by payment under the assurance. There are often upper age limits on this 'free' assurance.

13.7   Budget Accounts

Most householders are only too well aware that at certain times of the year their bills all seem to arrive at once. The first three months of every year are apt to bring heavy bills, such as those for gas and electricity which are higher

as a result of increased consumption during the winter; other bills too have a regular pattern—often the rates on a house are due in April and October, car tax and car insurance seem to come together, and so on. As an attempt to assist personal customers to even out their expenditure over the year, the banks introduced budget accounts during the late 1960s, a service that is normally only available to current account customers. A separate budget account is opened, and a cheque book specially printed for use with this account. The customer estimates his expenditure on items such as gas, electricity, car tax and insurance, season tickets, rates and so forth for the forthcoming twelve months, adding a little to allow for inflation and bank charges: the annual total is then divided by twelve and a standing order is taken to transfer this amount monthly from the customer's current account to the budget account. As bills which are included in the budget fall due, the customer settles them by using the special budget account cheque book. Charges are made on the account, consisting of interest for any overdrafts incurred during the year and the costs of operating the account—these are usually stated in leaflets advertising the service. If all goes well, at the end of the twelve-month period the balance of the account should be nil, standing order transfers of money into the account having been equal to payments made by cheque together with charges. The account is then reviewed and the customer asked to estimate his expenditure afresh for the next twelve months.

The budget account is only available for paying bills that do not come at regular monthly intervals and so items paid on a monthly basis, such as mortgage repayments or insurance premiums, would not be allowed to go through it, but would be debited to the customer's ordinary current account.

13.8   Revolving Credit Accounts

Some banks offer the facility whereby a customer makes agreed payments, usually from £10 upwards each month, from his current account into a special account. At any time the customer may overdraw the special revolving credit account up to (often) thirty times the agreed monthly payment: thus with regular payments of £10 he has available an overdraft of £300. He may use the full amount immediately if he likes; if he then makes regular repayments for say ten months, the balance of the account would be down to £200 and he could then draw on the account for a further £100. The advantage from the customer's point of view is that he may spend the funds available when and how he wishes without having to negotiate fresh loan arrangements every time. Interest and charges are normally debited to the revolving credit account, although they could be taken from the customer's current account on request.

13.9   Questions

1. Obtain some advertising leaflets from one of the major clearing banks and contrast the different types of accounts they offer.

2. Find out how the major clearing banks calculate charges on current accounts. Which one would work out the cheapest with different average balances and numbers of debit transactions? Also find out similar information for Trustee Savings Banks, National Girobank and a smaller clearing bank such as the Co-operative, and compare their charges with those of the larger clearing banks.

Banking Services: Personal Customers

14.1 Introduction

In this Unit we shall describe the services offered by the banks to their personal customers; some of these are equally applicable to business customers and a note is appended where this is so. Specialist business services are discussed in Unit 15, and certain specialized payment methods used by exporters and importers are considered in Unit 16.

Most of the services mentioned in this Unit are available to current account holders and most, but not all, can be used by those with deposit and savings accounts. Whether or not any particular service is available to one type of account holder or another varies from bank to bank and reference should be made to a bank's literature to find out exactly which services are offered and any restrictions that may apply.

14.2 Cheque Cards

All the major banking groups offer their personal customers a cheque card, which is signed by the customer upon receipt. The card states the maximum amount for which it is valid (at the time of writing £50), the name of the issuing bank, the sorting code number of the issuing branch, the name of the customer, the card number and the expiry date of the card. It can be used in two ways: to draw cash at other banks and branches, and to 'back' cheques used to pay for goods and services. In either case a cheque has to be drawn and the card presented as a guarantee of payment. The amount of each cheque must not exceed the limit stated on the card, and this is also the maximum amount of cash that may be drawn at a bank on any one day—there is usually a page at the back of each cheque book for banks to record amounts cashed and the date, to ensure that this maximum is not exceeded. Naturally the withdrawal limit does not apply at the branch where the account is maintained.

The bank issuing the card guarantees to a shopkeeper that any cheque not exceeding the limit of the card in any one transaction will be honoured subject to certain conditions, which are:

(i) the cheque must be signed in the presence of the payee;

(ii) the signature on the cheque must correspond with the specimen on the card;

(iii) the cheque must be drawn on a bank cheque form bearing the code number shown on the card (if the account is transferred to another bank or branch, a new cheque card must be obtained);

(iv) the cheque must be drawn before the expiry date of the card;

(v) the card number must be written on the reverse of the cheque by the payee.

The card can also be used to enable cheques to be cashed in Europe at banks displaying the 'Eurocheque' sign—the red and blue symbol is printed on the card—but not to back cheque payments to hotels, shops and so forth. Cheques that are cashed abroad are drawn in sterling and the foreign bank deducts commission before paying over the currency proceeds. Foreign currency obtained abroad under the Eurocheque scheme is subject to certain conditions to meet United Kingdom exchange control regulations, and these conditions are set out in the *Notice to cardholders*, obtainable from banks.

Of the 'big four' clearing banks operating in England and Wales, three—Lloyds, Midland and National Westminster—use the same design of card, the only difference being in the name of the issuing bank. Barclays uses its own distinctive Barclaycard as both a cheque card and a credit card (see Unit 14.4).

Cards are normally available only to current account customers aged eighteen and over, subject to the previous satisfactory operation of their account. Issue is usually at the discretion of the branch manager and, under certain circumstances, the card may be made available to customers under eighteen years.

14.3 Open Credits

Where amounts of cash beyond the cheque card limit are required to be withdrawn from another branch of the bank from that where the account is held, arrangements are made to establish an open credit. This withdrawal facility is made available by the customer's branch sending an authorization card, together with a specimen signature of the customer, to the branch concerned. If there is no convenient branch in the town where the customer wishes to cash his cheques, the arrangement can be made with a branch of some other bank. This service is particularly appropriate for business customers having factories or branches in more than one town and enables them to draw wages and petty cash locally. The encashing branch or bank will need to know the maximum amount to be drawn under the arrangement, either per week or per cheque. Often a specimen of the signature of the person who is to receive the payments at the encashing branch—the wages clerk, for instance—will be required for identification purposes.

14.4 Credit Cards

The credit card as a method of payment has already been described in Unit 11.5. The two major credit cards currently available in Britain are *Access* and

Barclaycard. The Access card is produced by the Joint Credit Card Co. Ltd., of which the major shareholders are Lloyds, Midland and National Westminster banks; Barclaycard (obviously) come from Barclays. Another credit card available is the Trustee Savings Bank's *Trustcard* which has strong links with Barclays and can be used at 100 000 Barclaycard retail outlets in the United Kingdom and 2 250 000 outlets of the international *Visa* credit card network with which Barclays and the Trustee Savings Bank are associated. Access claims 90 000 United Kingdom retail outlets and the card may also be used at the 1 500 000 worldwide outlets of the *Mastercharge* and *Eurocard* systems.

Each card carries embossed characters giving the name of the holder, his account number and its period of validity and, on the reverse, the holder's signature. The card can be used for making purchases of goods or for obtaining a cash advance from any member bank involved in the scheme. While the cash facility principally applies to branches of banks in Britain, advances can also be obtained at certain overseas bank branches. Each month a cardholder who has used his card receives a statement detailing purchases and cash advances. If he wishes, he may pay only a proportion of the total amount he owes and spread the remaining payments over a number of months, for which he will be charged interest. When calculating interest charges, the credit card company charges for cash advances from the date they are taken, but it makes no charge for purchases of goods if the full amount of the account is settled within twenty-five days of the date of the statement on which they first appear. Interest is currently charged at a rate of 2 per cent per month: this is equivalent to an annual interest rate of 26.82 per cent.

Cards are issued to persons aged eighteen and over and there is no requirement that cardholders should have a current account; therefore this service could be of equal use to deposit and savings account holders. Naturally, before issuing a credit card, the company would wish to have financial details of applicants, including details of previous credit transactions, so that references can be taken up. Each cardholder is given a credit limit—commonly £200—which must not be exceeded.

Critics of credit cards believe they encourage people to overspend; nevertheless, used sensibly, the card can be of great benefit as a flexible way of spreading the cost of purchases over a period of time, and the card companies have recently run advertising campaigns stressing this aspect. The card companies do rely fairly heavily, however, on income from extended repayment: about three-quarters of cardholders do not settle their accounts during the nil-interest period on purchases and therefore must pay interest charges. If this kind of income were to fall drastically, card companies might well be tempted to raise their credit limits.

The companies also receive income from the retailers and other outlets that accept credit cards: they are obliged to give the company a discount on purchases.

As credit cards are a means of creating money, controls on their use are imposed by the Treasury from time to time: these usually involve setting a maximum limit on the cash withdrawal facilities together with a minimum monthly repayment placed on all accounts, expressed as either a percentage of the balance outstanding or a fixed money amount, whichever is the greater.

The implementation of the Consumer Credit Act 1974 has created some difficulties for the card groups. From July 1977 what are called the 'connected lender' rules have applied. This means that if goods that have been paid for with a credit card turn out to be faulty, the purchaser has legal rights of recourse to the lender—the card company—as well as to the retailer. The Act renders credit card companies (as well as retailers) subject to claims by borrowers in respect of faulty goods bought on credit within the price range £30–£10 000. Claims cannot only cover the whole cost of the goods, but can also include consequential damages. The legislation is not retrospective, however, and existing cardholders on the effective date (1 July 1977) are not covered; but Barclaycard and Access have agreed, as an act of goodwill, to accept liability towards these cardholders, although only up to the amount of the debit to the credit card account.

The card systems mentioned so far are 'free' in the sense that, if they are not used by the holder, there is no charge. Other cards, such as *Diners Club*

'I'm sorry, madam—Barclaycard accepts liability for faulty goods, but it doesn't exchange them'

and *American Express*, make an annual charge but do not have pre-set spending limits. Neither of these cards is, in fact, a credit card, and they are more correctly described as *business cards*; cardholders are expected to pay their accounts promptly on receipt of each monthly statement and, provided they do so, there are no interest charges. The main benefit of this type of card is the convenience of being able to pay for goods and services without having to carry large amounts of cash.

14.5 Cash Cards

The 1970s have seen the development of both the cash dispenser and the multi-function 'service till'. Both of these are sophisticated machines that can be operated by current account customers who have been issued with special plastic cards. Unlike cheque and credit cards, where there has been a degree of co-operation between the major clearing banks, each bank has evolved its own systems for these services, which are not available for use by customers of other banks.

Cash dispensers are machines located on the outside walls of certain bank branches which enable a customer using a special card to obtain a fixed amount of cash, usually £10, at any time of day or night. The customer is given a personal number which he memorizes. To use the card, he inserts it into the machine and enters his personal number into the keyboard; if all goes well, the amount of money is delivered out of a slot and, depending on the bank's system, the card is either returned immediately or kept by the machine. Where the card is retained, it will be posted back to the customer within a few days; where it is returned immediately, it cannot be used again within twenty-four hours—if an attempt is made to use it too soon the machine, which 'reads' the card, will retain it and not pay out any cash. The cards can be used at any machine of the issuing bank, but are not interchangeable between banks. When the machine is used, it reads the card, pays out the cash and prints a debit to the customer's account; the branch staff who service the machine remove these vouchers and debit the accounts of their own customers direct, passing vouchers concerning other customers through the clearing system to the appropriate branches.

The cash dispenser is limited to simple encashment facilities of a fixed amount and its natural successor has been the development of computer-linked systems providing a wider range of banking services and operated by the latest generation of plastic cards carrying a magnetic tape recording all the card-holder's personal financial details. Lloyds call their service Cashpoint, Barclays' is Barclaybank, while National Westminster's is called a Service Till; Midland's version is to be introduced very shortly. Not all the machines have the same facilities; the most elaborate take the form of special tills, mostly in bank branches but sometimes in stores or in the outside walls of banks. The card-holder is given a personal number to remember, which he enters into the keyboard on the till; this action links the till with the bank's computer. The holder then inserts the card and the tape directs the computer to look up his account. It can then give him the amount of cash he wishes to withdraw—up to £100 in some cases—tell him his balance, enable him to place an order for a cheque book or a statement or carry out a transfer payment to another account, provided the payee's bank details are known.

It is hoped that the next few years will see the installation in shops of computer terminals that will enable a cardholder to pay for goods immediately by giving his payment instructions to his bank's computer. This would then, after checking that the customer had sufficient funds or the necessary overdraft facilities, transfer the sum straight into the shop's bank account. This is a step towards the 'cashless society', where there would be no need to carry round large sums of money and only small change would be needed; the *electronic funds transfer system* (EFTS) would certainly have benefits for the shops in allowing the instant crediting of money paid into them and in eliminating the problem of 'bouncing' cheques.

14.6   Travel Services

All the major banks offer a travel service consisting of the provision of travellers' cheques and foreign currency to customers and non-customers alike.

Travellers' cheques provide a safe way of carrying money both in Britain and abroad; all the banks offer travellers' cheques denominated in sterling and some offer them in other currencies as well, particularly US dollars. On their issue by the bank they are signed by the holder; when they are to be cashed the holder countersigns them in the presence of the cashier who checks the signatures before making payment. If they are lost, a refund service ensures that the traveller will never be stranded without money.

Foreign currency can be obtained from all banks, but as not every branch carries a stock of currency it is wise for intending travellers to place an order a week or so before going abroad. Unused travellers' cheques and foreign bank notes (though not usually coin) can be cashed upon return to Britain. The amount of money that can be taken out of Britain is subject to exchange control regulations, on which the banks can advise the traveller. Most other countries operate similar restrictions.

Most banks also sell *travel insurance* providing cover for emergency medical expenses, for accidental death or disablement, for loss of baggage, travellers' cheques, currency and money, together with personal liability cover. Application forms for *passports and visas* can also be obtained from banks and assistance given in their completion. The banks will also buy foreign currency and cash travellers' cheques for visitors to Britain.

14.7   Hire Purchase

All the major banks have links with finance houses that provide a range of hire purchase and other schemes, all of which enable the customer to pay for goods by making instalments over an agreed period of time. Goods on hire purchase remain the property of the finance company until the *hirer* (as the hire-purchase customer is known) has made all the payments; where other finance schemes are used the goods legally belong to the customer from the start. Interest charged on hire purchase and similar contracts is usually higher than the bank would charge on a personal loan and is normally calculated with reference to the capital sum borrowed: thus the true rate of interest (see Unit 13.6) is an important consideration.

Hire purchase and similar schemes operated by finance houses are available both to customers (with all types of accounts) and to non-customers. They are equally applicable to personal and business customers (see also Unit 15.2(*e*)).

14.8 Management of Investments

In Unit 6, we discussed the range of opportunities available to investors. One of the services provided by the banks is the management of a customer's investments: this is particularly appropriate to private customers who already have stock exchange investments or who wish to start investing in this way. To be managed properly investments need a certain amount of time and professional skill and this, for a fee, the banks are able to provide. Often there is a minimum portfolio valuation that they will accept (sometimes £20 000) and for sums below this figure they frequently recommend an investment in the bank's unit trust. It is often possible to exchange existing shareholdings for units in the trust.

Investments that are taken over by the bank are usually transferred into its name so that dividends and interest received, notice of rights issues and similar matters can be attended to promptly; naturally the investments can be returned to the name of the customer upon request. In managing a customer's investments, the bank pays over dividends received to the investor at intervals, regularly reviews the make-up of the portfolio, buys and sells shares as appropriate, and sends an annual statement to the investor giving a current valuation of the investments. Some customers, particularly those uninterested in investment or living abroad, give the bank a complete authority to deal with the investments as they think fit; others ask the bank to refer to them before making any changes in the portfolio. When following an investment policy the bank considers the special requirements of the individual customer, such as a need for a high income or for capital growth of the portfolio. This service is available to all personal customers who are long-term investors: it is not available to speculators seeking short-term gains and wishing to make frequent changes in investments.

Specialist investment management schemes have been developed for the business customer (see Unit 15.5).

14.9   Safe Custody and Safe Deposit

Share and unit trust certificates, life assurance policies, deeds of property, wills and other valuables can be left with the bank for safe-keeping. These may be left in 'open' safe custody, in which case the receipt given for them will detail the items deposited; alternatively a locked box or a sealed envelope, parcel or suitcase may be left, the contents of which will be unknown to the bank.

Certain large city branches offer a safe-deposit service whereby a customer can rent a compartment in a specially built safe. There are usually two locks to each compartment, one key being held by the customer and the other by the bank; duplicate keys are held by the bank in case of emergency but would only be used in the presence of the customer at his request.

Unless an item is held in open safe custody the bank normally has no idea of the contents of a package or a safe-deposit compartment and care should be exercised with items that could be damaged. Where a customer deposits articles or securities with a bank for safe custody a *contract of bailment* arises (the bailee/bailor relationship mentioned in Unit 12.1) and under this contract a bank is bound to take reasonable care of articles left with it. The standard of care expected depends on the circumstances at the bank's disposal, however: for example, if its premises are old and the safes are damp, a customer will not be able to claim damages if his property is affected by the conditions in the safe.

14.10   Status Inquiries

A customer can quote his bank as a financial reference (see Unit 15.8).

14.11   Insurance

The banks offer an insurance service to all their customers, either through specially set-up departments or subsidiary companies or through their own insurance brokers. Besides the specialist insurance for businesses (see Unit 15.6), personal insurance available includes life assurance (see Unit 6.9), mortgage protection policies for those buying their home by means of a mortgage, travel insurance (see Unit 14.6) and insurance protection of home contents, cars, caravans and boats.

14.12   Executor and Trustee Services

Specialized departments of the banks offer services on all aspects of wills and trusts. When making their wills, many people appoint a bank to act as executor in handling their estate when they die. The banks have the experience and knowledge to take on such a responsibility and to perform the tasks required quickly and efficiently. Like other executors, the bank will gather together the assets of the deceased, agree and pay the capital transfer tax (if any) and distribute the estate according to the terms of the will. If the will set up a trust for the benefit of others, such as a widow or children, the bank can administer the trust and make payments to the beneficiaries at the appropriate time.

'We'll arrange the insurance, of course, Mr. Jonah, but I assure you the chances
of being swallowed by a whale are very remote indeed'

If the bank has not been appointed as an executor, it is still possible for it to act where the executors or trustees appointed by the will find that they are unable to take on the work, and it can also take over or join in an existing trust where a trustee dies or wishes to retire. When a person dies without leaving a will—*intestate*—the banks' executor and trustee departments can also take on the task of handling his affairs by acting as administrator.

These services are available to all personal customers (corporate trust services for businesses are discussed in Unit 15.5).

14.13 Taxation

All the major banks offer the services of dealing with personal taxation problems, whatever their size. The service, which is often provided through a section of the executor and trustee department, provides advice on income and other personal taxes such as capital gains tax and capital transfer tax. This specialist department also acts as its customer's tax agent, dealing with all the tax forms and correspondence to ensure that he gets all the allowances to which he is entitled, and where necessary handles claims for repayment of tax. The department can also provide a service to persons who are non-residents of the United Kingdom, but who have income in this country.

The tax departments are also able to advise customers how to arrange their affairs to the best advantage of themselves and their family. This involves a full consideration of the customer's will, tax position, life assurance and investment of capital, so that a suitable scheme may be worked out to reduce taxation and meet his obligations and wishes.

14.14 Guarantees and Indemnities

It sometimes happens that customers—both personal and business—need the guarantee of a bank before being allowed to undertake certain actions. A common example of this is where a share certificate has been lost: before issuing a duplicate the registrar of the company concerned will require a bank to guarantee its customer's application for a new certificate. A bank is normally willing to do this but, in order to acknowledge the small risk of possible future loss, the customer will be asked to sign a counter-indemnity so that it may have a claim against him should it be called to make a payment under the guarantee.

14.15 Questions

1. What banking services might become useful to an accountant as he progresses from student to senior partner in a busy practice?

   (*The Institute of Bankers*)

2. In detail describe the work carried out and services offered by (i) a bank's executor and trustee department, and (ii) a hire purchase company.

3. List and describe the main services offered by a commercial bank which are likely to be of greatest use to personal customers.

   (*The Institute of Bankers*)

Banking Services: Business Customers

15.1 Introduction

A wide range of the major banks' specialist services designed to suit the needs of different sizes of business concerns are discussed in this Unit. Some of these services are also applicable to personal customers and are described elsewhere, this Unit only referring you to the relevant section.

The services that the banks offer to the business customer can be classified under seven broad headings:

(i) financing;
(ii) money transfer;
(iii) foreign transactions;
(iv) investment;
(v) insurance;
(vi) accounting;
(vii) advisory service.

15.2 Financing

(a) **Loans and overdrafts**
See Units 13.2 and 13.5.

(b) **Medium-term loans**
Generally loans and overdrafts are repayable on demand and are reviewed at least once a year, so that they are often regarded as relatively short-term finance. This does not suit the business that is seeking finance for an expansion and development plan lasting over several years: medium-term loans are offered by the banks to provide for this kind of borrowing requirement. The banks each offer slightly different facilities but normally such loans are made for periods of between three and seven years, although both shorter and longer periods (up to a maximum of about ten years) can usually be arranged. They are made available to businesses for the purchase or extension of premises, for re-equipment in plant and machinery or for other investment such as the acquisition of, or merger with, another business. The minimum amount lent on medium-term loans is £5 000 and generally there is no maximum, each case

being considered on its merits; as with usual loans and overdrafts, interest is calculated on the amount of the loan outstanding on a day-to-day basis and charged half-yearly. Repayments are fairly flexible and are agreed to suit the customer's requirements, either at an even rate during the period of the loan or to coincide with the receipt of cash benefits flowing into the business from the asset purchased with the aid of the loan. The big advantage for a business taking out such loans is that the finance will always be available over the agreed period and cannot be recalled as a result of restrictions imposed on bank lending or other intervention.

(c) Farming advances

All the major banks have many accounts of farmers and of businesses and individuals connected with the agricultural industry. Special finance arrangements can be tailored to suit the needs of this group of customers, either directly through the bank or indirectly through subsidiary and associated companies such as the Agricultural Mortgage Corporation Ltd. (AMC) which is jointly owned by the clearing banks and the Bank of England. The finance provided to the agricultural industry is on either a short-, medium- or long-term basis, depending on the purpose for which it is required. Short-term finance is provided from the banks by means of an overdraft or loan to meet working capital requirements and to cover the seasonal 'swing' of most farmers' accounts, reflecting the peak in their need for borrowing during late spring and summer when money is paid out to finance crops and animals, and its reduction during the autumn and winter as sale proceeds are received. Medium-term loans for three to ten years are provided by the banks or their hire purchase companies to finance the buying of machinery, equipment and buildings. For longer periods, AMC provides a source of finance for the purchase of land and for major long-term improvements.

(d) Leasing

This is a method by which a business can obtain items of plant, equipment and vehicles without the need for capital outlay; instead of buying them outright, it leases or rents them from the bank's leasing company, which is often associated with the finance house. A wide range of assets may be leased, from agricultural machinery to machine tools and computers, worth anything from £1 000 up to several hundred times as much. The procedure is for the business to choose the equipment it wants and this is purchased by the leasing company. An agreement is then drawn up between the leasing company and the business establishing the terms of the contract and the amount of rental payable. A fixed primary lease is established for a period of three, four or five years, at the end of which there is normally an option to renew for a further period at a much reduced rental or, sometimes, an option to purchase. Rentals may be payable monthly, quarterly or annually to suit the customer.

The advantage of leasing to a business is that, although the legal title of the asset remains with the leasing company, once the first rental has been paid the business has complete use of the asset without having to finance its acquisition out of valuable capital resources or to seek a loan to cover its cost.

'A word of advice. Never say "How's business?" to a farmer'

(e) Hire purchase
Hire purchase for personal customers has already been discussed in Unit 14.7. For the businessman, hire purchase provides an alternative way of obtaining a wide range of assets without the need for major capital expenditure. The advantage of hire purchase is that the cost of plant or equipment can be spread over a period of time by making regular payments; thus, apart from the deposit required, there is no need to use capital resources. The asset eventually becomes the property of the business.

(f) Block discounting
This facility, usually provided by the bank's finance house subsidiary, is a service for retailers who provide hire purchase and other facilities for their customers. Many retailers and other businesses offer hire purchase, credit sale and rental services, particularly on the sale of consumer durables such as television sets, washing machines and cars. Most businesses do not have the necessary finance to provide these facilities for themselves, so they discount a 'block' of hire purchase, credit sale or rental agreements that they have entered into with their customers to a finance house. Thus the retailer receives immediate cash for the block of agreements sold and acts as an agent of the finance house by collecting and passing on the amounts payable from his customers; in this way

he has no need to finance the agreements himself, but can nevertheless appear to be giving a personal financial service to his customers.

(g) Factoring and invoice discounting

Factoring companies provide their clients with a sales ledger accounting service and bad debt protection. Most companies also offer finance against the trade debtors of a firm. You will know from your accountancy studies that when a business sells goods, particularly to another business, it has to allow credit: this means that sales have been made but the payment is due to the seller. Depending on the terms that are usual within the trade concerned, it can be anything from one to three months, or even longer, before payment is received. Until then, valuable cash is tied up, restricting the growth of the business: a factoring company provides, among other things, an immediate amount of money against these debtors. Most of the large banks offer a factoring service to their business customers, usually through a subsidiary company. The services differ from one factoring company to another but most provide assistance in three main areas:

(i) As already mentioned, finance is provided by purchasing debtors and making an immediate payment. Often the payment is restricted to a certain percentage of the debt due, commonly 80 per cent, and debts must be approved by the factoring company. Naturally charges are made for this service but the increased liquidity position of a firm might nevertheless enable it to take advantage of discounts for prompt payment offered by its suppliers.

(ii) A sales ledger accounting service is also offered whereby the factoring company takes responsibility for all aspects of sales accounting within the business: this includes maintaining the sales ledger (that is, the personal accounts of all debtors), sending out regular statements of account and collecting payments as they become due. This service relieves the management of the business from the time and expense of running the sales ledger.

(iii) The factoring company provides a further service of guaranteeing full payment on approved sales to customers. The payment is made even if the customer is unable to pay as a result of insolvency.

The factoring service is only appropriate for businesses that sell to a wide range of customers at regular intervals and where the total annual sales figure is in excess of £100 000. The charges made by the factoring company vary depending on the services used: the sales ledger accounting and bad debt protection usually cost between 1 and $2\frac{1}{2}$ per cent of sales, depending on the complexity of the work involved. Where debtors are purchased and payment made by the factoring company to the business, interest is charged on the finance at rates slightly higher than current bank lending rates.

A simpler service is that of *invoice discounting*. When one business sells goods on credit to another, an invoice—a document containing details of the sale—is sent to the buyer. With invoice discounting this invoice is sold to the factoring firm which makes an immediate payment of the full amount, less discount charges, to the seller and then arranges to collect the amount due on the sale.

(*h*) **Performance bond**
Often bank customers in the building and contracting industry are required
to supply a performance bond before being permitted to tender for a contract.
The bond guarantees that the company has the financial resources and expertise
to see the contract through to completion, if its tender is successful. A bank
is commonly asked to provide such a bond and, when giving it, usually takes
a counter-indemnity so that in the event of failure to complete the contract
and a requirement for payment under the terms of the bond, it will be able
to make a claim against the contractor.

(*i*) **Export finance**
See Unit 16.

(*j*) **Merchant bank services**
See Unit 5.3.

(*k*) **Discounting bills of exchange**
See Unit 7.3.

15.3   Money Transfer

(*a*) **Cheque clearance**
See Unit 10.9.

(*b*) **Bank giro credits**
Operation of the bank giro credit system has already been described in Unit
11.3. The business customer can use the service to make payments to suppliers
and other creditors, and often finds it very useful for paying the wages and
salaries of employees direct into their bank accounts. Additionally the system
can operate for receiving payments: a businessman can advise his debtors of
the name and address of his bank, its sorting code number and his own account
number; alternatively he can include bank giro credit slips when sending out
statements advising customers of the amount payable in respect of sales. For
a business receiving large numbers of credits into its bank account, such as
a mail-order firm or the head office of a chain of shops, special paying-in books
of credits can be printed and sent to agents or customers. Banks give such
firms details of all credits received into the account day-by-day.
   Standing orders and direct debits (see Units 11.3 and 11.4) can also be of
just as much benefit to business as to personal customers.

(*c*) **Night safes**
Most bank branches have a night safe installed mainly for the use of their
business customers: the entrance to the safe can be seen on the outside wall
of the branch. This service is useful for business customers, particularly shops,
that receive quantities of cash after the banks have closed. The bulk of their

takings can be paid into the bank during mid-afternoon; any takings received after this are placed in a special lockable and numbered night-safe wallet, and at the end of the day are taken to the bank and deposited in the night safe, to which the customer is given a key when he is allocated a wallet. The entrance to the safe is unlocked, and the wallets drop down a chute into a separate safe in the strongrooms of the bank. Next day the safe is opened by bank staff and the wallets are taken to the counter. Here they may be collected during bank opening hours by the customer or his authorized representative and the contents either paid in to the account or taken back to the business premises. Normally the bank will not unlock the wallet unless special arrangements are made for the staff to open it and pay the proceeds in to the customer's account. The charge for the night safe service is usually based on the number of wallets in issue; in any case, it is a small price to pay for knowing that surplus cash is stored safely overnight. As the wallets are of limited size it is recommended that they should be used for bank notes and not coin; cheques and other valuables can also be included provided that they will not be damaged by the fall down the chute into the safe. While this service is mainly intended for business customers who will use the wallets on most working days, a group such as a church or a club organizing a fête or a fair at a weekend can also hire wallets for a few days; this avoids the risk to the organizers of having to hold large amounts of cash in their homes until the banks are open again.

Other valuables such as documents and share certificates can be deposited with the bank in safe custody or safe deposit (see Unit 14.9) in the same way as for personal customers.

(*d*) **Bank drafts**
See Units 11.6 and 11.9.

(*e*) **Overseas transfers**
See Unit 16.5.

(*f*) **Open credits**
See Unit 14.3.

15.4   Foreign Services

To a country like Britain, the import and export trade is very important. The role played by the banks in assisting foreign transactions is fully discussed in Unit 16.

15.5   Investment

From time to time businesses have surplus funds available for investment and the banks are able to provide a number of investment possibilities. Most have been described elsewhere as they are also applicable to personal customers: these include deposit accounts and money market deposits (Unit 6.2), finance house deposits (Unit 6.3), certificates of deposit, both in sterling and dollars (Units 7.11 and 7.13), Eurocurrency deposits (Unit 7.14) and stocks and shares (Unit 6.12).

Investment management and corporate trust services
The executor and trustee departments are able to provide specialist services to companies. Some large businesses have considerable funds invested on behalf of pension funds or employees' savings schemes, and banks can act as trustees of such funds and administer the investments. Additionally, most banks maintain specialist companies situated on the Channel Islands and the Isle of Man where services are available to customers, both private and business, who are able to take advantage of the differing taxation structures that apply in these islands.

Where very large companies and Government agencies issue debenture trusts, loan stocks and Eurocurrency issues, these invariably entail the appointment of a trustee under a trust deed to protect the interests of prospective stock or bond holders. Most major banks are able to accept appointment as trustee to such issues, adding their experience, strength and international credibility.

Trustee departments are also able to undertake the trusteeship of unit trusts and insurance company funds.

15.6   Insurance

The banks provide a wide range of insurance services for personal customers (see Unit 14.11) and also offer specialist insurance for the business customer. Such insurance can be arranged through a bank's own insurance department, through companies for which it acts as agent or through insurance brokers.

Most businesses will need to take out insurance against *fire*, *theft* and perhaps *flooding*. A policy which complements these is one that covers against the *loss of profits* which would be the result of, say, a serious fire: such a policy would cover continuing overheads such as salaries and rates, loss of trading profits and the cost of temporary premises, together with expenses in connection with replacing deeds, plans, business records and documents. *Credit insurance* may be taken out by most types of business, except retail shopkeepers, to provide against the possibility of bad debts. Insurance for *motor vehicles* can be arranged to cover against the usual risks.

It is now a legal requirement that businesses should have *employers' liability insurance* to guard against their liability for accidents to employees. Most firms also take out *public liability insurance* to cover any possible claims for damages from the public—for instance, where a member of the public is injured as a result of buying faulty goods or of negligence by an employee.

Life assurance (already described in Unit 6.9) is particularly relevant for small businesses such as partnerships and private limited companies where a small number of people, perhaps only two or three, play a major part in running the business. The death of one of these key people would have a serious effect on the future of the business and it is appropriate for such a firm to take out assurance policies on the lives of its partners and directors and, similarly, *permanent health insurance* to guard against their ill-health. The banks can also advise about *pension schemes* for the self-employed, company directors and employees.

15.7   Accounting

The banks have been able to make use of the surplus capacity of their computer systems by offering their business customers a range of accounting services, including payroll, sales and purchases ledger accounting and data service.

(a) **Payroll**

This is a service for the calculation of weekly and monthly pay for a firm's employees and pensioners. The business customer supplies a specialist department or subsidiary company of the bank with the information required for the calculation of its employees' pay; pay advices are calculated and printed, together with a printout for the firm's own use containing details of each individual's pay and a summary of the payroll. Where employees receive their pay in cash, an analysis is printed showing the exact quantities of different denomination notes and coin that will be needed to make up the pay envelopes; where employees require cheques, these can be printed and placed with pay advices; where bank giro credits are used, the bank's payroll department is given details of each employee's bank account so that the credits can be prepared and despatched. An additional service is that of producing the required information for submission to the Inland Revenue.

The benefit to a business using the service is that its payroll staff costs and time are considerably reduced although, of course, the saving must be balanced against the charge made by the bank for its services.

(b) **Sales and purchases ledger accounting**

Business customers can avail themselves of the banks' service of maintaining their sales and purchases ledgers: these contain the firm's own accounts recording transactions with its customers and suppliers. The *sales ledger* contains the accounts of debtors—firms and individuals that owe money to the business—and transactions record the value of goods sold on credit, cash and cheques received and allowances made for goods returned. The *purchases ledger* contains the accounts of creditors—firms and individuals that the business owes money to; transactions therein record purchases of goods on credit, payments made and allowances given for returned goods. The bank's computer services deal with keeping the accounts, recording transactions and, in the case of the sales ledger, preparing statements for sending out to customers; the business itself receives regular printouts of the balances of accounts within the ledgers. The service takes over a chore that is for any business a time- and expense-consuming necessity and gives the firm more freedom to concentrate on manufacturing and selling its products.

Factoring (see Unit 15.2(g)) could be combined with the accounting service as a means of providing a method of finance.

(c) Data service

Where a business operates its own computer system the bank can provide details of transactions passing through its account in the form of magnetic tape rather than conventional printed statements. This cuts down on paperwork by saving the bank from having to prepare normal statements from magnetic tape and sending them to the firm, where the details would then have to be input into its own computer system.

Other data services offered by the banks to their business customers include assistance with stock controls, financial assessments of company projects and the maintenance of registers of shareholders.

15.8 Advisory Services

Some of the banks have in recent years concentrated on providing an advisory service to meet the needs for financial and management advice experienced by small and medium-sized businesses. The specialist managers appointed by the bank to run this service provide advice and guidance on a range of financial planning and control systems such as budgeting, costing, pricing, capital investment appraisal, cash flow forecasting and current asset management. They also advise on business strategy such as capital raising and reorganization, takeover bids for other firms and mergers with, and acquisitions of, other companies.

With larger companies, the merchant bank subsidiary of the bank can give advice on business strategy (see Unit 5.3).

An advisory service provided mainly for businesses (but also for personal customers) is that of the *status inquiry*. This consists of a short report on a customer's financial standing and is given only to another bank. Thus if a customer is asked to supply a financial reference before being allowed to purchase goods on credit, he may give the name of his bank; the supplier will then ask his own bank to take up the reference. Similarly, a business customer allowing credit to his own clients may ask for bank references and request his bank to take them up, usually inquiring if the customer in question may be 'considered good for £x (the amount involved)' or 'considered good for £x per month for y months (the time period)'. The bank's reply would seem vague to someone unused to the jargon but is clear enough to the inquirer; it may say 'considered good for your figures and purpose' where the customer is considered creditworthy to the extent indicated or 'we cannot speak for your figures' where the bank does not regard the customer as satisfactory.

The range of services offered by a large bank for its business customers goes far beyond the basic banking services of paying in, drawing out and granting overdraft facilities. The owner of a business, particularly of a small business, meets many financial and management problems and the bank manager is often the only adviser to whom he can turn.

15.9   Questions

1. List and briefly describe the main services offered by the banks to business customers.

2. What forms of finance do the major banking groups in the UK provide to industry?

(The Institute of Bankers)

Banking Services for the Exporter and Importer

16.1 Introduction

For a trading nation such as Britain—a small industrialized country with a large population and few major reserves of natural resources—international trade is especially important. Many manufacturers are tempted to ignore world markets and to concentrate on selling in the home trade: sooner or later, however, an inquiry will be received from abroad and the firm will probably go to its bank to seek advice. Whenever a business trades abroad its bank is involved at some stage: handling the documentation, making or receiving payments, granting advances—perhaps at concessionary rates of interest—or interpreting the exchange control regulations. In this Unit we shall discuss the role of the banks in assisting businessmen engaged in trading overseas, beginning with the services offered to exporters and the documentation and procedures involved in the export trade.

16.2 Services for the Exporter

All the major banks have overseas departments that are able to provide information both to established exporters and to those who are considering exporting their products for the first time.

(a) Trade inquiries

Within an overseas department will be a specialist department in contact with bank branches established overseas and correspondent banks, which can assist customers to find potential markets for export goods and which can effect introductions to overseas buyers and agents.

(b) Credit information

In a similar way to the operation of the bank-to-bank status inquiry service within a country (see Unit 15.8), banks are able to obtain up-to-date credit information on buyers and agents anywhere in the world.

(c) Economic and political reports

Most large banks prepare reports on a wide range of countries and keep them regularly updated to show the current political and economic background.

Information is often included on import restrictions and other developments likely to be of interest to UK exporters. In particular, specialist information is usually available on trading groups such as the European Economic Community and the European Free Trade Association.

(d) Travel services
As well as providing foreign currency, travellers' cheques and assistance with passports and visas (see Unit 14.6), most banks can issue an exporter travelling abroad with *letters of introduction*. These are addressed to overseas correspondent banks in the countries that he plans to visit, requesting them to give assistance by way of information and advice about possible buyers of his goods and about local trading terms and conditions.

(e) UK exchange control regulations

There are no restrictions on the transfer of funds between United Kingdom residents and residents of the Scheduled Territories (see Unit 4.7). When goods are exported to countries outside the Scheduled Territories there should be no exchange control difficulties provided that the payment is to be made in a manner acceptable to the Bank of England. Special approval is required from the Bank of England in certain circumstances:

(i) when payment is to be deferred beyond six months from the date of shipment on a contract not covered by an ECGD policy (see Unit 16.11);

(ii) when goods are exported free of payment; or

(iii) when goods are exported on a consignment basis or on hire.

At the time of writing Bank of England approval is also required when goods are exported to Rhodesia; this requirement exists because of the political situation in that country.

To assist exporters, details of United Kingdom exchange control regulations are set out in a leaflet issued by HM Treasury entitled *Notice to Exporters*. All banks are able to advise both exporters and importers on the regulations and to assist with the completion of the necessary forms where reference to the Bank of England is required.

(f) Forward foreign exchange

Where payment for exporting goods is made in a foreign currency rather than in sterling, there is a danger that exchange rate fluctuations occurring between the date of shipment and the date of payment may reduce the exporter's profit or even turn the transaction into a loss. This problem can be overcome by the trader's entering into a *forward foreign exchange contract* with his bank. The essence of such a contract is that the bank agrees to buy the foreign currency from the exporter at the date of payment at a certain fixed exchange rate; thus whatever happens to exchange rates in the interim, he always knows how much he will receive. The risk of changes in the exchange rates can thus be removed from the businessman's calculations, while the bank covers its own position by matching deals.

16.3   Terms of the Contract

When exporters are arranging to sell goods to a customer overseas, the terms of the contract between them must be agreed. They always specify the following:

(i) **Goods:** a full description of the items to be supplied including the quantity and quality.

(ii) **Method of payment** (see Units 16.5–16.9).

(iii) **Insurance and shipping terms:** these will establish who is to be responsible for arranging and paying for the insurance (including stating the risks to be covered) and freight charges. The more common terms are:

CIF (cost, insurance and freight): this means that the exporter's price includes the cost of the goods together with all charges incurred up to delivery of the goods at the port or airport named in the contract; thus the exporter is responsible for arranging and paying for insurance and freight to the named destination.

C & F (cost and freight): here the exporter's price includes the cost of the goods together with freight charges, but he is not responsible for insurance, this being arranged and paid for by the purchaser.

FOB (free on board): the exporter is responsible only for arranging to put the goods on board the carrying vessel at the port of loading and so his price consists of the cost of goods together with any insurance and transport costs incurred in getting them to the port and loading them on the ship. Arrangement of and payment for shipping and insurance is thereafter the responsibility of the buyer.

It is important for a banker to understand these different terms of trade so that he may know what documents to expect when dealing with contracts having different terms. International rules have been established for the uniform interpretation of the principal delivery terms used in overseas trading contracts: these are known as *Incoterms* and are published by the International Chamber of Commerce.

16.4 Documents of International Trade

Documents are important in international trade because they control the movement of goods; in some cases, they are the legal title to the goods. It is important that the correct documents should be in the right place at the right time and, in order to speed delivery of the goods and subsequent payment, that they should all be correctly completed. A seemingly minor discrepancy in the documentation will almost certainly lead to a delay in receiving payment.

In the rest of this Unit we shall describe the information to be found on the basic documents of international trade and list the documents that are required when a contract specifies some of the more common terms mentioned in Unit 16.3.

(*a*) **Invoices**
An invoice (Fig. 16.1) is prepared by the seller of the goods and contains the following details:

    (i) name and address of the seller;
    (ii) name and address of the buyer;
    (iii) date of the invoice;
    (iv) a description of the goods together with the price;
    (v) details of the way in which the goods are packed—for instance, whether

BRITISH OVERSEAS ENGINEERING & CREDIT COMPANY LIMITED

WALKER HOUSE,
87 QUEEN VICTORIA STREET,
LONDON, EC4V 4AP

TELEPHONE
01-236 6544

TELEGRAMS
BOCONCORP LONDON TELEX

CABLES
BOCONCORP LONDON EC4

LONDON TELEX 887305

CODES
ACME BENTLEY

BOECC

MESSRS.   Lafco S.A.C.I.F.,
Buenos Aires,
Argentina.

1st August   19 77

INVOICE No.
1234/7891/ARG

Shipped for your account and risk from LONDON   to BUENOS AIRES

per S. S.
on.......... CORRIENTES II

Shipping Marks: LAFCO
BUENOS AIRES
ARGENTINA
7891/ARG
NOS: 1-2

Two cases containing the following:

Drake MK II Pulveriser. Serial No: 65432

Price F.O.B. London: £25,000.00

Consular Fees: 750.00

Total Price F.O.B. London: £25,750.00

SPECIMEN

We declare under oath that all the information
contained in this invoice is true and correct
and that the prices indicated are those really
paid. We further declare that there are no
agreements that allow alterations to the said
prices.

We hereby certify that this invoice is authentic and in accordance with
our books, also that the goods are of United Kingdom   origin.

For and on behalf of
BRITISH OVERSEAS ENGINEERING & CREDIT COMPANY LTD.

G.A. Youthed — General Manager Commercial

Fig. 16.1   An invoice

they are in crates, cases or drums—and shipping marks stamped or written on the packages;

(vi) the terms of sale (CIF, C & F, FOB and so forth); the charges for insurance and freight, if applicable, may also be detailed on the invoices;

(vii) if applicable, details of import licences and exchange permits required by the importing country; and

(viii) the total amount payable.

The details of the invoice should tie up with the contract of sale; if a documentary letter of credit (see Unit 16.7) has been opened, the invoice should conform exactly with its terms. Several copies of the invoice are normally required for the use of the buyer, HM Customs and the importing authorities abroad. Some countries may require a *certified invoice* or *certificate of origin* to confirm that the goods come from a particular country; in Britain certain Chambers of Commerce are authorized by the Department of Trade to make declarations of origin (see Fig. 16.2).

(b) **Bills of lading**

Where goods are transported by ship, the bill of lading (Fig. 16.3) is one of the most important documents. Depending on the terms of the contract, either the exporter or the overseas importer may arrange with a shipping company for the carriage of the goods. The bill of lading is then issued by the shipping company as a receipt for the goods and forms the evidence of a contract of carriage. It is especially important because it is also the document of title to the goods, that is, the legal holder of the bill is also the legal owner of the goods, subject to the payment of any freight charges due.

Bills of lading are normally 'clean' in that they do not bear any clause declaring a defective condition of the goods; a 'foul' or 'dirty' bill may bear a clause such as 'drums leaking' or 'one case damaged'.

(c) **Insurance documents**

Goods for export should always be covered by adequate insurance from the time they leave the factory to the time the buyer takes delivery. The terms of the contract establish whose is the responsibility for arranging and paying for insurance during transportation. The documents consist of either the insurance policy itself or, more likely, a certificate of insurance, and the details appearing on them include:

(i) the name and signature of the insurance company;

(ii) the name of the insured;

(iii) where applicable, the endorsement of the insured so that the right to claim under the policy may be transferred (for instance, the exporter might take out a policy but it could be the importer who makes any claim);

(iv) a description of the risks covered and the sum insured;

(v) a description of the goods together with any packing details; and

(vi) the place where claims are payable together with the name of the agent to whom claims should be directed.

Consigner: (Expéditeur:) British Overseas Engineering & Credit Walker House, Co. Ltd., 87, Queen Victoria Street, London E.C.4.	**C** 878571
Consignee: (Destinataire:) Lafco S.A.C.I.F., Buenos Aires, Argentina.	**EUROPEAN COMMUNITIES** (Communautes Europeennes)
Consignment by: (Expédition prévue par:) Sea. MV CORRIENTES II	**CERTIFICATE OF ORIGIN** (Certificat d'origine)
	CITY OF WESTMINSTER CHAMBER OF COMMERCE

THE UNDERSIGNED AUTHORITY certifies that the goods shown below
(L'AUTORITE SOUSSIGNEE certifie que les marchandises désignées ci-dessous)

Serial No.	Packages		Description of goods	Weight (1)	
	Number and kind	Marks and numbers		gross	net
	Two Cases	LAFCO Buenos Aires Argentina 7891/ARG Nos.1-2	One Drake MK II Pulverizer. Serial No: 65432 S P E C I M E N	9000 kilos	8500Kilos

originated in:

(sqnt originaires de:)   EUROPEAN COMMUNITIES –
UNITED KINGDOM

London, 1st August, 197	**City of Westminster Chamber of Commerce**
(Place and date of issue)	(Name, signature and stamp of competent authority)

(1) This entry may, where appropriate, be replaced by others allowing identification of the goods.
DTI/XP/i 107

Fig. 16.2   A certificate of origin

Shipper	B/L No. 1
British Overseas Engineering & Credit Company Limited, Walker House, 87, Queen Victoria Street, London, EC4.	Shippers Ref: F/Agents Ref:

E.L.M.A. LINE

**EMPRESA
LINEAS MARITIMAS ARGENTINAS S.A.
CORRIENTES 389
BUENOS AIRES**

Consignee (if 'Order' state Notify Party)

TO ORDER

AGENTS

**SOUTH AMERICAN PURCHASING
AGENCY LTD.**

Notify Party (ONLY if not stated above: otherwise leave blank)

LAFCO S.A.C.I.F.,
Buenos Aires, Argentina.

**CAP HOUSE 9-12 LONG LANE
LONDON EC1A 9EP**

The vessel's agents at the port of destination are desired to notify the party named of the arrival of the vessel, but it is agreed that no responsibility shall attach to the vessel or owners if there should be any failure to make such notification.

*Local vessel	*From (Local port of loading)			
Ocean vessel CORRIENTES II	Port of Loading Liverpool			
Port of Discharge Buenos Aires	*Final destination (if on-carriage)	Freight payable at Destination	Number of original Bs/L Three	
Marks and Numbers	Number and kind of packages; description of goods and origin		Gross Weight in Kilos	Measurement

Applicable only when document used as a Through Bill of Lading

Argentine Freight Tax instituted by Decree Law No. 6677/63 is payable by Importers

LAFCO
Buenos Aires
Argentine
7891/ARG
Nos. 1 –2

Two Cases said to contain

One Drake MKII
Pulverizer   Serial No.65432

9000kilos

SPECIMEN

THE ABOVE PARTICULARS ARE FURNISHED BY SHIPPERS UNDER ARTICLES III AND IV OF
THE RULES COMPRISING THE SCHEDULE TO THE CARRIAGE OF GOODS BY SEA ACT, 1924.

The shipper must declare the nature and the value of the goods prior to the issue of this Bill of Lading before shipment and insert such particulars therein paying the corresponding additional freight of 3½", 'ad valorem' in consideration of which the carrier shall respond for the total value of the goods. In the event that the value of the goods is not declared by the shipper prior to the issue of this Bill of Lading or that the additional 'ad valorem' freight thereon be not paid, the value of the cargo shall be deemed not to exceed £100 Sterling per package or unit and the shipper expressly agrees that the limit of the carriers' liability shall be £100 Sterling per package or unit in respect of any loss or damage to cargo.

SHIPPED in apparent good order and condition (unless otherwise stated herein) on board the above named Ship either belonging to this Line or to other persons sailing from the above named port on a voyage as described by Clause 5 of reverse hereof always without warranty of customary or advertised dispatch or route the PIECES AND/OR PACKAGES MER-CHANDISE (with leading marks as per margin but all other particulars as per margin unknown) to be carried and delivered subject to all the exceptions, limitations and conditions hereinafter referred to the last page of Discharge or as near thereto as the carrying Vessel may safely get and always lie afloat or not Carrier's option) as agreed in Clauses 10 to 13 of reverse hereof

BRITISH OVERSEAS ENGINEERING
& CREDIT COMPANY LIMITED

ON BEHALF OF SHIPPERS

SUBJECT   TO   ALL   TERMS
EXCEPTIONS AND CONDITIONS
Authorised Signature ON BOTH SIDES HEREOF

IN WITNESS whereof the Master or Agents of the said Ship and its connections have affirmed to the number of Bills of Lading stated above, all of this tenor and date, one of which Bills being accomplished, the others to stand void.

Number of Packages (in words)   TWO

Dated at LONDON

For THE MASTER AND OWNERS
For SOUTH AMERICAN PURCHASING AGENCY LTD.
(AS AGENTS)

Fig. 16.3   A bill of lading

The risks covered by the insurance should agree with those called for by the buyer in the contract.

(d) Air waybill

This takes the place of the bill of lading, when goods are sent by air; but unlike most bills of lading it is not a document of title to the goods, being only an acknowledgement of goods received for despatch. The details appearing on it are similar to those found on a bill of lading.

These four are the basic documents required in international trade: there are others, particularly in connection with trade between countries of the European Economic Community, but they are too specialized to be dealt with in this book.

In a CIF contract the exporter is responsible for providing invoices, the insurance policy or certificate, and a full set of bills of lading marked 'freight paid', the freight charge being his responsibility. A C & F contract would require the exporter to produce invoices and a full set of 'freight paid' bills of lading, insurance being the responsibility of the importer. For an FOB contract the documents required from the exporter are the invoices and a full set of bills of lading evidencing that the goods have been shipped on board the carrying vessel and stating that freight is payable at the destination.

16.5   Methods of Payment in International Trade

The terms of payment and the method by which settlement is to be effected are agreed between the exporter and his customer in their contract. The terms and method of payment required by exporter will depend very much on the previous experience, if any, that he has in the particular market, on his knowledge of the overseas customer and on the latter's financial standing. The main methods of securing payment (starting with the safest) are:

(i) payment in advance;

(ii) payment under a documentary letter of credit;

(iii) documents against payment or acceptance of the exporter's bill of exchange; and

(iv) open account.

We shall discuss these one by one.

16.6   Payment in Advance

This is undoubtedly the safest way to receive payment for exports but buyers are seldom prepared to pay for goods in advance of shipment, other than for small consignments. Any such payment is generally made by the buyer through his bank by means of a bank draft (see Unit 11.9) or by mail or telegraphic transfer (see Unit 11.8) in favour of the exporter.

16.7 Documentary Letter of Credit

After payment in advance this represents the safest and fastest way of obtaining payment for exports as the exporter can personally retain control of the documents of title to the goods until the moment of payment or acceptance of a bill of exchange. The parties to a credit are:

(i) the applicant (usually the buyer), who arranges to open a credit in accordance with the terms of the contract he has made with the beneficiary (usually the seller);

(ii) the beneficiary in whose favour the credit is issued;

(iii) the issuing bank which commits itself in accordance with the applicant's instructions;

(iv) the advising bank which is located in the country of the beneficiary and is usually the issuing bank's correspondent.

Where the terms of the contract call for payment under a credit, the buyer (or *applicant*) applies to his bank (the *issuing bank*) to open a credit in favour of the exporter (the *beneficiary*). Before issuing a credit the bank must make certain of its customer's creditworthiness; if this is satisfactory, the credit is then advised to the exporter through a bank in his own country (the *advising bank*). Under the terms of the credit, the issuing bank undertakes that the seller will be paid for his goods provided he complies with certain stated conditions: these will call for certain documents, such as invoices, bills of lading and insurance documents (depending on the precise responsibility of the exporter) covering the quantity and quality of goods agreed in the contract between the exporter and the overseas buyer. Provided that the documents presented to the advising bank agree exactly with the requirements of the credit, the exporter receives the payment due to him in exchange for the documents. The advising bank sends the documents to the issuing bank by air mail; upon receipt, they are handed to the buyer, who then awaits the arrival of the carrying vessel. When the ship docks, the buyer presents the bills of lading to the representatives of the shipping company and, in discharge of the shipping company's responsibilities under the contract of carriage, receives the goods. Payment for the goods by the buyer to the issuing bank is a matter of arrangement between them and of no concern to the exporter. The settlement between the banks for the amount paid by the issuing bank is carried out through their agency accounts: the issuing bank's account in the records of the advising bank is debited, and the account of the advising bank in the records of the issuing bank is credited.

Besides the advantage of a credit to the exporter, who knows that he will receive payment provided he complies with its terms, there are benefits to the buyer. He knows that payment will only be made by the advising bank when the exact documents specified have been received—as these are the documents of title, then once they are in the hands of the advising bank, it will only be a matter of time before they are sent to him, allowing him to collect the goods.

There is, however, a risk to the issuing bank because the credit only deals in documents and not in goods, so that provided the exporter complies with the terms and conditions of the credit he will be paid even though the crates supposedly containing the goods have been packed with sawdust and old newspapers. A status inquiry by the issuing bank on the exporter is therefore essential.

An example of a simplified transaction will show the sequence of events (Fig. 16.4):

(i) ABC Engineering Ltd. of London have entered into a CIF contract with XYZ Import Co. Ltd. of New Zealand to supply certain specialized machinery. The contract stipulates that payment is to be made under the terms of a documentary letter of credit, the required documents being:

1. invoice in triplicate;
2. certificate of origin issued by a Chamber of Commerce;
3. a full set of clean, on-board bills of lading made out to order and endorsed in blank, marked 'freight paid' and 'notify XYZ Import Co. Ltd.';
4. insurance policy or certificate in duplicate covering marine and war risks to the buyer's warehouse for invoice value of the goods, plus 10 per cent.

(ii) The machinery is manufactured by ABC Ltd.

(iii) Meanwhile the XYZ Co. Ltd. have asked their bank, the North and South Bank, to open a credit in favour of ABC Ltd. As their customers are creditworthy, the bank instructs its correspondent bank in London, National Barllands, to advise a credit in favour of ABC Ltd. for the invoice value (which will include insurance and freight charges).

(iv) Insurance and shipment details for the voyage are arranged by ABC Ltd.; the machinery is delivered to the shipping company and the freight charges paid. Once the goods are loaded, the shipping company issues a set of shipped bills of lading marked 'freight paid' and ABC Ltd. must ensure that the other details comply with the terms of the contract and the requirements of the credit.

(v) ABC Ltd. now presents the documents at the branch of National Barllands specified in the credit and, provided they agree exactly with the requirements of the credit, receives payment.

(vi) Meanwhile the goods are on their way to New Zealand by sea and the London bank sends the documents to the North and South Bank by air mail.

(vii) The North and South Bank in New Zealand releases the documents of title to their customers XYZ Ltd. and, when the ship arrives, upon presentation of a signed copy of the bill of lading to the representative of the shipping company, the goods may be taken away.

(ix) The banks involved then effect book-keeping transfers between themselves to record the transaction and, at the North and South Bank, the account of XYZ Ltd. is debited with the amount involved.

In this example the payment was made immediately upon presentation of the

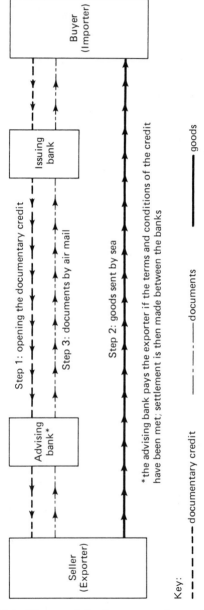

Fig. 16.4   The use of the documentary letter of credit

correct documents—the credit was *at sight*. It could equally well have been an *acceptance credit*: this would have meant that, instead of making an immediate payment, National Barllands Bank would have been authorized to accept a bill of exchange drawn by ABC Ltd. for a certain *tenor* or time period as specified in the credit. This bill could then have been held by ABC Ltd. until maturity or, if the company needed the money urgently, could have been discounted and the full value, less discount, received quickly.

Documentary letters of credit may be of two types: revocable or irrevocable. A *revocable credit* gives no undertaking to the exporter that payment will actually be made or a bill of exchange accepted because it may be cancelled or amended at any time without the prior knowledge of the exporter. An *irrevocable credit* does not suffer from this disadvantage and consequently is more often specified in contracts: under such a credit, the issuing bank gives its irrevocable undertaking to make the payment if all the terms of the credit are met, and can only amend or cancel the credit with the consent of all parties.

An irrevocable documentary letter of credit may be confirmed or unconfirmed. Where it is *confirmed*, besides having the irrevocable undertaking of the issuing bank, it also has the irrevocable undertaking of the advising bank in the exporter's country to make the payment under the terms of the credit. An *unconfirmed* credit still carries the issuing bank's irrevocable undertaking but the advising bank does not add its own, merely informing the beneficiary of the terms and conditions of the credit. From the exporter's point of view, the best payment method under a credit is by means of a confirmed, irrevocable documentary letter of credit because it contains the irrevocable undertaking of two banks, one of which is in his own country, and the terms of the credit cannot be altered without his knowledge; provided he complies with all the terms, he knows that he will either be paid or have his bill of exchange accepted.

Most documentary letters of credit are subjected to international 'rules' of interpretation issued by the International Chamber of Commerce and known as *Uniform Customs and Practice for Documentary Credits.*

16.8   Documents Against Payment or Acceptance

Where it is not possible in a contract between exporter and importer to agree that payment should be made under a documentary letter of credit, an alternative is to send the documents on a *collection* basis. Using this method the exporter ships the goods and arranges with his bank for the documents (invoices, bills of lading and, if appropriate, the insurance policy or certificate), together with a bill of exchange to be despatched to an appropriate overseas correspondent bank. Depending on the instructions from the exporter and the terms of his contract with the buyer, the documents are only released upon either payment or acceptance of the bill or exchange by the importer (Fig. 16.5).

If the documents-against-payment method is used, the exporter is able to retain a measure of control over his goods as he knows that the documents of

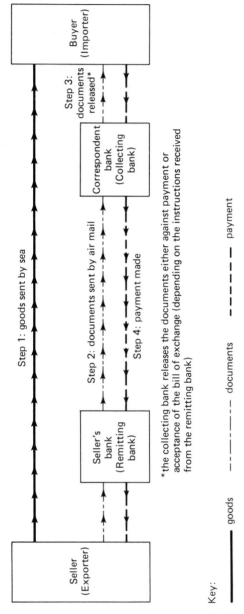

Fig. 16.5　Documents against payment or acceptance of a bill of exchange

title will not be released by the overseas bank until payment has been made. When documents are released against acceptance of a bill the exporter loses control of his goods and relies on the creditworthiness and integrity of his overseas customer to pay on the due date. Both methods have the advantage that the documents, and therefore the title to the goods, remain under the control of the banking system until either the bill is accepted or payment is made. However, if the buyer cannot pay or refuses to accept the bill, the exporter may be involved in considerable time and expense in recovering his goods; with an irrevocable documentary letter of credit, by contrast, the exporter knows that, providing he complies with the terms of the credit, he will receive his payment or have his bill accepted.

International rules also apply to documents of payment or acceptance and are known as the *Uniform Rules for Collections.*

16.9 Open Account

Where an exporter knows that he is dealing with a first-class overseas buyer he may be prepared to ship goods on an open account basis: this means that he simply sends the documents of title direct to the buyer and requests payment by a certain date. This is similar to the way in which credit sales are made between businessmen within the same country: provided their credit is considered satisfactory, goods are supplied and a regular statement of account sent out, payment being made by cheque. The only differences in international trade are that the distances involved are greater, making it more difficult to chase up any bad payers, and that an overseas buyer is more likely to settle his account by means of mail transfer or bank draft.

Very often the open account basis of international trade is forced on exporters because of short sea journeys which do not give time to process documents so as to enable more secure methods of payment to be used; bills of lading that do not constitute a transferable document of title are now being issued by shipping companies for goods on such short journeys. Similarly, with the increasing use of air and road transport (where there is no equivalent of a bill of lading to give the holder a legal title to the goods) exporting on open account is becoming more common.

16.10 Financial Problems in Exporting

There are two main financial problems for the exporter: the risk of non-payment, and the provision of finance.

The problems of collecting debts in the export trade can be troublesome. It is not as easy to telephone an overseas customer about non-payment as it is a customer in the home country, it is far less easy to visit a debtor with an overdue account and, if it should come to taking a customer to court, the difficulties are very great indeed.

Exports often have to be sold on extended credit and the terms have to be better than those offered by competitors. Compared with credit transactions in inland trade, which are usually settled within one or two months, the credit offered to export customers usually needs to be between three and six months. For large-scale capital projects up to five years' credit, or even longer, may need to be offered.

Solutions of both the main financial problems of the exporter are available: a Government department provides credit insurance to exporters (see Unit 16.11) and the banks offer special finance facilities, sometimes at reduced rates of interest (discussed in Units 16.12(*d*) and 16.12 (*e*)).

16.11   Credit Insurance

A British Government department called the *Export Credits Guarantee Department* (ECGD) assists exporters of both goods and services by providing a special type of insurance covering two main areas of risk: the creditworthiness of overseas buyers, and the economic and political risks arising from events in overseas countries. The department does not cover risks normally dealt with by commercial insurers, such as fire and marine risks.

ECGD classifies the export trade into two broad categories:

(i) trade of a repetitive nature involving standard or near-standard goods, and

(ii) projects and large capital goods business of a non-repetitive nature, usually of high value and involving lengthy credit terms.

Cover for the first category is provided on a 'comprehensive' basis: the exporter must offer for cover all or most of his export business on credit terms of up to six months for at least a year in both good and bad markets. This is known as the *Comprehensive Short Term Guarantee*. Where credit terms are longer than six months but not more than five years with standard goods, the business can still be insured under a comprehensive policy but an 'extended terms' endorsement is required.

The second category of export trade is not suited to the comprehensive treatment and specific policies are negotiated for each contract. Cover for this specific insurance is given in two main ways. In the case of *Supplier Credit*, the manufacturer sells on credit (which may be long-term) and ECGD will insure him against certain risks. With *buyer credit* the exporter receives a prompt payment from his overseas customer, the cash for which is provided by a loan from a British bank; the loan is by instalments, repayment being guaranteed to the bank by ECGD.

The major risks covered under the most widely used policy, the Comprehensive Short Term Guarantee, are:

(i) 90 per cent of the loss resulting from the insolvency of the buyer or the buyer's failure to pay for goods which he has accepted within six months of the due date;

(ii) 90 per cent of the loss that remains after the policyholder has borne the first 20 per cent of the loss himself, in the event of the buyer's failure or refusal to accept goods which have been despatched to him;

(iii) 90 per cent (if the cause of the loss occurs before shipment) and 95 per cent (if the cause of loss occurs after shipment) of losses resulting from war, political events, withdrawal of licences, export/import restrictions, etc.

Claims are payable at the following times:

For insolvency of the buyer: immediately upon proof of insolvency.

For failure to pay for accepted goods: six months after the due date of payment

For failure or refusal to accept goods: one month after resale.

For other causes: four months after the due date of payment or date of event causing the loss.

16.12 Finance for Exports

Several methods of finance are used by the banks to assist their exporting customers and a number of these involve ECGD giving a direct guarantee to a bank.

(*a*) Advances against shipping documents

Most banks are prepared to grant overdraft facilities to customers who export on credit terms of up to six months. Where the bank is handling the shipping documents by passing them to a correspondent overseas bank for collection, it is usually prepared to grant an advance based on an agreed percentage of outstanding collections pending receipt of the proceeds. In some cases acceptable security for the advance would be the shipping documents which give control of the goods, together with bills of exchange in course of collection. A bank may require an exporter to insure his overseas trade with ECGD (if he does not do so already) and to assign directly to it any benefits payable under the policy.

(*b*) Negotiation of bills of exchange

Banks are usually willing to *negotiate* (discount) sight bills of exchange or bills maturing within six months, whether denominated in sterling or in a foreign currency. The customer is credited with the sterling amount, less discount, and the bank collects the proceeds of the bill when it becomes payable. The bank usually retains a 'right of recourse' to debit the customer's account with the full amount in the event of non-payment.

(*c*) Documentary letter of credit

Provided the exporter complies with the terms of a documentary letter of credit, he may obtain either an immediate payment or acceptance of his bill of exchange by the advising bank (see Unit 16.7). In the latter case, after acceptance of the bill, the exporter may arrange with a discount house to have the bill discounted at the rate of ruling for that particular type of accepted bill (see Unit 7.3), and thus he can receive cash almost immediately.

(d) ECGD-backed short-term finance

Where an exporter has held an ECGD Comprehensive Short Term Guarantee for at least twelve months, he may be able to obtain finance from his bank at a concessionary rate of interest. There are two schemes, both available to assist exporters of consumer and light engineering goods: 'bills or notes' and 'open account'. For both of these the exporter must arrange with ECGD for the issue of a Banker's Guarantee covering the bank for 100 per cent of the finance made available. Interest on the advance is calculated at the concessionary rate of 0.5 per cent over base rate on a day-to-day basis: this compares with between 2 and 4 per cent over base rate for other advances.

Bills or notes scheme. As the exporter ships his goods, he gives the bank bills of exchange drawn on the buyer or the buyer's promissory notes, together with invoices and documents evidencing shipment. The bank then makes finance available to the extent of 100 per cent of the face value of the bills or notes. The bank subsequently handles the documents on a collection basis (see Unit 16.8) and receives the cash proceeds from the buyer.

Open account scheme. This is a little different: when goods are exported in this way (see Unit 16.9) the payment is made by the buyer direct to the exporter. ECGD is therefore guaranteeing a loan from the bank to its customer in respect of the transaction and the payment is not collected by the bank as it is under the bills or notes scheme. When the exporter wishes to borrow against the guarantee he produces to the bank a copy invoice and evidence of shipment. The finance is made available and, at the same time, the exporter gives the bank his own promissory note undertaking to repay the loan on a certain date, usually the last day of the month in which payment is due to him from the overseas buyer. Thus the sale proceeds are received by the exporter direct from his customer, and at the end of each month he repays the bank for the finance provided against the promissory notes. In the event of a payment not being received, the exporter would look to his ECGD guarantee to reimburse him.

(e) ECGD-backed medium-term finance

Where export credit is given for two years or more a finance scheme for exporters can be linked to an ECGD extended-terms or specific policy: such finance would also be provided at concessionary rates of interest. Unlike the short-term schemes already mentioned, however, each contract is considered separately and in approved cases ECGD issues a guarantee in favour of a bank. This covers the bank fully against non-receipt of payment three months after the due date.

An alternative arrangement to such supplier credit is buyer credit where finance is provided direct to the overseas customer. Under the scheme, he negotiates a financial agreement with the supplier's bank, so that he can borrow money to enable him to enter into a cash contract with the exporter. Payment is made to the exporter against documentation by the lending bank purchasing promissory notes made by the borrower. As these promissory notes fall due the proceeds are collected by the bank in repayment of its loan. This form of credit is only available for contracts valued at £1 million or more.

There are other, more specialized, forms of finance available involving the assistance of ECGD. These include *pre-shipment finance* to assist in the provision of working capital, and *buyer lines of credit*, which resemble buyer credit in that they take the form of a loan made by a British bank to an overseas borrower, but instead of being linked to a single contract, they may be used to finance the supply of a variety of British goods and services falling within specified groups of industrial products.

(*f*) Factoring
Nearly all the major banks offer a factoring service (see Unit 15.2(*g*)) and some have special schemes tailored to meet the needs of exporters. The amount of finance available is normally based on a certain percentage of sales; if an overseas customer should not pay his debt, the factor usually takes steps to recover it.

16.13   Services for Importers

Most of the material we have considered so far in this Unit relates to exports. While the banks do much to assist the exporter because of the importance of exports to Britain, they also provide a range of services for importers. These can be assisted to find overseas sources of supply and the names of potential suppliers, using information gathered from overseas branches and correspondent banks. In addition the banks are able to obtain status reports on overseas suppliers: this ensures that an importer who considers entering into an overseas contract can ascertain beforehand whether the supplier is of sufficient standing and creditworthiness to carry out his side of the contract and supply the goods required.

Where importing is concerned, the banks are most likely to be involved in handling payments. The methods of payment are the same as for exports except, of course, that the money flows in the opposite direction. An importer may request his bank to issue a documentary letter of credit (see Unit 16.7) in favour of an overseas supplier: the bank will be particularly concerned to ensure that its customer is sufficiently creditworthy for the commitment. Where other methods of payment are used, the bank may receive documents of title from overseas correspondent banks relating to goods being imported, for release against payment or acceptance of a bill of exchange. Where an importer is buying goods on open account (see Unit 16.9) the bank will be involved in making mail or telegraphic transfers to overseas suppliers. A bank's foreign department advises its importer customers on United Kingdom exchange control regulations and import controls, and the requirements for import licences and documentation.

An importer is almost always required to pay his supplier in a currency other than sterling: if the exchange rates between sterling and the foreign currency alter during the period between the date of contract and the date of payment, a potentially profitable contract could turn into a loss-maker. A bank is able to provide a means of eliminating this risk by entering into a forward foreign exchange contract with its customer (see Unit 16.2(*f*)). Such a contract may be taken out by either an exporter or an importer wherever payment is to be received or made in a currency other than sterling, but is more likely to be used by importers. The benefits of a forward foreign exchange contract are that the trader can eliminate the risk from future exchange rates fluctuations and he can calculate the exact sterling value of an international trading transaction even though the payment will be received or made at some time in the future in a foreign currency.

16.14   Questions

1. Your customer, J. Smith (Manufacturing) Ltd., has received a first export order. Describe to him the main methods that might be used for receiving a payment from overseas.

2. What are the main financial problems facing an exporter? How are these solved in Britain?

3. What advisory services can a bank offer to its exporting and importing customers?

4. Describe the services offered by ECGD.

5. Describe the details to be found on (i) an invoice, (ii) a bill of lading, and (iii) an insurance policy or certificate.

Unit Seventeen

Bank Lending

17.1 Introduction

In Unit 1.1 we said that one of the basic functions of a bank is the lending of surplus deposits to those who wish to borrow. For most customers, both personal and business, the banks represent one of the cheapest and most flexible sources of finance available; for the small business in particular, the bank is often the only source of advice and additional funds. The banks' lending policies have to operate in accordance with the Bank of England's qualitative directives and other controls (see Unit 4.9) while at the same time adequate reserve asset ratios and cash in the tills must be maintained. During periods when the supplementary special deposits scheme operates, the banks must bear in mind the fact that each new advance granted necessitates the buying-in of additional deposits which may result in them exceeding their guidelines.

Regulated agreements. The Consumer Credit Act 1974 seeks to control these agreements, which can be defined as loans to the non-corporate sector not exceeding £5 000. In particular, the Act prohibits canvassing for a regulated agreement outside what are called 'trade premises' without having received a prior invitation for that purpose. It is not unusual for a bank manager to visit his customer at his home and chance meetings occur on many a social occasion, the Act means that the manager would commit an offence if the question of credit were discussed in these circumstances. However, the Act recognizes the continuous nature of a bank manager's relationship with his customer and probably no offence would be committed if the manager 'solicited' an agreement enabling his customer to overdraw on current account. Thus, to agree overdraft facilities on current account with an existing customer at the golf club is permissible under the Act, but to arrange a new personal loan with the same customer is not. The trade premises referred to in the Act can be either those of the banker or his customer. This means that there is no problem if the discussion with the customer takes place inside the bank, and equally no difficulty if the conversation is held in the customer's office.

Ultimately a considerable amount of documentation will be required for regulated agreements but at the time of writing the regulations have not yet been drafted.

17.2 The Basic Questions

The bank manager faced with a request for loan or overdraft facilities must always remember the four basic questions:

(i) how much does the customer want to borrow?
(ii) what does he want it for?
(iii) how long does he want it for?
(iv) how is it to be repaid?

None of these questions mentions security for an advance: the question of security is a secondary one, and is discussed in detail in Units 17.4–17.9.

We shall consider each of the basic questions in turn.

(a) How much?
Among the things the manager should bear in mind are the customer's own resources and whether the bank is being asked to lend too much in comparison with these resources: most managers agree that if the customer has a reasonable amount of his own money invested in the project he will have plenty of incentive to see it through to a profitable conclusion. Although no hard and fast rules can be laid down it is often thought that the bank should not have more invested in the business or project than the customer. This rule does not necessarily apply to personal borrowing, but some contribution from the customer is still required. When a personal loan is being granted to buy goods, the manager must bear in mind any current Government restrictions: these usually take the form of specifying a minimum deposit and a maximum repayment period.

'Jackson, could you adopt a more suitable expression?'

Above all, the manager should look at the proposition, check any figures given and attempt to see that the bank advance will fit into the scheme and that the amount being requested is sufficient to carry out the project. If the advance is inadequate the manager may later find himself in the difficult position of having to lend more money to protect previous lending.

(b) What for?

Naturally a lender of money is entitled to know the purpose for which the advance is required. A manager must bear in mind Bank of England qualitative directives (see Unit 4.9(a)) and the purpose of the advance should also be within the terms of the bank's own policy. For personal advances the purpose is usually easy to understand—for example, to buy a car—but for companies the proposition may form part of a complex scheme which the manager needs to understand and assess.

(c) How long for?

Most of the deposits of a bank are repayable either on demand or at seven days' notice. It makes commercial sense that where the sources of advances are repayable at such short notice, the lending should similarly be repayable at short notice. Technically all bank overdrafts and loans, except for medium-term loans, are repayable on demand. In practice it is not possible to call in advances at such short notice and provided a customer 'plays ball' with his bank, financing arrangements are not withdrawn without agreement.

Advances for capital expenditure, such as the purchase of a car or a piece of machinery, are usually arranged on a loan or personal loan account. Such advances are required to be repaid within an agreed period of time; a manager always expects the borrowing to be repaid well before the equipment becomes due for disposal, and on certain goods Government controls fix a maximum repayment period. Where additional machinery is being purchased for a business, the manager would expect to see increased cash flowing into the bank account. For personal borrowing, such as for the purchase of furniture or central heating or finance for a holiday, the repayment terms are agreed at the time of granting the advance.

Businesses often require working capital finance to help them over the period between commencing to manufacture their product and receiving cash from their customer. During this time they have to buy raw materials and to pay other costs involved in the manufacturing process such as wages, factory rent and rates, heating and lighting, together with the expenses involved in selling the goods; even when the goods are sold, payment is not received instantly. The length of time it takes to start with cash, go through the manufacturing and selling processes and, when payment is received, return to cash again is known as the *working capital cycle*. Banks are prepared to assist approved customers with finance for working capital and this is usually done by placing a 'limit' on the current account and permitting an overdraft up to this limit. Some businesses, such as those concerned with agriculture, are seasonal and require working capital only at certain times of the year; others require the same facilities throughout the year for a number of years.

(d) How is it to be repaid?

The repayment of every advance can only come from the customer's future earnings. Where an individual wishes to borrow by way of a personal loan, perhaps in order to buy a car, repayments must come each month from his wages or salary. In order to assess his proposition the manager asks for details of his earnings and normal outgoings, including any existing mortgage and hire purchase repayments: this information is needed because often a customer asks for a loan without having calculated whether or not he can make the repayments. For businesses too, the advance can only be repaid from future profits (unless the business is to cease trading and sell off its assets to pay its creditors). Therefore the manager needs to ensure that lending the bank's money will increase the profits of the business, after allowing for the interest and charges to be made on the advance. Nowadays a bank manager is trained to consider the future profitability of business customers and it is usual for him to ask the customer for a cash budget and projected profit and loss account and balance sheet for the forthcoming year. A *cash budget* gives a month-by-month estimate of future cash receipts and payments and shows the estimated closing bank balance at each month-end for the period for which it is prepared and can thus provide a guide to the maximum overdraft that is likely to be needed. It relies for its accuracy on the estimates made by the business itself, however; moreover, the longer the period of the budget, the less accurate it will be in the more distant months. A manager soon comes to know those customers that stick to their forecasts and those that produce a budget simply to keep him happy. The *projected profit and loss account* and *balance sheet* for a future accounting period incorporate much of the information contained in the cash budget and also show the estimates of gross and net profits; these too may be used to assess the future profitability of the Business. Unit 18 gives a detailed description of customers' accounts and their interpretation.

Where security is taken it should never be looked upon as the source of repayment, but only as something to fall back on if the expected source of repayment should fail.

17.3   The Customer

There is one highly variable factor in any lending proposition: the customer. One of the tasks of every branch manager is to get to know his customers— very often, though, he only meets those customers who wish to borrow money. To help in the task of knowing the customer all branches maintain reference sheets and files which contain details of past lending, letters received from customers and copies of letters sent out, and summaries of telephone conversations and interviews held; where business customers are concerned the file should contain copies of sets of accounts for past years. The manager refers to all this information prior to an interview with a customer. He takes into account the borrower's health and age and the value of connected family and business accounts held at the branch. With a personal customer he looks particularly to see if any past advances were repaid in accordance with the arrangements made. With a business customer, besides being concerned with the past history of the account, the manager wants to satisfy himself that the customer has experience at his job, has the necessary degree of management ability to run the business and is ploughing back profits into the business. Always, he is looking for a degree of integrity in his customer and must be constantly on the watch for the small percentage of rogues and the somewhat higher percentage of muddlers and eternal optimists that are among the customers of most branches.

17.4 Security for an Advance

Although every lending proposition should 'stand up by itself'—that is, it should be good enough not to need any security—a manager often asks for suitable security from the customer in case the advance should go wrong. There is a wide range of securities to cover a bank loan, and the main types are considered in more detail later in this Unit. There are three main requirements of any security acceptable to a bank:

(i) it should be easy to value;
(ii) it should be easy for the bank to obtain a good legal title;
(iii) it should be readily marketable or realizable.

A fourth requirement, though a less essential one, is that it is useful if the value of the security increases as time goes by.

Security may be either direct or collateral: it is *direct* when it is deposited by the customer to secure his own account; *collateral* security is deposited by another person to secure a customer's account. There are four main securities that are often taken:

(i) a mortgage of stocks and shares;
(ii) an assignment of a life policy;
(iii) a mortgage over land;
(iv) a guarantee.

The first three may be either direct or collateral security, but the fourth is always collateral because it is given by one person to secure another person's account. In each case a legal document has to be signed in the favour of the bank and the customer's or guarantor's signature witnessed. If you work in a bank you should ask the security clerk to let you see the bank's mortgage, assignment and guarantee forms: they look very complicated, being full of legal language and have been developed over many years to cover most eventualities. These forms have to be completed and certain other procedures carried out when taking securities: the bank's regulations are taught on training courses for security clerks and are contained in bank instruction manuals.

A *mortgage* is the conveyance or transfer of an interest in land or other assets as security for a debt. Where a bank takes a *legal mortgage* of property or shares, it has ownership of the property and can sell or do anything it likes with it; under an *equitable mortgage* the bank does not have such powers and the mortgage deed merely establishes a claim on the land or other assets. Upon repayment of the advance the mortgage is reconveyed and ownership of the land or other property reverts to the 'true' owner. A legal mortgage is taken where the bank wants to make absolutely certain that in the event of a forced sale of the security it will receive all the sale proceeds; an equitable mortgage is taken where the bank is prepared to rely less on the security concerned, because it could happen that others might have similar equitable claims on the property.

Whereas a mortgage transfers an interest in assets, an *assignment* is the making over to another person of rights under a contract. For instance, under a contract of life assurance, the beneficiary of the policy has a right to receive a sum of money when a certain event happens (after a certain number of years from the date of the policy, for example) and this is the right that is assigned or transferred to the bank by means of a legal document—that is, the life assurance company is asked to pay the benefits to another party, the bank.

The methods of taking each of the four major types of security are briefly described in turn in Units 17.5–17.9. Although these procedures may sound complicated, they are fully explained to members of the bank's staff who attend a securities course at a training branch. The following details are, therefore, intended only as a general introduction to taking security.

17.5 Stocks and Shares as Security

Stocks and shares that are quoted on a stock exchange are generally acceptable to banks as security for an advance.

(a) Valuation
They are easy to value: the *Financial Times* gives the prices of most of the well-known stocks and shares and the *Stock Exchange Daily List* contains an even wider range.

(b) Obtaining a legal title
It is usually easy to obtain a good legal title over stock exchange securities: the transfer of stocks and shares from one person to another is effected by means of a stock transfer form. The bank has the choice of taking either a legal or an equitable mortgage. In the former case, the customer deposits his share certificate with the bank and signs and has witnessed the bank's form of mortgage, together with a stock transfer form covering the shares in question. The bank then sends the share certificate and the completed stock transfer form to the registrar of the company whose shares are concerned; the registrar thereupon prepares a new share certificate in the name of the bank. Thus the

bank becomes the owner of the shares and receives any dividends paid by the company; these are normally credited to the customer's account. When the advance is repaid and the customer wishes to receive back his security, the bank transfers the shares back into his name by completing another stock transfer form and sending it, together with the certificate in the bank's name, to the company registrar who then prepares another new share certificate.

An equitable mortgage over stocks and shares is somewhat simpler in that, while the customer still deposits his share certificate and completes the bank's form of mortgage together with a stock transfer form, the share certificate is not transferred into the name of the bank but is held in the bank's safe together with the signed mortgage and stock transfer form. If necessary, at a later date, the bank can use the transfer form to put the shares into its own name. Upon repayment of the advance, the equitable mortgage form is filed at the bank and the share certificate returned to the customer (unless he wishes it to be held in safe custody).

Equitable mortgages may also be taken over Premium Savings Bonds, British Savings Bonds, National Savings Certificates and deposits with building societies and savings banks. The bank's mortgage is executed and signed, but an uncompleted but signed withdrawal or encashment form is held also. Such items are less satisfactory as security because the terms under which they are issued do not allow a legal mortgage to be taken over them, and also because it is relatively easy to obtain duplicate bonds, certificates and pass books. It is much more difficult to obtain duplicate share certificates since a registrar will only issue these if an indemnity is signed, usually by a bank (see Unit 14.14).

Most stocks and shares require a stock transfer form to be completed to effect a change of ownership; one type of stocks and shares, however, may be transferred without completion of such a form. These are called *bearer securities* because the certificates do not name the owner but are designated in the name of 'bearer'; such certificates, like bearer cheques or bank notes, are transferred by passing them from one person to another. When a bank takes these as security, a mortgage form is signed to show the customer's intentions, but there is no need for a stock transfer form.

(c) Marketability

Stocks and shares are usually readily marketable and can be sold through a stockbroker, the proceeds being received within a week or so. Some shares, even though they are quoted on a stock exchange, are more difficult to sell: these are usually the shares of small companies for which there is a limited market. The shares of public limited companies that are not quoted on a stock exchange and those of private limited companies are especially difficult to realize, either because the market is limited or, in the case of private companies, because of restrictions placed on the transfer of shares: as security for an advance, therefore, shares in these kinds of company are usually unsatisfactory.

Premium Savings Bonds, British Savings Bonds and so on are marketable in that, if a signed repayment or encashment form is held, this can be completed and sent to the appropriate authority together with the certificates or other documents and the funds will be received within a few days. However, some of these investments may require a period of notice before repayment will be made.

(d) Increase in value

Unfortunately, from the security point of view, stocks and shares fluctuate in value according to supply and demand on the stock market and other factors. This means that a bank must exercise considerable care when shares are deposited as security to ensure that, when stock market prices are falling, the value of the security does not fall below the amount of the advance. One of the tasks of the security clerk is to value shares deposited at regular intervals.

The values of National Savings Certificates and of building society and National Savings Bank deposits increase over a period of time as the benefits of interest are received. Interest may not, however, be added to the value of the security but may instead be paid direct to the customer: this is true of British Savings Bonds and, in some cases, deposits with building societies and finance houses. With Premium Savings Bonds there is always the chance that the customer will win the top prize, pay off the advance from the bank and require investment advice!

17.6   Life Policies as Security

Besides being a good method of long-term saving, most endowment and whole-life policies having a surrender value can be assigned to a bank as security for an advance. Some policies, known as *industrial policies*, are unsuitable as security because they often contain a clause prohibiting assignment: these are similar to endowment and whole-life policies except that they are for much smaller amounts, perhaps £100 or so, and the premiums are collected weekly by the insurance agent.

When a life policy is taken as security it should be read very carefully and the following points noted:

(i) *The name of the assurance company issuing the policy:* banks prefer to take a policy issued by a reputable company. British banks prefer policies of companies domiciled in the United Kingdom; where a company is domiciled overseas there could be problems of obtaining payment in the event of a claim.

(ii) *The type of policy:* there are various types of life policy issued (see Unit 6.9), and the best, from a banking point of view, are endowment or whole-life policies. The former are payable at a certain time in the future or on the earlier death of the assured; the latter are payable on the death of the assured.

(iii) *The names of the life assured and the beneficiary:* with most policies these are the same person, probably the bank customer. However, there are policies where the beneficiary is different from the life assured and it is important that this should be noted, as all interested parties will have to 'join in' the bank's form of assignment.

(iv) *Restrictive clauses:* policies may contain clauses which restrict travel by air to scheduled flights only or exclude dangerous occupations and hobbies.

(v) *'Age admitted':* Before paying a claim on a policy, all assurance companies require proof of the age of the life assured. This is to prevent the assured stating to the company that he is younger than he actually is, which would result in cheaper premiums. It is quite common to find policies where the age is not admitted and this is unsatisfactory from the bank's point of view because the assurance company would not pay out on such a policy in the event of a claim. Where a bank takes a policy as security it is usual to make sure that it is 'age admitted', if necessary by obtaining the customer's birth certificate and sending this to the assurance company for its attention. (In any case, the customer would have to do this at some time before the policy was due for payment.) As this needs the customer's co-operation, it is a good idea to get it done before any borrowing is allowed: once he has taken the advance he will become distinctly less co-operative in helping the bank to complete the security satisfactorily. This also applies to anything else that the customer needs to sign: it is always advisable to get his signature before allowing the borrowing to commence.

We will now consider how well life policies meet the four basic requirements of any security.

(*a*) **Valuation**

Life policies are easy to value: most endowment and whole-life policies, except perhaps in the first year, have a surrender value and this may be ascertained by writing to the assurance company. Naturally, the longer the policy has been in force, the more premiums will have been paid, and the higher will be the surrender value relative to the sum assured. When a policy is used as security for an advance it is usual for the security clerk to write to the assurance company at regular intervals—perhaps every two or three years—and ask for an up-to-date surrender value.

(*b*) **Obtaining a legal title**

It is a relatively simple matter to obtain a good legal title to a life policy, but it should be remembered that all interested parties must join in the assignment. If, for example, a policy is on the life of a husband and in the favour of his wife, then both should join in the assignment form and have their signatures witnessed before the policy can be taken as security for the husband's account. As a life policy is not a negotiable instrument it is necessary to give notice to the assurance company of the assignment in favour of the bank and to ask if there are any prior assignments. Suitable records must be maintained to ensure that the customer continues to pay the premiums on the policy, and from the bank's point of view it is useful if premiums are paid by standing order or direct debit. If the customer stops paying premiums before maturity of the policy the bank must consider whether to make the payments itself and debit the customer's account, thus increasing his indebtedness, or to allow the assurance company to make the policy 'paid up' on the basis of the premiums already paid. As life policies, like all insurances, are contracts of utmost good faith (*uberrimae fidei*) between the assurance company and the life assured, there is a danger that the contract could be rendered invalid, with consequences on the bank's security, if incorrect statements were made by the assured. For example, if the assured at the time of taking out the policy stated that he was in good health and did not disclose the information that he knew himself to be suffering from an incurable disease, the contract could be set aside because he did not state facts about which the assurance company should have been told. The principle of utmost good faith also requires the assured to disclose material facts even though the assurance company has not asked about such facts.

When the customer repays his advance and requests the return of his policy, the bank must reassign its rights back to the original beneficiary.

(c) Marketability
A life policy can always be realized by the bank surrendering it to the assurance company and the proceeds will be received quickly, with a minimum of formality.

(d) Increase in value
Provided the premiums continue to be paid, life policies increase in value as time goes by. In addition, every year or sometimes every two or three years, the assurance company sends out bonus notices to those policyholders who have 'with profits' policies, stating how much of the profits earned by the company in investing its surplus funds has been allocated to the policy. Such bonuses will be paid in addition to the sum assured when a claim is made on the policy or upon maturity.

17.7   Land as Security

A mortgage over land is a fairly complex affair and taking it as security for an advance may involve the bank's customer in the expense of legal fees. A person owning land, which includes anything on it such as houses and other buildings, always holds evidence of his legal title, which in Britain takes one of two forms: either a land certificate or a bundle of deeds and documents. Where a land certificate is held the land is known as *registered land* and the details of the land and its owner are kept at the Land Registry (a central register); otherwise the land is *unregistered land* and no central record is maintained. The system of registering the title to land started in 1925 and eventually the whole country will be registered. As it will be some time before the system is completed, bankers taking a mortgage over land need to know how to obtain a good legal title over both types.

Irrespective of whether the land is registered or not, there are two main classes of title: freehold and leasehold. Where the title is *freehold* there is no time limit on the owner's possession: it is his until he chooses to sell it. With a *leasehold* title, however, the leaseholder pays a sum of money (known as the ground rent) to the freehold owner of the land and holds it in return for a set period of time, often initially either 99 or 999 years but usually less in the case of older property. Apart from the ground rent and any restrictions imposed in the lease, there is little difference from the bank's point of view between a freehold property and a leasehold property with a long lease still to run.

(a) Valuation

Land is much more difficult to value than stocks and shares or life policies: it is the branch manager who usually carries out an inspection and gives an estimated valuation. The figure he decides on may be reasonably accurate if the land includes a building of a standard design, such as a semi-detached house, but his valuation could be considerably inaccurate if it consists of a farm or factory premises. It is rare for a bank to use professional valuers; minor inaccuracies are not of great importance because the security is taken as a form of insurance against possible future difficulties and, when arranging the advance, neither the customer nor the bank wishes to have to realize the security.

(b) Obtaining a legal title

The method of obtaining a legal title over land differs between registered and unregistered land.

(i) **Unregistered land.** The procedure is not very different from the taking of stocks and shares or life policies as security. For unregistered land, the legal title of the owner is evidenced by a bundle of deeds, which when held as security must be kept in the bank's safe. The bank prepares a mortgage form—which may be either legal or equitable (see Unit 17.4)—for signature by the customer, and the completed form is held with the deeds. Where the bank is taking a legal mortgage, the deeds are commonly sent to the branch solicitor who inspects them in order to prepare a *report on title*, stating whether the customer has a good and marketable title to his property. At the same time the solicitor may carry out various searches against the customer's name on the Land Charges Registry (nothing to do with the Land Registry) and the local planning registers. The former reveals any matters outstanding such as a bankruptcy order against the customer or claims against the property; the latter, known as *local searches*, indicate whether the property is likely to be affected by local authority developments such as the building of a new road. If the branch solicitor does not make these searches, the security clerk will carry them out. Where the property is leasehold it is necessary to check that the ground rent has been paid to date and a note made to check this annually.

When the advance is repaid the title of the legal mortgage is reconveyed to the customer and the deeds together with the bank's reconveyed mortgage are handed back; an equitable mortgage is filed at the bank among the old security papers and the deeds returned to the customer.

(ii) **Registered land.** There are two ways in which a bank may take registered land as security for an advance: either by deposit of the land certificate, protected by notice of deposit, or by registered charge. These methods are the equivalent of an equitable mortgage and a legal mortgage respectively.

When the *notice of deposit* method is used the customer deposits the land certificate and signs the bank's mortgage form. The bank then sends the certificate to the Land Registry where the details of all registered properties are maintained, requesting it to write the certificate up to date: the Registry then compares the certificate with existing records and makes any necessary alterations. At the same time the bank also encloses the special Land Registry form giving notice of deposit. This is recorded at the Registry and the bank's interest in the property noted in the charges (or mortgages) section of the certificate which is then returned to the bank. Thus the bank's interest is noted both at the Registry and on the land certificate; the bank is protected by its notice of deposit and will be immediately advised of any attempted dealings in the land. It is still necessary for local searches to be carried out and, if the property is leasehold, for ground rent receipts to be obtained.

Upon repayment of the advance the bank withdraws its notice of deposit and again has the certificate sent to the Land Registry for writing up to date. Thus the bank's interest is removed and the certificate can then be handed back to the customer.

If a *registered charge* is to be taken the customer deposits the land certificate at the bank and signs a mortgage form. The bank then sends the completed mortgage form to the Land Registry, together with the land certificate. The certificate is withdrawn and a new one, called a charge certificate, is issued: this has the bank's mortgage form stitched inside. Local searches and checks on the payment of ground rent, where appropriate, are also carried out.

When the advance is repaid the bank returns the charge certificate to the Land Registry who withdraws it and re-issues the land certificate, which can then be either kept at the bank in safe custody or handed back to the customer.

Whenever there are buildings of any value on land that has been taken as security it is essential to check that they are insured against fire risk. This is, of course, primarily the customer's responsibility, but the bank should ensure that the fire insurance is of a sufficient amount and that the premiums are paid to date; a note should also be made to check future payments.

A person will only be in possession of the deeds or land certificate relating to his land and property if it is free from mortgage. As we have seen, when the bank takes a mortgage, it takes possession of the relevant documents of title; a building society acts similarly. Most personal customers and a number of business customers have a mortgage outstanding on their property; this is the *first mortgage*. Such a customer can still use the value of his property as security for an advance but the bank, instead of being able to take a mortgage as previously described, must take a *second mortgage*. Suppose that a customer bought a house five years ago for £10 000 by paying a deposit of £1 000 and borrowing

£9 000 on mortgage from a building society; if the house is now worth £14 000 and the mortgage outstanding is £8 500, then he has an *equity* of £5 500 in his house, an amount that could be used as security for an advance by giving the bank a second mortgage. A special second mortgage form is signed by the customer; the deeds, of course, remain with the first mortgagee. In the event of the customer's default, the house would be sold, the first mortgage paid off and the balance (in theory, of £5 500) would be paid to the second mortgagee, any surplus after that being paid to the customer. Reference should be made to a more specialist book for further consideration of second mortgages.

(c) Marketability

Technically, land and property is easily realized provided the bank has taken a legal mortgage over unregistered land or a registered charge over registered land. In practice, however, a bank is generally reluctant to realize such security particularly when the customer's own house is concerned, and will only sell the property as a last resort when all else has failed. Other land and property may be put up for sale very quickly; owing to the vagaries of the property market, however, it may be some time before it is sold and the proceeds received. Stocks and shares and life policies can be realized much more quickly than can land.

(d) Increase in value

Over a period of time most land and property rises in value, especially houses of a type for which there is a steady demand, such as semi-detached and smaller detached properties. Factory premises also rise in value provided that they are well maintained and are easily converted to other uses; large, highly specialized factories that would be difficult to convert do not rise in value very much, and should their sale be forced, may be worth less on the property market than they are to the firm owning them. Farm land and buildings usually rise in value as time goes by.

17.8 Guarantees as Security

A guarantee is a collateral security involving three parties, in which the third party, the guarantor, agrees to be liable for the debts of a second party, the bank customer, if he doesn't pay the first party, the bank. Guarantees are often taken from the directors of a limited company as part security for the company bank account, thus preventing the directors from hiding behind the 'shield' of limited liability (see Unit 12.5) for at least a part of the company's debts. They may also be taken from members of a club or society to guarantee an advance to the club, and from friends and relatives to guarantee a personal account. One company from a group of companies may guarantee the bank accounts of the other companies in the group: where all group companies guarantee each others' accounts this is known as an *interlocking guarantee*.

(a) Valuation
Most guarantees are easy to value in that the money amount is usually stated on the guarantee form. How much a bank would actually receive from the guarantee if the security was realized is a different matter (see paragraph (c) below).

(b) Obtaining a legal title
The mechanics of taking a legal guarantee are very simple. When a person offers himself as a guarantor of an account the manager usually explains to him that in the event of the customer's default, he will be liable to pay up to the amount of the guarantee. The guarantor then signs the bank's form and, if he does not maintain an account at the same bank and branch as the account being guaranteed, the bank takes steps to check his financial standing by making a status inquiry on his bank and branch; if the reply is satisfactory the advance is granted to the customer. Regular, perhaps annual, status inquiries continue to be made on the guarantor as long as there remains a liability under the guarantee, and the bank also writes at regular intervals, possibly every five years, to remind the guarantor of his liability. A bank could ask a guarantor, besides signing the bank's form, to deposit security, such as stock and share certificates, life policies or deeds of land, as support to the guarantee.

(c) Marketability
The major problem of guarantees is that, however hard the bank tries to explain the potential liability, the guarantor never expects to be called upon to pay. There can be serious ill-feeling between the guarantor and the bank if this should happen; it may be difficult to persuade him to pay without taking court action, something that a bank would only undertake as a last resort. Thus although the bank may hold a guarantee for, say, £500, the manager may in his own mind consider that the bank would receive less if it asked the guarantor to pay. Where additional security has been deposited in support of the guarantee, this may be realized as part or full payment of the guarantor's liability.

(d) Increase in value
Where a guarantee is for a fixed sum, as is generally the case, it does not, of course, go up in value over a period of time: in fact, with inflation, the purchasing power of the money will fall. In future years, if borrowing on the customer's account continues, it might be necessary for the guarantor to sign a guarantee for an increased amount.

There is often some confusion among banking students between a guarantee and an indemnity. With a *guarantee*, as already mentioned, there are three parties, the guarantor agreeing to pay the bank if its customer does not. With an *indemnity* there are two parties: the bank and the indemnifier who is primarily liable for the debt of the customer. Contrast the following statements: *'if Joe does not pay you, I will'* and *'lend Joe £50 and I will see that you are repaid'*.

The former is a guarantee, with a secondary responsibility being taken by the guarantor if Joe does not pay; the latter is an indemnity whereby the person making the statement assumes primary responsibility for the money. The distinction may seem a fine one but there are certain circumstances in which a guarantor could not be forced to pay, whereas an indemnifier could. Therefore, to be on the safe side, most banks incorporate an indemnity clause into their guarantee forms.

Besides taking guarantees and indemnities to secure the accounts of customers, the banks also join in indemnities on behalf of their customers (see Unit 14.14), the commonest example being where a customer has lost a share certificate.

'Very well then—two hundred and fifty million—my coffee's getting cold!'

17.9 Other Securities

There are other securities that may be acceptable to a bank granting an advance. These include a *letter of set-off*, which formalizes the bank's right to set off a credit balance on one account with a debit balance on another account of the same customer. Thus a customer with money on his deposit account might be permitted to overdraw his current account on the basis of the right of set-off. A similar situation might exist where a group of companies maintains accounts at the same branch: some individual company accounts might be overdrawn, while others have credit balances but by arrangement with the bank the group might be charged interest only on the 'net indebtedness'.

A security commonly taken from companies is a *fixed and floating charge* which takes all the assets of the company including stocks, debtors, machinery and plant. The floating part allows the company to buy and sell assets without restriction—the charge only 'crystallizes' when certain events take place, such as default on an advance.

It is inappropriate in this book to describe these in detail; they are covered in the more specialized books dealing with securities for advances.

17.10   Special Lending Situations

There are certain special situations in which a banker may be asked to lend, and it is appropriate to consider some of these now.

(a)   Bridging loan

This is an advance sometimes needed by customers moving from one house to another. It involves the bank advancing the deposit or the purchase price of the new house to the buyer pending receipt of the sale proceeds of the old house and/ or the provision of a building society mortgage.

The first principal step in house purchase is that the prospective purchaser agrees to buy 'subject to contract'. This may involve payment of a deposit which is returnable should the transaction fall through, but there is no binding contract at this stage. If the purchase proceeds, contracts are signed and exchanged by the buyer and the seller: at this stage the buyer pays a 10 per cent deposit to the seller's solicitors. A legal contract now exists and within the contract, a completion date is fixed when the balance of money will be paid in return for vacant possession of the property.

Normally a bank only agrees to a bridging loan for the purchase of a property when a binding contract exists for the sale of the customer's old property. If such a contract does not exist, however, the bank may be prepared to grant an advance that is 'open-ended' in the sense that the repayment date of the loan is not known and will be dependent on the sale of the customer's existing property.

In any bridging loan involving the transfer of property it is necessary for the bank to work closely with the customer's solicitor and the usual security taken is a solicitor's letter of undertaking. Before granting a bridging loan the bank must firstly look closely at the lending proposition to see if the customer has done his calculations correctly with regard to the sale and purchase prices; in particular, the bank needs to know that any building society or other mortgage that the customer plans to take out on the new property will actually be available. Secondly, the bank needs to hold a solicitor's undertaking agreeing to pay the net proceeds of sale direct to the bank. Thirdly, if the solicitor giving the undertaking is not known to the bank, an inquiry must be made as to his integrity, through his banker. Fourthly, the bank will wish to obtain control over the deeds of the property being purchased by the customer. This is achieved by the customer instructing his solicitor to give the bank an undertaking to hold the deeds of the new property to the order of the bank. The bank then allows the customer to pay over the purchase monies and, at the same time, checks that he has adequately insured his new property against the risk of fire. (Fire insurance is the responsibility of the purchaser from the date of signing the contract). Where the customer is arranging a building society or other mortgage on his new property, the solicitor's undertaking agrees to hold the deeds to the order of the bank pending release to the building society and to pay the amount of the new mortgage, when received, direct to the bank.

While the change from one house to another is the most common occasion for bridging loan finance, other types of bridge-overs are sometimes needed to cover urgent temporary finance pending the receipt of funds from another source; for instance, the bank might grant a temporary loan which will be repaid by the receipt of funds from the sale of investments or the surrender of a life policy. A company might require temporary finance pending the receipt of the proceeds of a share or debenture issue.

The very nature of a bridging loan—temporary finance to be repaid from a known source—means that the customer's account may be overdrawn only for a short period; a house bridge-over, for example, may be for no more than two or three days. As such the interest charged by the bank for the facility will be low in comparison with the costs of setting it up. It is usual for a special charge—an *arrangement fee*— to be made to cover the administrative costs of arranging a bridging loan.

(b) Produce advances

These are advances where goods (produce) are taken as security. Such an advance is self-liquidating in that the goods which form the bank's security are sold to repay the advance. The bank must be certain of the commercial integrity of its customer, especially with regard to the quality and marketability of the goods.

The security taken by the bank consists of either obtaining the documents of title to the goods or arranging for the goods to be warehoused in the bank's name, rather than by the bank taking actual delivery of the goods—no manager wants the banking hall cluttered up with his customers' goods. The customer is required to sign a *memorandum of pledge* (sometimes known as *a letter of hypothecation*). While the customer cannot obtain the goods, the documents of title or the goods themselves are sometimes released against a *trust letter*, in which the customer acknowledges the bank's security rights in the goods and undertakes to hold in trust for the bank the goods and the sale proceeds and to pay the latter in to the bank.

(c) Other types of advance

These include probate advances to enable executors and administrators to pay capital transfer tax on a deceased's estate (see Unit 12.7). More specialized advances include ships' mortgages, agricultural charges, discounting bills of exchange and the assignment of debts; further details of these would be found in any book on banking practice.

17.11   Questions

1. What are the basic requirements of any security? How are these met in the case of (i) life policies, and (ii) guarantees?

2. If you, as a lending banker, had the choice of taking either shares or land as security, which would you prefer? Give reasons for your decision.

3. You work at a small bank branch. The second officer (accountant, chief clerk) is ill and you are deputizing for him. His diary shows the following:

    '2.30 J. Smith—requires loan to exchange car.'

   The manager asks you to take this interview. What information would you collect beforehand, and what questions would you ask at the interview before making your decision?

4. Describe what is meant by (i) a bridging loan, and (ii) a produce advance. Give an account of the operation of each.

5. What are the main criteria which govern a banker's decision to lend money to a prospective borrower? What part does security play in his final decision?

(The Institute of Bankers)

Interpreting the Accounts of Customers

18.1 Introduction

We saw in Unit 17.2 how it was important for the bank manager to consider the future profitability of his business customers when considering any request for an advance. Banks are constantly lending money to businesses of all sizes and types and every time that a manager grants a loan or allows an overdraft facility, he takes a risk—the risk of not getting all the money back, or at least, the risk of having difficulty in recovering some of it. The main problem for the manager is in assessing the degree of risk he is taking with his depositors' funds.

How then does the manager set about assessing this risk? We have seen that the manager has his own impressions of his customer as to reputation, financial standing, business ability, prospects and so forth, these impressions have been acquired through their past dealings together. In addition to those impressions the manager will want to study his customer's accounts in order to interpret them and draw out of them some conclusions which will aid him in assessing the risk.

18.2 What Accounts will the Bank Manager See?

Obviously the manager is less concerned with the day-to-day book-keeping transactions of his customers than with the accounts that are made up at the end of the trading year. These *final accounts*, as they are called, will consist of the following:

Trading account: This compares the purchases and sales of the business for the year, together with an adjustment for change in the stock level from the beginning to the end of the year, and shows the gross profit for the year.

Profit and loss account: This shows all the expenses of the business for the year and deducts them from the gross profit to give net profit.

Appropriation account: This is used by partnerships and limited companies to show how the net profit has been *appropriated*, or divided, among the partners or shareholders; a sole-trader business does not include this account among its final accounts as all the net profits belong to the trader himself.

Balance sheet: This shows what the business owns and owes at a certain stated time. The balance sheet is not an 'account' as it doesn't form a part of the double-entry book-keeping system, but is a statement of the assets and liabilities at a given date. It has been likened to a snap-shot taken of the business at an instant in time: next day it could look totally different.

Trading account of J. Smith Ltd. for the year ended 31 December 19–9

	£		£
Stock at 1 Jan. 19–9	15 000	Sales	130 000
+ purchases	90 000		
	105 000		
− Stock at 31 Dec. 19–9	14 000		
Cost of goods sold	91 000		
Gross profit	39 000		
	130 000		130 000

Fig. 18.1   A trading account

Profit and loss account of J. Smith Ltd. for the year ended 31 December 19–9

	£		£
The various expenses of the business, e.g. wages and salaries, rent and rates, heating and lighting, etc., together with provisions for depreciation and bad debts would be listed here, totalling for example	30 000	Gross profit	39 000
Net profit	9 000		
	39 000		39 000

Fig. 18.2   A profit and loss account

A manufacturing business will precede the trading account with a *manufacturing account* which shows the factory cost of producing the goods that are subsequently sold. The factory cost is made up of materials, labour and the overheads incurred in running the factory and this total cost is brought into the trading account instead of, or in addition to, purchases of finished goods for resale.

An example of a simple set of final accounts, excluding a manufacturing account, is shown in Figs. 18.1–18.4.

Appropriation account of J. Smith Ltd. for the year ended 31 December 19–9

	£		£
Corporation tax	3 500	Balance of unappropriated	
Transfer to general		profits brought forward	
reserve	1 000	from previous year	2 000
Proposed dividend on		Net profit for year	9 000
ordinary shares	5 000		
Balance of unappropriated			
profits carried forward			
to next year	1 500		
	11 000		11 000

Fig. 18.3   An appropriation account

The balance sheet in Fig. 18.4 is presented in a horizontal form with the captial and liabilities on the left and the assets on the right. It is not uncommon, however, for the assets to be presented on the left-hand side and the liabilities on the right. Alternatively, balance sheets, especially those of companies, can be presented in a vertical form as shown in Fig. 18.5.

However different this presentation may look, the figures going into it are exactly the same and a banker must be able to read and find his way about differently presented sets of accounts. While all businesses produce a set of final accounts once a year it is common to find that interim accounts are prepared half-yearly, quarterly or even monthly by larger organizations.

Before we examine a set of accounts in detail a brief word of explanation about some of the items appearing on the balance sheet is appropriate.

Capital: This is the amount that the owners of the business have invested in it. Limited companies can issue various types of shares (see Unit 12.6(*b*)) and the authorized and issued share capital of the company is normally stated on the balance sheet.

Revenue reserves: These are the profits of the company that over the years have been kept in the business and not distributed to the shareholders. The

Balance sheet of J. Smith Ltd. as at 31 December 19–9

	£		£
Authorized share capital		*Fixed assets*	
100 000 £1 ordinary shares	100 000	Premises	
		(net of depreciation)	45 000
		Fixtures and fittings	
		(net of depreciation)	4 000
		Motor vehicles	
		(net of depreciation)	5 000
			54 000
Issued share capital			
50 000 £1 ordinary			
shares, fully paid	50 000		
		Current assets	
Revenue reserves		Stock 14 000	
General reserve 15 000		Debtors 22 000	
+ transfer 1 000		Cash 500	
	16 000		36 500
Balance of appropriation			
a/c	1 500		
Ordinary shareholders'			
interest	67 500		
Current liabilities			
Creditors 12 000			
Bank overdraft 2 500			
Proposed dividend			
on ordinary			
shares 5 000			
Corporation tax 3 500	23 000		
	90 500		90 500

Fig. 18.4   A balance sheet

Balance sheet of J. Smith Ltd. as at 31 December 19–9

	£	£	£
Fixed assets			
Premises (net of depreciation)			45 000
Fixtures and fittings (net of depreciation)			4 000
Motor vehicles (net of depreciation)			5 000
			54 000
Current assets			
Stock	14 000		
Debtors	22 000		
Cash	500		
		36 500	
Less current liabilities			
Creditors	12 000		
Bank overdraft	2 500		
Proposed dividend on ordinary shares	5 000		
Corporation tax	3 500		
		23 000	
Working capital			13 500
			67 500
Authorized share capital			
100 000 £1 ordinary shares			100 000
Issued share capital			
50 000 £1 ordinary shares, fully paid			50 000
Revenue reserves			
General reserve .	15 000		
+ transfer	1 000		
		16 000	
Balance of appropriation a/c		1 500	
			17 500
Ordinary shareholders' interest			67 500

Fig. 18.5   A balance sheet (vertical presentation)

'He has this thing about changing his cell round so that the debit side is nearest the window'

cash which represented them has been invested in the assets of the business. In the case of a sole trader or a partnership there would be no specific revenue reserves but the profits not withdrawn from the business would represent reserves. A limited company also often has capital reserves (see Unit 8.2(*b*)) which, unlike revenue reserves, cannot be distributed to the shareholders in the form of dividends.

Current liabilities: This section of the balance sheet contains those liabilities that are normally due to be paid within twelve months from the date of the balance sheet. It always contains creditors, the bank balance (if overdrawn) and, for companies, the amount of a dividend proposed but not yet paid, and corporation tax which will be paid during the next twelve months.

Creditors: These are amounts owing by a business to its suppliers at the date of the balance sheet.

Proposed dividend: Obviously this item only appears on a company balance sheet and represents the amount of dividend that the directors propose should be paid to shareholders in the near future.

Corporation tax: Another item that is only found in company accounts (although, of course, individuals running their own businesses also have to pay tax).

Fixed assets: This section of the balance sheet comprises those items that do not change daily and are likely to be retained for use in the business for some time to come. They have been described as the 'means by which companies produce the goods or services they offer to customers and clients', for without premises, fixtures and fittings, motor vehicles and machinery the business would not be able to function. It is usual for fixed assets, with the exception of freehold land, to be depreciated over a period of time or with use. Thus the value of the assets is reduced and the amount of depreciation is charged as an expense of the business in the profit and loss account.

Current assets: This section of the balance sheet contains stock, debtors, bank (if the business has a credit balance at the bank) and cash. The current assets are sometimes described as the *circulating assets* because, unlike the fixed assets, they are changing from day to day throughout the working capital cycle.

Stock: This item on the balance sheet represents the estimated valuation of the stock of the business. A manufacturer may well have different sorts of stock to include under this heading: raw materials, work-in-progress and finished goods, for example. A business that both buys and sells the same goods, such as a shop, does not have these different categories of stock although it may have many thousands of different lines of goods in stock. Whatever the complexities most stock will be valued on the basis of either cost or net realizable value, whichever is the lower.

Debtors: The figure for debtors records the total amount owing to the business by its customers at the balance sheet date. A provision for bad debts is usually deducted from this figure and any bad debts written off are charged to the profit and loss account.

18.3   Interpretation of Accounts

This involves understanding what the accounts tell us and is not, in itself, difficult. The problem is knowing where to start because we are faced with a mass of figures and information and some logical method is needed to extract the information. However, before we start, a word of warning! It is easy to think that interpretation of accounts consists solely of calculating a number of ratios, percentages, and so forth: there is more to it than this and it is a waste of time to make these calculations unless useful and significant information can be derived from the answers.

There are six main areas to consider when looking at a set of accounts: the *shareholders' stake*, any *long-term loans* made to the business, the firm's *working capital*, its *liquidity*, the *trading figures* and *other items*. We shall consider each of these in turn.

(a) Ordinary shareholders' stake

This means the ordinary share capital and reserves of a limited company or, for sole traders and partnerships, the balance of the capital account. In the balance sheet of J. Smith Ltd. referred to earlier, the ordinary shareholders' stake amounts to £67 500. A bank is unlikely to be prepared to put more money into the business than its owners have done, without a very good reason. The accounts will show if profits are being retained in the business, which is an indication of a good policy. The profits figure for the current year can be compared with that of the previous year—most sets of accounts show, in a separate column, the previous year's figures. A banker looks to see how the figures compare and will want to know the reason for a fall in profits. He may be able to see from the profit and loss account that the reduction in profit is due to a large increase in a particular type of expense, such as general expenses. If sales have increased by 60 per cent and general expenses have also increased by 60 per cent then something is wrong because, although some expenses may rise as sales increase (variable expenses), few will increase exactly in proportion and many expenses remain the same (fixed expenses) and do not, in the short term, vary with sales.

The percentage return on capital employed can be worked out and the trend can be discovered by comparison with previous years. The calculation is made as follows:

$$\text{Percentage return} = \frac{\text{Net profit before tax}}{\text{Shareholders' stake} + \text{Long-term loans (if any)}} \times \frac{100}{1}$$

A fall in the percentage from one year to the next would indicate that the business was not using its capital as effectively. A banker who has several customers in similar types of business can, for himself, make a direct comparison of their effectiveness in using their capital employed.

(b) Long-term loans

If a business has long-term loans (not a bank overdraft which is technically repayable on demand) they are listed after the capital and reserves. A banker needs to know when any such loans are due to be repaid and whether they are secured on the assets of the company—that is, is there any security left for the bank? If they are loans from the company's directors and they are for substantial amounts, a *letter of postponement* could be taken from the directors, whereby they postpone their own repayment in favour of the bank's.

(c) Working capital

The amount of working capital may be calculated as follows:

Working capital = Current assets − Current liabilities

Sufficient working capital ensures that the business is able to pay its creditors without difficulty, hold adequate stocks and allow its debtors a reasonable time for payment. As a business expands it needs to carry larger stocks and increased debtors and will need an increase in the amount of its working capital rather than trying to delay payments to creditors.

The method of calculating working capital stated above gives an answer in pounds and, if calculated year by year, can show the trend of a particular company's business. The working capital requirements of a small shop are totally different from those of a large departmental store, however, and in order to make a comparison between businesses more meaningful the *working capital ratio* or *current ratio* can be calculated:

$$\text{Current ratio} = \frac{\text{Current assets}}{\text{Current liabilities}}$$

A satisfactory current ratio is usually regarded as being about 2:1; that is, for every £1 of current liabilities there should be £2 of current assets. Thus if a creditor demands immediate payment there are sufficient current assets to be realized to meet his requirements.

When a manager lends money to a business customer he often attempts to estimate what the working capital will be if he grants the advance. The bank overdraft will form a part of the current liabilities and thus help to reduce and worsen the current ratio; the ratio will be further aggravated if the advance is used to assist with the purchase of a fixed asset. Consider the following balance sheet:

Balance sheet of ABC Co. Ltd. as at 31 December 19–9

	£		£
Capital	30 000	*Fixed assets*	23 000
Current liabilities		*Current assets*	
Creditors	7 000	Stocks 4 000	
		Debtors 8 000	
		Bank 2 000	
		——	14 000
	——		——
	37 000		37 000
	═══		═══

The current ratio is 2:1 (£14 000 ÷ £7 000) which is reasonably satisfactory. Suppose the company now approaches the bank for overdraft facilities of £5 000 to purchase a machine (a fixed asset) costing £7 000; if the advance is granted the balance sheet will appear as follows:

Balance sheet of ABC Co. Ltd. as at 31 December 19–9

	£			£
Capital	30 000	*Fixed assets*		30 000
Current liabilities		*Current assets*		
Creditors 7 000		Stocks	4 000	
Bank 5 000		Debtors	8 000	
	12 000		——	12 000
	42 000			42 000

The current ratio has thus altered to $1:1$ (£12 000 ÷ £12 000) and if the overdraft limit is strictly adhered to the company could have difficulties in paying pressing creditors.

(d) Liquidity

When referring to the liquidity of an asset we mean the ease and speed with which it can be converted into cash. The balance of the bank account and cash on hand are, of course, perfectly liquid, whereas debtors are 'near-liquid'. Stock is not as liquid as debtors because it has to go through the process of being converted into debtors before it becomes cash.

In any business, certain liabilities have to be paid off in the very near future and part of the interpretation procedure must be in seeing that payments which are due can in fact be met. This is why bankers are interested in the liquidity of assets. It may be that the bulk of the current assets are in the form of stock, which means that cash cannot be forthcoming for some time, especially if the stock is turning over slowly and the business sells only on credit and has no cash customers. It should not be too difficult to determine whether the assets are sufficient and liquid enough to meet pressing liabilities. A banker must also be concerned as to future liquidity in deciding whether the repayments to the bank will be maintained as promised by the customer or in deciding how repayments are likely to be made. If he suspects that the facilities being requested are inadequate and that the customer will soon be back asking for more, it would be appropriate to ask the customer to prepare a cash budget (see Unit 18.4).

A general impression of the liquidity position can be obtained by seeing how far current assets less stocks go towards repaying the current liabilities. When expressed as a ratio this is known as the *liquid* or *quick ratio* and is calculated as follows:

$$\text{Liquid ratio} = \frac{(\text{Current assets} - \text{Stock})}{\text{Current liabilities}}$$

Thus for the ABC Co. Ltd. mentioned earlier the liquid ratio is 1.43:1 (£10 000 ÷ £7 000) in the first balance sheet and 0.67 : 1 (£8 000 ÷ £12 000) in the second.

A liquid ratio of 1 : 1 is quite reasonable: it means that the business, without selling its stock, could cover its current liabilities in full. A ratio of 1.5:1 is even better but a ratio any higher than this could indicate that too much is tied up in debtors and bank—idle money that is not working for the business.

(e) Trading figures

In comparing the sets of accounts from two or three years, any large fluctuations in debtors, creditors and stocks should be noted.

A banker should find out how many debtors' accounts there are: it is better to spread the risk of bad debts widely, rather than have a few large debtors. From the year-end accounts it is possible to calculate the period of credit being allowed by the business by comparing debtors with sales. For example, suppose that debtors are £6 000 and sales for the year are £36 000: the average period of credit being allowed is 1/6 of a year (two months).

Similarly, the make-up of creditors needs to be known: are there many small creditors' accounts or one or two very large ones? If one large creditor exerts pressure for repayment this could create financial difficulties for the company. The period of credit being taken by the company can be calculated by comparing creditors with purchases. For example, if creditors are £4 000 and purchases for the year are £40 000, the average period of credit being taken is 1/10 of a year (about five weeks).

The bank manager must consider if the figures for credit allowed and taken are reasonable, bearing in mind the type of business—if the customer were running a sweet and tobacco shop one would not expect to see substantial debtors on the balance sheet! If possible, the figures calculated should be compared with those of the previous year; if the period for creditors is increasing while that for debtors is decreasing this would indicate that the firm's resources were being stretched.

The banker needs to know certain points about the stock of the business. He needs to find out if the stock includes any 'dead' or unsaleable items; he needs to know how it is valued—as already mentioned, a common valuation is at the lower of cost and net realizable value. In particular the banker should find out how fast it is being 'turned over', that is, how many times the average amount of stock held is sold and replaced in a year. This may be calculated from a trading account by dividing the total cost of goods sold in a year by the average cost of stock held. Suppose we find that the average stock is sold (turned over) six times in a year, that is, stock remains in the stores, on average, for 1/6 of a year (2 months) before being sold and replaced. Is this a good turnover? It is for a furniture dealer but not for a fishmonger! In other words, it depends on the type of business. As stock 'turns over' profits are made, so obviously a quick turnover is very desirable.

In addition to looking at debtors, creditors and stock, the banker can calculate the *gross profit percentage* from the trading account and the *net profit percentage* from the profit and loss account as follows:

$$\text{Gross profit percentage} = \frac{\text{Gross profit}}{\text{Sales}} \times \frac{100}{1}$$

$$\text{Net profit percentage} = \frac{\text{Net profit}}{\text{Sales}} \times \frac{100}{1}$$

These figures indicate the profitability of the business for each £100 of sales both before and after deduction of expenses. Comparative figures for previous years should indicate a steady trend and any sudden fall in the percentages warrants further investigation.

(*f*) **Other items**
When looking at a set of accounts a banker must be alert to many things. In particular he should check whether the business has any investments listed on the assets side of its balance sheet: if so, there is the possibility that they could be sold to provide additional funds or could be used as security.

Any large item in the accounts should be inspected and considered and particular attention paid to any major changes that have taken place since the previous set of accounts.

18.4   Projected Accounts

One problem with interpreting customers' year-end accounts is that such accounts look to the past, in that they record what has gone on in the previous year, whereas it is from the future trading that profits will come to repay any proposed advance. The other problem is that by the time year-end accounts are prepared and sent to the bank manager, another six months could have elapsed so that the accounts are well and truly historical. This is not to say that accounts from the past are of no value to the banker: they are of considerable value in recording the progress of the business and establishing trends for the future which are, apart from any major change in trading, likely to continue.

To assist both bank and customer in planning for the future it is common for the manager to ask for the production of a month-by-month *cash budget*. This records the anticipated monthly cash receipts and cash payments and estimates the closing bank balance at the end of each month. An example of a cash budget is shown in Fig. 18.6.

A cash budget shows clearly the extent of the need for bank overdraft or loan facilities. In the example in Fig. 18.6 the company would realize that it needs a maximum of about £4 500 and could approach the bank manager in plenty of time to make the arrangements.

It follows that as a cash budget is a projection into the future, it is only as good as the figures going to make it up. When a bank manager asks for a cash budget some customers put down a few hastily thought-up figures to

Cash budget of XYZ Trading Co. Ltd. for the six months ending 30 June 19–0

	Jan	Feb	Mar	Apr	May	June
Cash receipts	£	£	£	£	£	£
From debtors	2 000	2 500	2 750	2 250	3 000	3 000
Cash sales	500	750	1 000	750	1 000	1 000
Sale of old machinery					250	
	2 500	3 250	3 750	3 000	4 250	4 000
Cash payments						
To creditors	1 500	2 000	2 500	2 000	1 500	1 500
Wages	1 000	1 250	1 500	1 250	1 000	1 000
General expenses	500	1 000	1 000	500	500	250
Purchase of new machinery				2 000		
	3 000	4 250	5 000	5 750	3 000	2 750
Opening bank balance	1 000	500	(500)	(1 750)	(4 500)	(3 250)
Add cash receipts	2 500	3 250	3 750	3 000	4 250	4 000
Deduct cash payments	3 000	4 250	5 000	5 750	3 000	2 750
Closing bank balance	500	(500)	(1 750)	(4 500)	(3 250)	(2 000)

Fig. 18.6   A cash budget (note: bank balance in brackets indicates an overdraft)

'keep him happy', although most give the matter more thought. It is a simple matter for a manager to check the progress of the customer's forecasts by inspecting the balance of the bank account at each month-end to see if the trend anticipated by the budget is reflected in the working of the account: he thus soon gets to know those customers whose forecasts are wildly optimistic and those who are consistently nearer the mark. No cash budget can be completely accurate, however: so many variables are involved, ranging from the unknown future rate of inflation to an unexplained change in sales.

Any business that seriously attempts to produce a realistic cash budget must involve itself in estimating future sales, purchases and expenses. These can be combined to make up a set of *projected* or *budgeted accounts* which show what the trading profit and loss account should be like for the next six or twelve months, together with a balance sheet at the end of the period. These can be of great use to both bank manager and customer as an indication of future profitability and also as an early warning of impending difficulties so that corrective action can be taken well in advance. Also, as time goes by, the actual results for the accounting period can be compared with the projected figures and any major discrepancies investigated. Nearly all large companies already prepare these projected accounts and have sophisticated control systems to highlight any variances from the actual results. However, the further ahead in time the projections are made, the less accurate they usually turn out to be in practice; for example, a slight increase in the buying price of materials not anticipated by the projected accounts will scarcely affect the budgeted accounts for the forthcoming three months, but will have a greater effect on accounts for the next six months and a considerable effect on the accounts for the next year.

18.5   'Going Concern' and 'Gone Concern'

Most balance sheets are prepared on a *going concern* basis which means that the business will continue to trade and, under such circumstances, the values shown in the balance sheet are those that the assets are worth to the company. No banker intentionally lends money to lose it, but sometimes a company's plans go wrong for a variety of reasons and a manager may have to look critically at a business balance sheet and estimate what the assets might realize in the event of a forced sale. Such an exercise involves going through the company's assets as shown on the balance sheet and reducing them by different amounts in an attempt to estimate their sale value. Often a bank's head office can give guidelines as to how much assets should be reduced by, if a balance sheet must be studied from the *gone concern* point of view.

Land and premises. These will be reduced by varying amounts depending on the specialized nature of the premises. It may be that the bank has taken the property as security and wishes to sell it: if the proceeds of sale do not fully repay the overdraft, the bank could claim as a general creditor of the business for the remaining indebtedness.

Motor vehicles. If these have been satsifactorily maintained they may well realize something approaching the figure shown in the balance sheet provided that suitable provision for depreciation has been made. It is inevitable that as a business gets into financial difficulties, it will reduce repairs and maintenance of vehicles, (and of plant and machinery as well) to a minimum.

Plant and machinery, fixtures and fittings, office equipment. These assets usually realize no more than a very small proportion of their balance sheet valuation. As there is only a limited secondhand market for them, a banker will often consider them at scrap value.

Stock, work-in-progress, raw materials. The stock of finished goods generally has some resale value but must be considerably reduced from the balance sheet figure. Work-in-progress is usually of no use to anybody except as scrap and is valued accordingly. The stock of raw materials, provided it does not comprise highly specialized items, can be valued at nearer the balance sheet figures.

Debtors. Most should be collectable but a check should be made to ensure that the figure comprises current or 'live' debtors and is not made up of badly overdue debts that should have been written off long ago.

Bank and cash. When a company is in financial difficulties there is one thing of which you can be certain: at the end, the bank overdraft will be at its limit or beyond, and there will be no float of cash.

Creditors. As mentioned previously the bank must prove its debt along with all the other general creditors of the business where it has lent unsecured or where, after realization of its security, there remains an amount of indebtedness.

Lending money is a complex affair and the interpretation of a customer's accounts is only one of the lending banker's considerations. Above all he should remember that, while it is the depositors' funds that are being lent, behind every set of accounts showing cold facts and figures there stands a group of human beings who make up the business that seeks new or continued bank facilities.

The four questions in Unit 18.6 present the kind of problems that a bank manager meets when lending to his business customers. Outline answers to these questions are given at the back of the book. You should realize that in practice, in a bank branch, you would have far more information about these customers than it is possible to give here.

18.6   Questions

1. Johnson Brothers Ltd. owns a number of do-it-yourself shops in and around the town where you work. The brothers have always followed an expansion programme, buying suitable premises and altering the layouts of their existing shops to enable a greater range of stock to be displayed. In the past they have had overdraft facilities which have been satisfactorily cleared; the company bank account is currently in credit. The latest balance sheet shows the following position:

Balance sheet of Johnson Brothers Ltd. as at 31 December 19–9

	£		£
Issued share capital		*Fixed assets*	
100 000 £1 ordinary		Freehold premises (net)	90 000
shares, fully paid	100 000	Leasehold premises (net)	55 000
Reserves		Shop fixtures	
Profit and Loss a/c	60 000	fittings (net)	5 000
		Delivery vans (net)	6 000
			156 000
Long-term liabilities			
Loans from directors	10 000		
Current liabilities		*Current assets*	
Creditors 8 000		Stock 23 000	
Corporation Tax 7 000		Debtors 3 000	
	15 000	Bank 2 500	
		Cash 500	
			29 000
	185 000		185 000

Relevant figures from the trading and profit and loss accounts for the year:

Sales	£143 000
Purchases	£100 000
Gross profit	£46 000
Net profit	
before tax	£20 000

The brothers come to you in February 19–0 seeking an overdraft facility of £10 000 for six months to enable them to carry out extensions at one shop at a cost of £3 000, and to allow them to build up their stocks in readiness for the spring when there is always a big increase in demand for do-it-yourself products.

How would you treat their request?

2. Your customer Elizabeth Adams Designs Ltd. has been trading for two years. The directors are Elizabeth Adams, who holds a majority shareholding and her husband David, who owns the remaining shares. The company sells handmade dresses to small shops and boutiques, most of the manufacturing and selling being carried out by Elizabeth herself, assisted in production by a few outworkers. The balance sheet for the second year of trading is as follows:

Balance sheet of Elizabeth Adams Designs Ltd. as at 31 December 19–9

	£		£	
Issued share capital		*Fixed assets*		
1 000 £1 ordinary shares,		Machinery (net of		
fully paid	1 000	depreciation)		500
Long-term liabilities		Delivery van (net of		
Loans from directors	1 000	depreciation)		750
Current liabilities		*Current assets*		
Creditors 3 000		Stocks:		
Bank 350		raw materials	200	
	3 350	work-in-		
		progress	900	
		finished		
		goods	500	
		Debtors	1 500	
			——	3 100
		Fictitious assets		
		Profit and loss a/c		1 000
	——			——
	5 350			5 350
	══			══

Relevant figures from the trading and profit and loss accounts for the year:

Sales	£10 000
Purchases of raw	
materials	£8 000
Gross profit	£1 000
Net loss	£500

Although there is no official overdraft limit on the account, cheques have recently been paid to meet pressing creditors. Despite the loss that was made last year, Elizabeth Adams is convinced that if she can organize production properly, she can make profits and she comes to you with the following proposition: she requires an overdraft limit of £10 000 to pay a year's advance rental of £3 500 on vacant factory premises on the Industrial Estate, to buy new machinery and fixtures for £2 500, to carry out alterations to the new premises at a cost of £2 000 and to provide additional working capital of £2 000.

How would you treat this request and what suggestions would you make to the directors?

3. Your customer, Bill Harris, comes to the bank and hands you the set of accounts shown below which he has prepared himself. The bank account has only been open a matter of months and, during the course of the inter-

view, you learn that he is self-employed and makes wooden toy cranes which sell in the shops at £5 each. He does everything from manufacturing to selling, employing no workers.

Profit and loss statement for the six months ended 31 December 19–9

	£	£
Sales		2 340
Materials purchased	1 250	
Wages	3 000	
Rent	400	
	4 650	
Less stock unsold 31 December 19–9	3 250	
Cost of goods sold		1 400
Gross profit		940
Advertising and selling expenses	350	
Interest on loan	40	
		390
Net profit		550

Balance sheet as at 31 December 19–9

	£	£
Assets		
Cash at bank	50	
Debtor*	100	
Stock	3 250	
		3 400
Less liabilities		
Loan from father	1 000	
Creditors	1 050	
		2 050
Net worth of Bill Harris		1 350

*Debtor was for a sale made on 15 October 19–9

He asks you for an overdraft limit of £1 000 for twelve months to help the business become better established. How would you treat this request?

4. Your customer, the Inbetween Co. Ltd., sells a range of convenience foods to retail outlets in the Midlands area. The foods are Chinese meals that only need to be boiled or put in the oven for half an hour or so and are then ready to be eaten. They are very popular with busy housewives and sell well. The company does not make the products itself, but buys from a manufacturer at 80p per pack and sells to the shops at £1 per pack. Sales have been fairly static for the past few years and the company has made profits of between £5 000 and £10 000 each year.

A new managing director has recently been appointed. He is determined to expand the sales of the company over a much wider area and has already taken on an extra sales representative. Sales are currently running at 20 000 packs per month but he confidently predicts a cumulative increase in sales amounting to 5 000 packs each month commencing in June. He tells you that the financial position now (1 April) is:

	£		£
Capital	50 000	Stocks	16 000
Creditors	16 000	Debtors	40 000
		Bank	10 000
	66 000		66 000

He asks for an overdraft limit of £5 000 for the next six months to cover the expansion in sales—he says it won't be needed after that because the extra profits from increased sales will bring the bank balance into credit.

In conversation you learn that as the manufacturer is a large organization, the Inbetween Co. Ltd. has to pay for purchases in the month after purchase. On the other hand, to be competitive with other food wholesalers, it has to allow its customers two months' credit. In order to give a good service to its customers, the company maintains an anticipated month's supply of food packs in stock to cover the expected sales in the succeeding month. Operating costs are £3 000 per month and are paid as they fall due; they are not expected to increase with the expansion of business.

How would you treat this request? (A clue: try to calculate the closing bank balance at the end of each month until the end of December.)

Unit Nineteen

The Institute of Bankers

19.1 Introduction

No book on 'Elements of Banking' would be complete without mentioning The Institute of Bankers, which is the professional body for bankers. It was founded in 1879 and has two broad aims:

(i) to provide the educational foundation on which any man or woman can build a banking career; and
(ii) to keep its members in touch with the latest developments in banking and business generally.

An elected Council, comprising senior bankers, decides the policy of the Institute, and most local centres (see Unit 19.5) are entitled to elect representatives to the Council. The headquarters of the Institute are in the heart of the City of London in Lombard Street, but membership and other records are now maintained at an administrative centre at Canterbury in Kent.

19.2 Membership

The members are men and women engaged in banking at all levels from the junior clerk working at a small branch to chief general managers and chairmen of large international banks. At present the membership stands at over 110 000 from 1 800 different banks in 100 countries. There are three grades of membership:

(i) *Ordinary members* are those who have not yet passed their Associateship examination.
(ii) *Associates* are those members who have passed the Associateship examinations and have been elected by the Council. They are entitled to use the letters AIB (Associate of the Institute of Bankers) after their name.
(iii) *Fellows* of The Institute of Bankers (FIB) are elected by the Council from Associates who have achieved senior professional status and have performed services on behalf of the Institute.

Bank staff wishing to become members of the Institute should write for application forms to:

> The Institute of Bankers,
> 10 Lombard Street,
> London EC3V 9AS.

19.3   Examinations

In recent years the Institute's qualifications have been completely reviewed to ensure that they continue to meet the modern banker's educational requirements. There are two stages in the examinations leading to Associate membership (which is regarded as the basic qualification for most career bankers). For those who have passed the Associateship examinations or who have a recognized degree, there is a further, more advanced, course of study, the Financial Studies Diploma.

Stage One. In Britain this stage may be completed by taking either a Business Education Council (BEC) National level course or a 'conversion' course.

The entry requirement for BEC National level courses is usually a minimum of four GCE 'O' levels (normally of grades A, B or C) or CSE grades one passes, or successful completion of a BEC general level course. It is also possible for those without these entry requirements to join the course if they are aged nineteen or over (at the college principal's discretion). The National level course is of two years' duration and may be either full-time or part-time. Most staff joining the bank straight from taking 'O' levels at school take the part-time course which usually involves attendance at the local college of further education on the basis of one day or two half-days each week; some, however, take the full-time course at a local college to complete their Stage One qualification before joining the bank. Whether the student takes the full- or part-time national level course, he studies areas which include economics, accounting, law, English and, usually, elements of banking. Other study areas may also be included, particularly on the full-time courses which explore topics in greater depth. Upon successful completion of the course a full-time student is awarded the BEC National Diploma, and the part-timer the BEC National Certificate. Both these awards are 'public sector qualifications' and are, in their own right, accepted by a large number of employers in the commercial world.

The conversion course entry requirement is that the student should have passed one or more GCE 'A' levels plus 'O' level English language or equivalent. There are also facilities for students aged twenty or over to join the course even if they do not have these qualifications. The conversion course is of one year's duration based on attendance at college for one day (or equivalent) each week. Subjects studied include accounting, law, economics and elements of banking. While there is no award, successful completion of the course permits a student to go on to Stage Two of the examinations.

Staff in Britain who live and work inconveniently far from a college can study for their conversion course examinations through certain correspondence colleges.

Overseas, Stage One may be completed by taking an equivalent local qualification, approved by the Institute, of the BEC national level course or by taking single subject examinations at Royal Society of Arts Stage III or London Chamber of Commerce Higher levels.

Stage Two. The entry requirements to this stage are the Stage One qualification or two or more relevant GCE 'A' levels (law, economics or accountancy) or a recognized degree. Holders of degrees who are admitted directly to Stage Two are expected to undertake a course of background study in law, economics, accounting and elements of banking. In addition students aged twenty-five years and over who do not have any of these qualifications may be permitted to take the BEC Higher National level course (see below) subject to the requirement that they have experience to enable them to benefit from the course.

'We had to call in the Fraud Squad to look at this answer to one of the questions'

Stage Two consists of Parts A, B and C and is normally studied on a day-release/evenings basis. All students take Institute of Bankers' examinations in the following subjects:

Part A
Applied Economics
Accountancy
Law Relating to Banking

Part B
Nature of Management
Investment
Finance of International Trade

After 1980, it is possible that in Britain parts A and B may be taken by completing a BEC Higher National level course which includes certain approved areas of study. Such a course will usually be taken on a day-release basis, although a full-time course will be available, successful completion of which will allow exemptions to be claimed from Stage Two. It is also possible that some overseas courses which compare favourably with the Institute's Stage Two may also be accepted for exemptions.

Part C of Stage Two consists of two Institute papers (normally taken in the third year):

Practice of Banking 1
Practice of Banking 2

For staff working in the trustee departments of banks there is a separate set of examinations for Parts A, B and C.

Upon successful completion of Stages One and Two, members of the Institute qualify to be elected as Associate members and use the letters AIB provided that they also have at least three years' banking experience and have been members of the Institute for at least three years.

19.4 The Financial Studies Diploma

This is quite separate from the Associateship examinations; its object is to provide a degree-level qualification in banking and management subjects for those who are expected to reach senior management levels. The entry requirements are either AIB or a recognized degree or professional qualification, these last two subject to being of a standard and content acceptable to the Institute. Where a person is allowed direct entry as a result of possessing a degree or professional qualification, he is required to sit and pass two introductory papers before being allowed to take the Diploma course. The introductory papers, which do not have to be taken by AIBs, are:

(i) Financial Institutions and the Monetary System, and
(ii) Practice of Banking.

The Diploma course, which all candidates are normally required to take, is in two sections and the subjects in each are;

Section 1:
Practice of Banking 3
Human Aspects of Management
Business Planning and Control

Section 2:
Marketing of Financial Services
Practice of Banking 4
Practice of Banking 5

All papers in these two sections are examined by the Institute and tuition is available at a number of colleges and polytechnics, mainly on an evening basis, or from a correspondence college. The Financial Studies Diploma is awarded to candidates who have successfully completed both sections in a period of not more than five years, have at least three years' banking experience and have been members of the Institute for at least three years.

19.5   Local Centres

The Institute has developed a number of local centres both in Britain and overseas where members can meet one another and also keep up-to-date in their careers. There are currently 106 local centres, of which eight are overseas. Local centres run programmes of seminars, debates, group discussions, lectures and industrial visits which are open to all Institute members. These meetings are on a variety of topics, some (though not all) connected with banking, but in each programme, there are some meetings chosen especially with the examination candidate in mind. Certain meetings are held jointly with the local centres of other professional organizations and thus bring bankers into social contact with other members of the local business community. Each local centre is concerned with the tuition facilities available in its area and an education officer is appointed to liaise with local colleges and to advise student members on all aspects of examination matters.

19.6   Other Services of the Institute

Each member receives a copy of the Institute's professional magazine, the *Journal of the Institute of Bankers.* This is published six times each year and contains articles on a wide range of banking and related topics and, in every edition, articles to help banking students with their examination work. The Institute publishes a range of books on banking and these are available from the Lombard Street headquarters either by post or by personal call.

Also in Lombard Street, the Institute maintains a specialist library consisting mainly of financial and commercial books and periodicals; this can be used by personal callers and also operates a postal service within the United Kingdom. In addition, the library provides an information service for members and others who require answers to banking problems.

The Institute organizes a number of lectures and seminars on a national level. Of particular note is the regular management seminar for Associates in the 30–45 age-group at Christ's College, Cambridge. This usually lasts for one week and enables managers and potential managers from a variety of different banks to consider a specific theme and to widen their outlook on professional problems. In recent years the themes of the Cambridge seminars have included 'The Banks and Industry' (1976), 'Banks and the British Exporter' (1977) and 'The Banks and Small Businesses' (1978).

Internationally, the Institute sponsors the International Banking Summer School which was first held in 1948 at Christ Church, Oxford. This is now held annually and cities all over the world have played host to it. It is attended by a large number of senior bankers from many different countries and a specific theme is chosen each year, as for the Cambridge seminars. These have recently included 'Banking in a Changing Environment' (1976) and 'The Effective Use of Global Capital Resources' (1977).

The Institute also organizes two major scholarships: the Transatlantic Banking Scholarship, which enables certain members to undertake a three-month tour of the USA, and the Bank of England European Banking Scholarship which provides for three months in a selected European country.

Further Questions

1. Outline the significance for British banking of any *two* of the following:

   (*a*) Bills of Exchange Act 1882;
   (*b*) National Board for Prices and Incomes Report on Bank Charges (1967);
   (*c*) *Competition and Credit Control* (1971).

   (*The Institute of Bankers*)

2. Write brief explanatory notes on the following and indicate the relationship between them:

   (*a*) a London clearing bank's base rate;
   (*b*) the Bank of England's minimum lending rate.

   (*The Institute of Bankers*)

3. What is the significance of a crossing on an order cheque?
   Is this affected in any way if the words 'not negotiable' are included?

   (*The Institute of Bankers*)

4. Compare and contrast the respective roles of commercial banks and savings banks in the economy of a country with which you are familiar.

   (*The Institute of Bankers*)

5. Write brief explanatory notes on any *two* of the following, indicating their special characteristics and the institutions to which they are attractive investments:

   (*a*) sterling certificates of deposit;
   (*b*) Treasury bills;
   (*c*) prime bank bills;
   (*d*) short-dated Government bonds.   (*The Institute of Bankers*)

6. Describe *three* of the following bank services:

   (*a*) bridging loan;
   (*b*) personal loan;
   (*c*) documentary credit;
   (*d*) forward exchange.

   (*The Institute of Bankers*)

Assignments

1. Research a detailed history of monetary notes and coin in your country.

2. If you work for a bank, trace the development of that bank from its beginnings to the present day.

3. Research the history of banking in your locality (your library will have books on local history).

4. From an up-to-date copy of the *Bank of England Quarterly Bulletin* prepare the balance sheet of the Bank of England (both the Issue and Banking Departments) and a balance sheet for the London clearing banks (calculate the reserve asset ratio).

5. Obtain leaflets and newspaper advertisements on savings and investment schemes. Prepare a report stating in summary form the advantages and disadvantages of each scheme. Compare current rates of interest making clear the income tax position.

6. Obtain leaflets on bank services. Categorize these under the following headings:

    (i) for personal customers;
    (ii) for business customers (exclude export/import services);
    (iii) specialist export/import services.

    Summarize the advantages to bank customers of a number of the less well-known services.

7. You have just been appointed General Manager (Domestic Banking) of National Barllands Bank, one of the major clearing banks. What new services would you like to see introduced? Draft a memorandum of your ideas to the Chief General Manager and prepare a draft of an advertising leaflet for one of these services.

8. If you work for a bank, prepare a summary of the staff (by job title) at your branch; list the tasks that each performs.

9. Imagine that you have been given £10 000 to invest. From the *Financial Times* (or similar paper) make up an imaginary portfolio of shares. Keep

accurate records and value your 'portfolio' at regular intervals (perhaps fortnightly or monthly). The aim is to maximize capital appreciation and you may 'buy' or 'sell' shares as appropriate. Ignore expenses and taxation.

(See also the questions at the end of Unit 18).

Further Reading

Anthony, V.: *Banks and Markets.* Heinemann (London, 1972).

Bank of England: *Competition and Credit Control 1971–78.* Bank of England (London, 1979).

Central Office of Information: *British Banking and other Financial Institutions.* HMSO (London, 1975).

Committee of London Clearing Banks: *The London Clearing Banks: Evidence to the* [Wilson] *Committee to Review the Functioning of Financial Institutions.* Longman (Harlow, 1978).

Crockett, A.: *Money: Theory, Policy and Institutions.* Nelson (Sunbury-on-Thames, 1973).

Dyer, L. S.: *A Practical Approach to Bank Lending.* The Institute of Bankers (London, 1978).

Hutchinson, H. H.: *Interpretation of Balance Sheets.* The Institute of Bankers (London, 1972).

Jones, J. P.: *The Money Story.* David and Charles (Newton Abbot, 1972).

McRae, H. and Cairncross, F.: *Capital City.* Eyre Methuen (London, 1973).

Mather, L. C.: *The Lending Banker.* Waterlow (London, 1972).

Pringle, R.: *Banking in Britain.* Methuen (London, 1975).

Revell, J. R. S.: *The British Financial System.* Macmillan (London, 1973).

Sayers, R. S.: *Modern Banking.* Oxford University Press (Oxford, 1967).

Shaw, E. R.: *The London Money Market.* Heinemann (London, 1975).

Watson, A. J. W.: *Finance of International Trade.* The Institute of Bankers (London, 1976).

Articles of interest to the student are regularly published in the *Bank of England Quarterly Bulletin, The Bankers' Magazine*, the *Journal of the Institute of Bankers* and in bank reviews and leading newspapers.

Answers to Questions

Unit 12

	Debentures	Cumulative preference	Non-cumulative preference	Ordinary
5. Year 1	£7 000	£4 000	£5 000	£10 000
Year 2	£7 000	£2 000	nil	nil
Year 3	£7 000	£6 000	£5 000	nil
Year 4	£7 000	£4 000	£5 000	£19 000

Unit 18

1. This seems to be a highly successful and profitable business. As overdraft facilities have been granted in the past, it is likely that the bank has copies of earlier sets of accounts so that comparisons may be made.

(*a*) **Shareholders' stake.** The balance of the profit and loss account tells us that profits are being retained in the business. The shareholders' stake is £160 000 out of total assets of £185 000; the shareholders are thus financing 86 per cent of the total assets—a very healthy position from the point of view of the lending banker. The return on capital employed is:

$$\frac{£20\,000}{£160\,000 + £10\,000 \text{ (long-term loans)}} \times \frac{100}{1} = 11.76 \text{ per cent.}$$

This seems generally perfectly satisfactory and could be compared with the return calculated from previous sets of accounts.

(*b*) **Long-term loans.** These are from directors and, as liabilities are low in comparison with assets, it hardly seems appropriate to ask for Letters of Postponement.

(*c*) **Working capital.** The working capital is £14 000 (£29 000 − £15 000) and, as a ratio, is 1.93:1 which seems satisfactory. If the overdraft facility of £10 000 was granted the total of current liabilities would increase but, equally, there would be an increase in stocks to compensate although £3 000 of the advance would be spent on extensions to one shop and this will be reflected in an increase in the fixed assets. Overall there would be a reduction in the current ratio but it would not be too severe.

(d) **Liquidity.** The liquid capital (working capital less stocks), is *minus* £9 000 or (£9 000); as a ratio, this is 0.4:1. This is not such a good position and could indicate that the company would have difficulty in paying its way if a major creditor demanded repayment. The corporation tax is payable in one lump sum, and, depending on the date of the formation of the company, this will be due either at the end of September or at the end of December in 19–0. A low current ratio is not unusual for the retail trade where most sales are made on a cash basis (confirmed by the low figure for debtors) and with sales of £143 000 per year or £2 750 each week it would not take long to raise the money through sales to pay creditors.

(e) **Trading figures.** The credit period being taken by the company is just over four weeks [(£8 000 ÷ £100 000) × 52]. This seems quite a short period of time and indicates that the business pays its bills promptly.

Without knowing the amount of credit sales made by the company during the year the period of credit being allowed to debtors cannot be calculated.

To calculate the stock turnover requires the figure for cost of goods sold, which may be found by deducting the gross profit from sales; this gives £97 000. The closing stock is £23 000 and the opening stock for the year is £20 000 (found by constructing a trading account). Thus the average stock is £21 500 and therefore the stock turnover is approximately 4.5 times per year, which means that the stock remains in the shops for just over eleven weeks before being sold and replaced. For the type of business that Johnson Brothers Ltd. run, this seems to be perfectly satisfactory.

The gross profit percentage is 32 per cent which seems satisfactory for the trade. The net profit percentage is 14 per cent.

The figures calculated in this section can be compared with those for previous years and any major changes could be taken up with the directors.

(f) **Other items.** Inevitably, before making the decision about granting the facilities, the manager will consider the previous conduct of the account (we are told that previous overdrafts have been satisfactorily cleared) and the ability of the directors—from the information given, they seem to be hard-working and prepared to plough profits back into the business.

A further point is the consideration of security (if required) by the bank: the shop premises appear to provide an ideal form of security.

This would seem to be a good lending proposition and the facilities should be granted.

2. The company so far has been unprofitable in both years of trading. There is a net loss of £500 in the second year and, as the balance of the profit and loss account of £1 000 is shown as a fictitious asset, there must also have been a net loss of £500 in year 1. (Contrast the position of the profit and loss

account on this balance sheet with that of Johnson Brothers Ltd.—the difference between losses in past years and profits, respectively).

(*a*) **Shareholders' stake.** Although there is the issued share capital of £1 000, this is cancelled out by the debit balance on the profit and loss account. Therefore the shareholders' stake is nil. As the company has made a loss for the year there is no return on capital employed.

(*b*) **Long-term loans.** The assets of the business are partly financed by loans from directors. If any lending is to be considered Letters of Postponement would be essential.

(*c*) **Working capital.** There is a deficit of working capital of £250 and the current ratio is 0.92:1—hardly a satisfactory position. Granting the proposed overdraft would make the matter even worse.

(*d*) **Liquidity.** If there is a lack of working capital, there is an even greater lack of liquid capital—a deficit of £1 850—and a liquid ratio of 0.45. The ratio might not be too bad if there was a substantial element of cash sales but, in selling to shops and boutiques, the company has to allow credit and there will be a time lag between making the sale and receiving the cash.

(*e*) **Trading figures.** The credit period being taken by the company is nearly twenty weeks—little wonder that the bank had to pay the account overdrawn without facilities to meet pressing creditors.

Debtors, on the other hand, pay their accounts in just under eight weeks; this seems to be a satisfactory figure.

As this is a manufacturing business stock turnover is difficult to calculate on the information given; in order to reach a figure we would need to know the details of the costs of manufacture, such as the wages paid to outworkers.

The gross profit percentage is 10 per cent and there is a net loss of 5 per cent of sales. The percentage gross profit figure is rather low and a suggestion might be made that the selling prices could be increased without jeopardizing sales.

(*f*) **Other items.** If the bank lent the money as proposed, the company's balance sheet would be in an even worse state than it is now. There would also be the additional costs of bank interest which, depending on interest rates and the amount the facility is used, would probably amount to approximately £1 000 per year. There is no source of repayment apart from possible future trading profits; there is no security, apart from the possibility of taking directors' personal guarantees.

This is probably the type of business that could be made profitable if it operates in a small way and puts up its selling prices, but to consider expanding by renting a factory would seem to be foolhardy. The request should be turned down and steps taken to get the bank account into credit as soon as possible.

3. The set of accounts needs careful interpretation because they have been prepared by the customer himself and are, presumably, unaudited. The following points should be queried:

(i) As he employs no one, the wages at £3 000 for a half-year must be Bill's own drawings and seem somewhat excessive!

(ii) The closing stock figure is high in terms of both money and number of cranes, especially as this is the stock at 31 December (a toy manufacturer's stock would be at its lowest just after Christmas).

(iii) The method of valuing the stock should be ascertained.

(iv) The debtor can, presumably, be written off.

(v) The terms of the loan from his father need to be known: is the bank going to grant an overdraft limit of £1 000 so that Father can be repaid?

(a) **Shareholder's stake.** If the stock valuation is correct, total assets are £3 300 (ignoring the debtor—see (iv) above) and Bill's stake in this is 41 per cent which is rather on the low side. The return on capital employed is:

$$\frac{£550}{£1\,350 + £1\,000 \text{ (loan)}} \times \frac{100}{1} = 23.4 \text{ per cent.}$$

This seems to be quite a healthy figure.

(b) **Long-term loans.** As mentioned in (v), the terms of the loan need to be known.

(c) **Working capital.** Ignoring the debtor and treating the loan as a long-term one, the working capital is £2 250 which seems satisfactory. However, all but £50 of the current assets is stocks—see 'liquidity'. The current ratio is 3.14:1.

(d) **Liquidity.** Liquid capital is (£1 000) and, as a ratio, is 0.05. This is disastrous and probably one reason why he needs an overdraft—the creditors are pressing for payment.

(e) **Trading figures.** The accounts show that the credit being taken by Bill's business is no less than 22 weeks! No wonder he needs an overdraft. In fact, things may not be as bad as they seem because of the seasonal nature of his business: the majority of purchases on credit may have been made in the month or two leading up to Christmas which should have been a busy period for him.

Stockturn is very low at times (£1 400 ÷ £1 625) for the six months, even allowing a 'nil' figure for opening stock and thus calculating average stock at £1 625. This indicates that Bill has concentrated too much on production and not enough on selling the toy.

The gross and net profit percentages are 40 per cent and 23.5 per cent respectively. These seem to indicate that he has a good product provided he can sell the cranes. The danger with these two figures on this set of accounts, however, is that they are reliant on the closing stock value. If this has been calculated incorrectly these percentages could be totally misleading. (Try re-working them with the stock valued at £2 500!)

(*f*) **Other items.** The whole credibility of this set of unaudited accounts relies on the stock figure. Inquiries must be made to find out more about the method of valuation and the reason why there should be so much stock left after Christmas: the stock could be valued at cost and Bill could have concentrated too much on production. It might well be that he has a good marketable product and only needs some basic financial guidance to put him on the road to good profits. His main task is to concentrate on selling for the next few months, even though the period just after Christmas is not the best time for a toy manufacturer. He could consider taking on a partner to take over the selling side of the business and to inject some extra capital. Bank assistance could be made available provided it is not used to repay the loan from Father and provided Bill returns some of his wages for the last half-year and reduces substantially the amount he pays himself in the next half-year. Security is non-existent: the only possibility, unless he has other assets, is a guarantee from his father.

4. This question is different from the preceding ones, in that the company operates to fixed standards and, if these standards continue to apply, it is possible to anticipate the future profitability of the business. Thus we are told that the creditor (manufacturer) is paid one month after purchase and that the shops are allowed two months' credit. The Inbetween Co. makes a gross profit of 20p per pack and once it has paid the monthly operating costs of £3 000, the rest is net profit. Therefore, on the figures given, it will take sales of 15 000 packs to cover operating costs and at present sales levels there will be a profit of £1 000 per month. It is quite likely that an increase in sales will have little or no effect on the operating costs: there may be extra transport costs or salesman's commissions but there is no direct comparison between sales and operating costs. In such circumstances it is a temptation to expand the business as much as possible.

At present the gross profit margin is 20 per cent and the net profit margin is 5 per cent. With an increase in sales the net profit margin will increase because the operating costs are, in the short term, fixed. There is working capital of £50 000 with a current ratio of 4.125:1; liquid capital is £34 000 (liquid ratio 3.125:1): these are very good figures. The shareholder's stake is over 75 per cent of total assets—again very good.

Thus far, the company looks an excellent lending proposition, although there is no obvious security to take (if it is even necessary). Presumably the company rents offices and a warehouse and the costs of these are included in the operating costs. We, as bankers, are in a position to check the future financial position of the company because we have the facts and figures available (we shall have to take the managing director's word for the increased sales figures). We need to prepare a cash budget for the company until, say, the end of December. This will appear as follows:

	April	May	June	July	Aug	Sept	Oct	Nov	Dec
	£	£	£	£	£	£	£	£	£
Cash receipts									
From debtors	20 000	20 000	20 000	20 000	25 000	30 000	35 000	40 000	45 000
	20 000	20 000	20 000	20 000	25 000	30 000	35 000	40 000	45 000
Cash payments									
To creditor (manufacturer)	16 000	16 000	20 000	24 000	28 000	32 000	36 000	40 000	44 000
Operating expenses	3 000	3 000	3 000	3 000	3 000	3 000	3 000	3 000	3 000
	19 000	19 000	23 000	27 000	31 000	35 000	39 000	43 000·	47 000
Opening bank balance	10 000	11 000	12 000	9 000	2 000	(4 000)	(9 000)	(13 000)	(16 000)
Add cash receipts	20 000	20 000	20 000	20 000	25 000	30 000	35 000	40 000	45 000
Deduct cash payments	19 000	19 000	23 000	27 000	31 000	35 000	39 000	43 000	47 000
Closing bank balance	11 000	12 000	9 000	2 000	(4 000)	(9 000)	(13 000)	(16 000)	(18 000)

Pity the manager who granted the company an overdraft limit of £5 000 until the end of October! He might not have started to get worried until the end of September, but by the beginning of January he would have some explaining to do to head office. The balance sheet of the company as at 31 December is as follows:

	£		£
Capital	50 000		
+ Net profit (for the nine months)	37 000		
Current liabilities		*Current assets*	
Creditors 48 000		Stock	48 000
Bank 18 000		Debtors	105 000
	66 000		
	153 000		153 000

The company has vastly improved its profits: £37 000 for nine months instead of £5 000–10 000 per year. Working capital is now £87 000 with a current ratio of 2.3:1 and liquid capital is £39 000 with a liquid ratio of 1.59:1. Both of these figures are still perfectly satisfactory. Credit allowed and credit taken remain at two months and one month respectively. The shareholder's stake in the business is reduced to 57 per cent but this is still quite a good figure. So what has happened? The company has *over-traded* —it has tried to expand too quickly with insufficient capital. It is 'caught' between its credit-taken and credit-allowed terms neither of which, presumably, it can do anything about because of the size of its supplier and the need to remain competitive with other wholesalers. The way out of the problem for the bank manager is to insist that the present high rate of expansion is levelled off (as surely it must anyway with this type of product). If this happens the backlog of debtors will soon put cash into the bank account. An alternative would be for the company to seek extra capital or a long-term loan.

The answer is, of course, to check the financial data given by the company and anticipate what the overdraft will be. If you wished to lend to this company it would need a maximum overdraft of £19 000 in January and, after this, even if the expansion continued, the end-of-month overdraft would start to fall and the balance would be in credit by the end of July in the following year.

Index

268   Index